RED CARPET
AT THE
WHITE HOUSE

Red Carpet
at the
White House

**FOUR YEARS AS CHIEF OF PROTOCOL
IN THE EISENHOWER ADMINISTRATION**

By WILEY T. BUCHANAN, JR.
with Arthur Gordon

NEW YORK   E. P. DUTTON & CO., INC.   1964

Introduction

"No man ever 'saw' a government," said Woodrow Wilson at Pittsburgh during his campaign for re-election in 1916. "I live in the midst of the government of the United States, but I have never seen the government of the United States." There are, however, those privileged few who have "seen" the *sources* of government (which are human beings) at first-hand, shirt-sleeved and in action. And the memoirs of such observers are the raw material of history.

For that reason alone this book would qualify for the category, which is invaluable to contemporary generations and posterity alike. But there are other reasons, not always found in memoirs of official service, for the special distinction of Mr. Buchanan's account of his experiences as President Eisenhower's Chief of Protocol.

It is good and thorough reporting. It is a set of penetrating analyses of the characters and purposes of the men and women in this glittering parade who rule or reign in many nations. Moreover, Mr. Buchanan relates hitherto unknown incidents of contacts of the members of his cast with American officials and the people of the United States that are meaningful to the assessment of history. And the writing is lively and always readable. Yet no breach of confidence or taste can fairly be charged by those who entrusted Mr. Buchanan with an office whose importance to the conduct of foreign affairs is masqueraded under the stuffy diplomatic title of Chief of Protocol.

The objective of that assignment is to create good-will toward this government and this people among the representatives of foreign nations. When the attainment is not possible, the job is to "see that none . . . was in danger, or insulted or made to feel anything but welcome." But in his very successful official performance of this responsibility, Mr. Buchanan noted and meditated upon such incidents as these:

Premier Khrushchev's vocabulary of denunciation or complaint was toned down by his interpreter when it got too rough. . . . At an official function, a Soviet security officer switched to another guest a plateful of food on its way to the Premier. . . . The visitors from the U.S.S.R. showed no interest in anything created by Americans, remarking only on the natural beauties of the United States. . . . At a buffet luncheon Mrs. Roosevelt gave for Mr. Khrushchev at Hyde Park, the Premier took only "a sip of champagne," but before abruptly departing he snatched a bread-roll and stuck it in his pocket. . . .

When Mr. Khrushchev availed himself of a choice of air transport that was offered him, between the Soviet plane he arrived in and a Boeing, and chose the American craft, an official purpose was achieved. This was to give President Eisenhower the same option when he made the visit to Russia he was planning. The plan was abandoned when Mr. Khrushchev denounced the President on the U-2 flight at the Paris Summit conference—a denunciation which Mr. Buchanan believes was made for this very purpose, because the Kremlin feared the warming effects toward the United States of an Eisenhower pilgrimage among the Russian people.

A Hungarian refugee whose questioning angered the Premier during his visit to San Francisco was found beaten up afterward in a side street. . . . In Iowa Mr. Khrushchev said to Mr. Buchanan: "You know, I talk a lot about how in seven years we'll surpass your country. But that's not really true. It will take us years to catch up. Years and years." . . .

The African chief of an "emerging" nation "emerged" in person when his tribal robes caught up to the small of his back as he awaited an audience with President Eisenhower. . . . A Mideastern potentate, informed he could not bring to a White

House function a female secretary to whom he was very attentive, protected himself from her wrath by appointing her his "Secretary of State" on the spot. In this role, of course, she became eligible as a White House guest. . . .

These are only a few of the host of characters in the book. Like the narratives of Mr. Khrushchev's doings, they supply merely the hors d'oeuvres of the solid feast it provides of facts and portents of the international relations of the United States. In point is the following extract from a profile of Premier Khrushchev in a state of real or assumed rage, when asked at a National Press Club luncheon how he justified Soviet military intervention in Hungary:

> Instantly a change came over the Russian leader, a change that we were to see repeated many times in the next few days. A tide of red crept up his bull neck; his little eyes glared with a ferocity that reminded me unpleasantly of a wild boar I once had seen, too close for comfort, while shooting in the forest of Ardennes. His voice rose, snarling in Russian. As translated, he was comparing the Hungarian question to "a dead rat that sticks in some people's throats," but I had the feeling that the interpreter was moderating much stronger language. In fact, sitting near me, Mrs. Gromyko leaned over and murmured dryly, "The Chairman's remarks are not being translated literally."
>
> Then, almost as abruptly as it had started, Khrushchev's rage subsided, leaving observers to wonder whether it was genuine or simply contrived, a part of the familiar Russian tactic of being tough one moment and conciliatory the next.

Since foreign policy must be based in part on speculations like this, it is more likely to be sound when "observers" as acute as Mr. Buchanan occupy the office of Chief of Protocol.

Arthur Krock

Washington, D.C.

Contents

Illustrations

Foreword

This book is not an exposé. It reveals no government secrets, though I was privileged to hear many. It tells no tales out of school. Its purpose is simply to give an accurate and (I hope) entertaining account of one of the most colorful and fascinating jobs in government, a job I was fortunate enough to hold for four exciting years, the job of Chief of Protocol of the United States.

In those four years I found myself dealing with some of the most powerful people in the world—and some of the most unpredictable. They came from every country under the sun, drawn by the great political magnet that is Washington.

During such visits it was my department's responsibility to see that everything went smoothly—that no one was in danger, or insulted, or made to feel anything but welcome in the capital of the free world. We had other functions, too, but in essence we were dealing constantly with the most mysterious and elusive and complicated of all commodities: human beings.

Here, then, is the passing parade as I saw it.

WILEY T. BUCHANAN, JR.

I   The Man Who Came to Bury Us

We stood alone in the brilliant autumn sunshine, the President of the United States and I. Ahead of us were the broad runways of Andrews Air Force Base, some fifteen miles from Washington. Behind us one of the longest red carpets I had ever seen—and I had seen some long ones—stretched back to a waiting group of dignitaries. There was our tall, distinguished Secretary of State, Christian Herter, crippled by arthritis and resting his weight on the little portable device that he used on such occasions. There was our handsome Representative to the United Nations, Henry Cabot Lodge, towering over Llewellyn Thompson, our Ambassador to Russia who had been recalled especially for this occasion. There was silver-haired General Nathan F. Twining, Air Force Chief of Staff. There were Russian diplomats and the wives of various dignitaries, including my own wife, Ruth. Flanking them were the military band and honor guard. Farther back, behind a wire fence, was a crowd of several hundred curious Washingtonians.

We were there, all of us, on a mission that a few months earlier would have been inconceivable—to me, at least. We were there to welcome, with full honors, the leader of a nation that was our chief rival and deadly enemy in the atomic age. We were there to offer our hands and hospitality—if not our hearts—to Nikita S. Khrushchev, former Ukrainian sheepherder and miner, now Chairman of the Council of Ministers of the Soviet Union.

Already the huge Russian turbo-prop transport was coming in for its landing. It had flown nonstop from Moscow, fighting head winds that had made it late. President Eisenhower watched it somberly; I had never seen him so serious. Walking out with him to the edge of the main runway I had ventured the somewhat obvious remark that this first visit of a Russian ruler to our shores was an historic and momentous occasion. Either he sensed the doubts and reservations I felt, or else he shared some of them himself. "Wiley," he said, "in these times, if there is anything at all that a person can do to advance the cause of peace, he had better do it."

Puffs of blue smoke spurted from the tires as the TU-114 touched the runway. It swept past us, going very fast, engines roaring as the pilot reversed the pitch of his propellers to slow it down. It looked gigantic, this product of Russian technology; the tail fin seemed as high as a five-story house. Indeed, it was Russian technology that had made necessary my splendid isolation with the President. The landing gear of the TU-114 was so wide that it could not use the taxi strip that would have brought it closer to the customary unloading area.

As I stood there in my dark suit, dark glasses protecting me from the airport glare, a thousand thoughts seemed to be boiling through my mind. Outwardly, I was only doing my job—doing it correctly and efficiently, I hoped. On that particular morning, September 15, 1959, as Chief of Protocol of the United States, my job was to introduce to each other the two most powerful men in the world—and to see that the complicated machinery underlying such a ceremony ran smoothly. This included everything from inspecting the endless red carpet itself (I had been amused to observe one young soldier furtively sweeping some cigarette butts *under* the carpet) to arranging the precedence and timing of the fleet of automobiles that would be required to take all of us back to the capital.

I was sure that all such details had been taken care of by my able and devoted staff. What I *was* worried about (although I had no official right even to question it) was the wisdom of the decision to invite Khrushchev to the United States in the first place.

It seemed to me that I was worrying about it on three different levels. As Chief of Protocol, I knew already that Russians were not exactly the easiest people in the world to deal with. Whatever it was you wanted them to do, they had a standard and instinctive reaction, which was to do something else. If plans were made and agreed upon, they seemed to take a fiendish delight in demanding last-minute changes. Only the night before, for example, with all arrangements made and precedents established, General N. S. Zakharov, chief of the Russian Secret Service in Washington, had come to my office demanding that the order of precedence be changed (he wanted to move himself up several notches, naturally, and Ambassador Menshikov down). I had refused the request, as he doubtless knew I would. But it was all part of an endless game they played, a game that might well have been called: "Let's harass the Americans."

In addition (still worrying as Chief of Protocol), I felt we had already made two serious mistakes. The first was to treat Khrushchev as if he were a Head of State, which in fact he was not. Voroshilov was President of the USSR; Khrushchev was only Prime Minister. Technically, our own President should not have been meeting Khrushchev at the airport; our Secretary of State should have welcomed him. But here was President Eisenhower waiting patiently, and a battery of cannon ready to fire a twenty-one-gun salute.

A second mistake, I felt, was due to an oversight by our Under-Secretary of State Robert Murphy, who first discussed the proposed Khrushchev visit with Russian Ambassador Menshikov. Murphy failed to set a limit on the size of the Russian party (ten or twelve individuals was the customary number).

I was in Europe when the first conversations concerning this visit took place. Bob Murphy told me later that he had simply overlooked this important factor—which was understandable enough since, to my knowledge, this was the first time Murphy had ever arranged a state visit.

While this oversight was unfortunate, I was astounded to

learn upon my return to Washington that, outside of a few conversations between Murphy and the Russian Embassy, not one detail of the coming visit had actually been planned. This unhappy state of affairs existed because Menshikov refused to return repeated telephone calls from Assistant Secretary Foy Kohler.

Khrushchev was due to arrive on September 15, only two weeks away. I immediately telephoned Menshikov and, to my surprise, was put through to him at once. I explained the urgency of our getting together to plan this complicated tour, but he hesitated to set a definite date. Whereupon I stated politely and firmly that unless he was in my office at two o'clock that same afternoon, it would be impossible to plan *any* program. Promptly at two o'clock, Ambassador Menshikov and two of his staff arrived.

I learned that, accompanying Khrushchev, were to be not only his family, including his wife, two daughters, a son, and a son-in-law, but a large assortment of writers, editors, educators, and so on—a total of some fifty people in the party. The more of them there were, the more complicated arrangements for their visit became. I was braced for thirteen days of administrative headaches.

In addition to this "official" uneasiness, I was not very happy on a personal level. It was my job to meet Mr. Khrushchev and introduce him to our Chief of State, a man I admired profoundly. But this did not keep me from remembering just who Mr. Khrushchev was. This was the man who first attracted attention by helping to direct the planned starvation in the Ukraine during the 1930s that resulted in the death of some five million people. This was the man who, only three years earlier, had ordered the massacre of the patriots in Hungary who tried to regain their freedom from the Red Army. This was the man who had lured the Hungarian patriot, General Pal Meleter, into negotiations under a flag of truce—and then had had him arrested and shot. This was the man responsible for the secret trial and execution of Premier Imre Nagy—after assuring him safe conduct out of the Yugoslav Embassy in

Budapest where he had taken refuge. This was the man who had led and was leading the attack of atheistic Communism on religion everywhere . . . and had watched approvingly Stalin's merciless persecution of the Jews.

This was the man whose airplane at this very moment was making the turn at the far end of the runway that would, within a few seconds, bring us face to face. It was my duty to be gracious and cooperative and polite, but there was a strange unreality about the whole thing. I thought of the poem Rudyard Kipling had written almost sixty years ago, warning his own nation against the Russian menace, the "bear that walks like a man." I wondered what the fiery little Englishman would have thought if he could have witnessed the scene that I was witnessing.

Finally, I was troubled—deeply troubled—on the political or, perhaps more accurately, the patriotic level. It seemed to me that the Khrushchev visit was putting the American people squarely on the spot. Either they had to welcome a man whom the vast majority detested, or they had to appear surly, un-gracious, guilty of hindering the foreign policy of their own government. Moreover, what would the rest of the non-Com-munist world think? Wouldn't they feel that by literally rolling out the red carpet the United States of America was negating their efforts, was coming to terms with the hated enemy?

I was sure that they would. And I was equally sure that the Russians would squeeze every drop of propaganda value out of the situation. They were past masters at this. They would flood their wretched satellite countries—flood the whole world, for that matter—with pictures of their leader being wined and dined, welcomed and applauded by the statesmen and people of the United States. "Look," they would cry, "they accept us, they condone us, they've capitulated!"

Already they had seized and held world attention, on the very eve of Khrushchev's flight to Washington, by firing a rocket to the moon. With the 800-pound lunar probe went a red flag, the hammer and sickle . . . and just to ram this achievement farther down our throats, Khrushchev had blandly announced that he was bringing a replica of his hated symbol as a gift for his host, President Eisenhower.

Now the TU-114 had swung around at the far end of the runway and was lumbering back toward us. I realized with a start that this maneuver would mean that the exit of the big plane would now be on the far side, away from the crowd. This meant that the waiting photographers and television cameramen would not be able to focus their long-range lenses on the door of the plane as Khrushchev stepped out onto the tall, movable staircase that we had had specially built for this occasion. It was not exactly a matter of life or death, but I knew the photographers would be exasperated, and it was typical of the minor frustrations that I had learned to expect in dealing with Russians.

I glanced once at the President, dressed as usual in business suit and homburg. His eyes were narrowed against the glare; he still looked serious, almost grim. But I knew that when the moment came, he would do his job conscientiously and well. No one, when he wished to, could radiate more warmth and charm than this man. I had seen him do it countless times in the White House with tongue-tied ambassadors arriving for the first time to present their credentials. In such moments, the President was not merely the Chief Executive, he was the United States—the embodiment of all the hospitality and friendliness of a generous and open-handed people. He would be no less here on this sun-drenched airfield—regardless of whom he was meeting.

And maybe he's right, I said a little desperately to myself, maybe he's right. Maybe a visit like this will break down some of the barriers, bring about a real thaw in the cold war. Maybe if Khrushchev sees for himself how peaceful this country is, how disinterested in conquest—and yet how strong—maybe the chances of war will diminish and the chances of peaceful coexistence will increase. . . .

I said this to myself, but I didn't really believe it.

I didn't know then—and I don't know now—whose idea the Khrushchev visit was. It all came about very suddenly. Vice-

President Nixon told me that there was no discussion of the matter in the Cabinet or Security Council. He was told of the invitation by President Eisenhower just as he was about to take off for Moscow on the trip where the famous "Kitchen Debate" took place. There were, no doubt, highly placed people in the government who honestly felt that the obvious disadvantages of giving Khrushchev the keys to the citadel of freedom were outweighed by the faint possibility of reciprocal concessions in such critical areas as Berlin and elsewhere. One thing was clear to me: whoever obtained the President's consent must have persuaded him that the gesture, however distasteful, was a step in the direction of world peace.

This hope—and it was a noble one—was to be brutally smashed six months later at the Summit Conference in Paris. But we could not read the future on that sparkling September morning. At exactly 12:30 Eastern Daylight Time, twelve hours and twenty minutes out of Moscow, the huge transport came abreast of us and stopped. The ramp was pushed into position. The door opened and Khrushchev stepped out.

Twelve hours in the air certainly had not affected the Russian's vitality: he came down the stairs with a springy stride, a chunky little bald-headed man who looked more like a teddy bear than the monster Kipling had in mind. His handshake, I remember, was curiously limp, almost weak. He, too, was carrying a black homburg and wearing a dark suit. Two Hero of Socialist Labor medals gleamed on his left lapel; on the right was the Lenin Peace Prize. He was smiling broadly, but his sharp little eyes were shrewd and appraising. Behind him came his wife Nina, a rumpled but amiable-looking woman wearing a two-piece gray rayon suit with black dots and a small black hat perched on the back of her head. Her hair, arranged in a long page-boy bob, was held firmly in a hair net.

"Welcome to the United States, Mr. Chairman," said the President, offering his hand. Still beaming, Khrushchev replied in Russian that he was glad to be with us. The President greeted Mrs. Khrushchev, Foreign Minister Gromyko, and the rest of the official Russian party. Then we all walked back to the reviewing stand where further introductions were made, the national anthems were played, and the two leaders read short prepared statements.

It was while President Eisenhower was speaking that I noticed for the first time (but certainly not the last) what an accomplished scene-stealer Khrushchev was. He wriggled, he watched a butterfly, he held his homburg over his head like a sunshade. When his turn came to speak, he included a few patronizing remarks about the American space effort. Surely, he said, we would get to the moon someday—and our American pennant would find the Russian pennant waiting to welcome it. Eisenhower looked grim. Later, at a press conference, he was to say disgustedly that he assumed the Russian pennant would have been burned up in landing on the moon—not a very educated guess in view of the absence of any atmosphere on the moon, but still indicative of his reaction to this sort of propagandizing.

A moment later, the President was in his car with the Khrushchevs, looking uncomfortable and cramped between his two wide-beamed guests. I knew that every security precaution had been taken, and yet I couldn't help remembering what J. Edgar Hoover had told me: that there were at least 25,000 potential assassins in America, men and women from lands overrun by the Red Army, fugitives from Russia itself, former Hungarian Freedom Fighters. One expert rifleman hidden somewhere with a telescopic sight, just one . . . My mind shied away from the thought, and as we know now, the possibilities were all too real.

As we neared Washington, the crowds of spectators increased—silent, mostly; impassive. Here and there a faint handclap or two from people applauding the hope of peace and friendship, no doubt, not the visitor himself. He would get some genuine applause later, on the West Coast. But not here in the heart of the nation. A few onlookers waved black skull-and-crossbones flags, although the police discouraged this. I saw the Russian Secret Service men snap pictures of

these demonstrators, and wondered if the faces of these Americans would henceforth be on file in the Kremlin. Later I heard
that one of his aides explained the silence to Khrushchev by
saying that a car had preceded us through the streets with
signs urging the people not to applaud. This was nonsense,
but perhaps he believed it.

We came at last to the President's Guest House, the old
Blair mansion diagonally across Pennsylvania Avenue from
the White House. I must confess, it gave me an odd feeling to
see the hammer and sickle floating from the flagstaff. The
housekeeper, Mrs. Victoria Geaney, had been a fixture ever
since the days of the Blairs. Indeed, there were times when
she seemed to feel that she was *still* working for the Blairs,
and weighed all State Department suggestions accordingly.
But she was a grand person. I knew she was going to have her
hands full. Blair House can accommodate ten or twelve guests
comfortably; the Russians were packing it with twenty-two.
So crowded were they, indeed, that not even Gromyko could
stay there. He and his wife were going to a hotel—an odd
arrangement since a Foreign Minister is almost invariably
housed with the head of his government while on a state visit.

As he took leave of the Russian leader, the President gestured toward me. "You've met Ambassador Buchanan," he
said, "our Chief of Protocol. He will go everywhere with you
during your visit and try to make your stay a pleasant one."

Khrushchev gave me a droll look. "Ah, yes," he said through
his interpreter, "Chiefs of Protocol are always the saviors!"

His remark came back to me later as I drove home to dress
for the formal dinner being given for the Russians that night
at the White House. I had been called many things in my
time, but never a savior. Actually, my job as Chief of Protocol
had many facets. Not only was I charged with welcoming
visiting dignitaries and seeing that all details of their visits
ran smoothly, but I also had to handle the accreditation of
foreign ambassadors, receive them on their arrival to the
United States, and present them with their "letters of credence"
to our President. I had to supervise the complicated system of

diplomatic immunities that make resident diplomats and visiting VIPs exempt from our laws and taxes. I had, on occasion, to decide complicated problems of precedence—who preceded whom on official occasions. The job brought with it ambassadorial rank and sometimes king-size headaches. I shall attempt to describe it in more detail in a later chapter.

Certainly it was a fascinating, colorful, and stimulating way of life. An exhausting one, too. On a typical day I might leave the office soon after 5, but usually I had to make an appearance at two or three receptions in various embassies, then return to the office, and finally dash home at 7:15 or 7:30. Virtually every night Ruth and I had to be at some official dinner. Our three teen-age children, Bonnie, Dede (Diane), and Bucky, were resigned to seeing us mainly in moments snatched between appointments, or on weekends which diplomats everywhere fight ferociously to preserve for themselves and their families. The closest thing to a family hour that we had was during the children's supper. Ruth and I would get dressed (both of us had learned to be phenomenally fast dressers; I needed only ten minutes to change from business clothes into full dress, and Ruth was just as quick); then we'd sit down with the children while they ate or until it was time to leave. Fortunately, diplomatic evenings always break up at 11, so sometimes we'd find the children still up, doing their homework, when we came home.

At the time of the Khrushchev visit, I had been Chief of Protocol for more than two years. One of the main requirements, I had learned, was plenty of stamina. It was also essential to be gregarious, to like people, to respect dignitaries without being awed by them. It helped to be a fluent conversationalist, ready to fill an awkward silence with an easy remark. It certainly was an advantage to have—as I did—a lovely wife who was a good organizer and a good linguist: Ruth spoke both French and Italian. In the early stages of the job I had indicated to the Secretary of State—then John Foster Dulles—that on trips where the visiting dignitary's wife was with him, I would like to take Ruth along. He had endorsed the idea with enthusiasm. As a result, we were able to be together much of the time.

As we dressed for dinner that night, I remember, one of the children asked if the Russians were going to wear full dress to the White House. It was a white-tie affair; all state dinners are. I said that I would be rather surprised if they did. The Russian Ambassador, Mikhail Menshikov, often wore white-tie. But to my knowledge Khrushchev had never worn full dress, and I was fairly sure that he wouldn't now. For one thing, he hardly had the ideal figure. For another, he probably considered full dress a symbol of decadent capitalism. I didn't expect him to make any such concession to American etiquette.

Nor did he. When I arrived at Blair House to escort him to the White House he was wearing a dark suit with a white shirt and a gray four-in-hand tie. Mrs. Khrushchev wore a long blue gown shot sparingly with gold and a simple black cloth coat. Her only jewelry was a handsome emerald-and-diamond brooch set in antique gold—quite capitalistic-looking, I thought.

Although the distance was very short, the Khrushchevs and I drove in a limousine with motorcycle escort to the White House, where I escorted them to the Eisenhowers' private apartments on the second floor. This procedure was often followed with state visitors if there was time. The Chief Executive would offer his guests refreshments—alcoholic or nonalcoholic. Then he and Mrs. Eisenhower would show them various rooms: the Lincoln Room, which was one of the President's favorites, or the oval study with his fascinating collection of curios and mementos. Visitors were often interested in the President's own paintings, but he almost never showed these. Chancellor Adenauer of Germany was one of the few who actually asked to see some of them—and did.

Meanwhile, downstairs, the other guests were gathering under the great crystal chandeliers in the East Room. Almost always there were a few who were self-conscious or ill at ease; the aura of the Presidency is an impressive thing. The warmth of the Eisenhowers always melted the ice, once they appeared, but waiting for them could be nerve-racking if you had never been in the White House before and weren't sure what was expected of you.

The procedure, which never varied, was as follows. Each man, as he came into the White House, was given a card telling him who his dinner partner would be and a diagram indicating where he would be seated in the State Dining Room. As each arriving couple entered the East Room, their names were called over a public-address system, a custom that enabled the people already in the room to identify newcomers or spot their dinner partners. A White House aide then took each couple to their proper place in the line that would move past the President and Mrs. Eisenhower and the guests of honor when they appeared. Here they were supposed to remain, in their assigned order of precedence.

White House aides—personable young bachelors in dress uniforms of the different branches of the armed services—moved through the crowd of men in full dress and splendidly gowned women, answering questions and making introductions when necessary. Often these tactful young men spoke several languages fluently. Drinks were never served at this time. No one was supposed to smoke, either. This was hard on chain smokers, who sometimes would be seen cupping a cigarette furtively in their hands or looking frantically for a potted palm to dispose of one.

At least half of the conversation among the ladies, according to my wife Ruth, dealt with the burning question of whether to fold back the right hand of their long white gloves or to keep it on when being presented to the visiting head of state. In general, we tried to follow the custom of the country from which the distinguished visitor came, but this could be confusing because in some countries it was considered perfectly proper for a lady to shake hands with her glove on, while in others it was frowned upon. Some heads of state—the Queen of England, for example—let it be known before their arrival that they preferred the guests to leave their gloves on. But sometimes the preference was not so clearly stated, and the whispered discussion among the ladies grew quite vehement.

When all the guests had arrived—and no one is ever late for a White House dinner—an aide would notify the President, and he would bring the distinguished visitors to the ground floor in his private elevator. Here, photographers were usually allowed to take a few pictures under the watchful eye of Jim Hagerty, the Presidential Press Secretary, who had a built-in radar that enabled him to know when the Presidential patience was wearing thin. Then the Marine string band in the hall on the main floor would strike up "Hail to the Chief," the President's four military standard-bearers would enter the East Room, and the President, Mrs. Eisenhower, and the guests of honor would take their places just inside the door and greet the guests as they moved past.

On this particular evening, two of the most nervous people in the room were Mr. Khrushchev's daughters, Rada and Julia. They were half-sisters, Julia being the daughter of Khrushchev's first wife, Rada the child of the present Mrs. Khrushchev. Wearing short white dresses, while all the other women were in long gowns, they clung to each other looking like a pair of lost teen-agers, although Rada was in her twenties and Julia forty-two. We were to notice this timidity among the Russian women throughout their stay in the United States. With the exception of Mrs. Khrushchev herself, who had considerable poise, they acted as if they lived in constant dread of making some mistake for which they might be held accountable.

The President and Mrs. Eisenhower always made the final decision on who should be invited to state dinners. In the State Dining Room, seating arrangements were generally—but not rigidly—controlled by protocol. There were always a few unattached men in the visiting group, and Mrs. Eisenhower usually tried to add interest and variety by seating them next to the wives of industrialists or other prominent civilian dinner guests. She was a marvelous hostess, gracious and poised, with a charm that matched her husband's. In my opinion, she is much more handsome than most of her photographs, with lovely skin, sparkling eyes, and a winning smile. Her favorite color is pink. At formal dinners she usually wore pastel gowns with matching gloves. She loved to play bridge with such friends as Grace Gruenther and Rosemary Silvercruys, wife of the former Belgian Ambassador. She also loved flowers and kept the White House full of them.

For the Khrushchev dinner, the flowers were chrysanthemums, glowing like miniature golden suns and matching the handsome gold draperies. The table was set with the gold vermeil service originally purchased in France in 1817 by President Monroe. In the center were the fabulous vermeil urns and candelabra left to the White House in 1956 by the late Margaret Thompson Biddle. At the head table, President Eisenhower and Chairman Khrushchev sat side by side, flanked by their wives. Since the Russian was being treated as a Head of State, he and Mr. Eisenhower would be served simultaneously. In not-so-remote times, no doubt, the ruler of Russia would have brought along a taster to make sure that his soup was not poisoned by some disgruntled cook or waiter. On one occasion later, I saw a Russian Secret Service man swoop down on a random table in a large dining room, snatch up a plate of food, and exchange it for the one his boss was supposed to eat. But this is a standard security precaution in all countries.

The White House menu that night was strictly American, the entree roast turkey and sweet potatoes, the dessert lady fingers and lime sherbet. Four wines were served with the meal, beginning with a dry sherry and ending with champagne. The entertainment afterward was strictly American, too: Fred Waring and his Pennsylvanians in a program of "best-loved American songs," including "The Battle Hymn of the Republic." ("Heavens," murmured one irreverent guest, watching the Russians, "are we trying to convert them?") But the Communists enjoyed it, and said so. Seated next to Ruth, their Chief of Protocol Malenchkov beamed and tapped his foot. He had thought all American music was rock 'n roll, he said, but he liked this very much. Malenchkov, who spoke fluent French, was the most refined and cultured of the group.

The President's after-dinner speech was grave and dignified and cautiously optimistic. Khrushchev's held the note of cockiness and combativeness that was to become so familiar to me before his visit was over. America might be richer than Russia at the moment, he said, but soon Russia would be as rich—and eventually richer. This sort of boasting was hardly good manners, coming from a guest, but Mr. Khrushchev was speaking to a world audience, and he knew it.

Driving home after dinner with Ruth, I could not help reflecting on what an extraordinary day it had been, not only in Washington but throughout the world. In Russia, no doubt, people were being told that their leader was receiving an enthusiastic welcome from the downtrodden workers of the United States. In Manhattan, according to the evening paper, a former Hungarian Freedom Fighter had tried to chain himself to a railing in front of the UN building as a protest against Khrushchev's visit. When the police carted him off to Bellevue, he issued a defiant statement from the psychiatric ward saying that he would go on a hunger strike until the Russians left. Down in Mississippi a pair of bemused parents, having produced their eighth child, had decided to name it Nikita.

At home, the telephone rang for a while, as it always did—members of the press seeking every detail that either of us could remember about the dinner. It was well after 1 when we got to bed, and even then I was awakened at 2 by a call from a morning paper seeking one more item before going to press. I gave the required information and sank wearily back to sleep. For the next twelve days, I was going to be virtually handcuffed to Khrushchev. I knew I'd need all the rest I could get.

Next day, without delay, the fireworks started. The first question put to Khrushchev publicly indicated plainly that the American press was not going to be deterred by his guest-status. At a luncheon given by the National Press Club, William H. Lawrence, president of the club, opened a question-and-answer session by asking Khrushchev, in effect, where he had been and what he had been doing while Stalin committed his crimes. The Russian refused to answer, on the grounds that the question was provocative. Later he shrugged off his famous "we will bury you" remark by claiming that it was a metaphorical reference to the superiority of Communism over capitalism and was not intended as a threat to bury anyone physically.

It was evident to me that Khrushchev was endeavoring to speak over the heads of his questioners to the American people and create an image of reasonableness that ultimately might cause us to lower our guard. But one question did get under his skin. "You spoke, Mr. Khrushchev," said the questioner, "about the need for avoiding outside interference in the affairs of other nations. How, then, do you justify armed intervention in Hungary?"

Instantly a change came over the Russian leader, a change that we were to see repeated many times in the next few days. A tide of red crept up his bull neck; his little eyes glared with a ferocity that reminded me unpleasantly of a wild boar I once had seen, too close for comfort, while shooting in the forest of Ardennes. His voice rose, snarling in Russian. As translated, he was comparing the Hungarian question to "a dead rat that sticks in some people's throats," but I had the feeling that the interpreter was moderating much stronger language. In fact, sitting near me, Mrs. Gromyko leaned over and murmured dryly, "The Chairman's remarks are not being translated literally."

Then, almost as abruptly as it had started, Khrushchev's rage subsided, leaving observers to wonder whether it was genuine or simply contrived, a part of the familiar Russian tactic of being tough one moment and conciliatory the next.

That night, when the Russians gave a dinner for President and Mrs. Eisenhower, they were all caviar and smiles. Their "golden hall," as they called the dining room in the old Pullman mansion that was now their Embassy, had been freshly gilded. I couldn't help wondering what the inventor of the sleeping car would have thought if he could have seen the gathering in the house his money had built. I was also amused to observe that the Russians had rented the gold service of the

Mayflower Hotel for the occasion, and so the food in this outpost of Communism was served on dishes bearing tiny replicas of the ship that brought the Pilgrims to America in search of freedom.

This time the President wore a tuxedo and Mrs. Eisenhower a short formal. The food, as might have been expected, was as Russian as the dinner the previous night had been American, borsch and shashlik and Caucasian wine. Ruth sat next to Senator Fulbright of Arkansas and traded her vodka, which she didn't like, for his black bread and caviar, which she did.

The next morning we left by special train for New York. With us on the train to New York were three American couples who were to be our constant companions for the next ten days: our Ambassador to the United Nations, Henry Cabot Lodge, and his wife Emily; our Ambassador to Russia, Llewellyn Thompson, and his wife Jane; and Foy Kohler, Assistant Secretary of State for Western Europe, and his wife Phyllis.

These six Americans had been chosen for their very special qualifications. During the past seven years, representing the United States brilliantly in the United Nations, Cabot Lodge had become a past master at recognizing and refuting Russian propaganda. Towering four inches over six feet, Cabot was not only a very handsome man but an excellent speaker with a keen sense of humor. His wife Emily, tall and blonde, had a wonderful, sparkling smile, and together they made a striking couple. Cabot generally wore dark suits and sometimes colored shirts, and I was amused at times to see this "capitalist," as Khrushchev loved to call him, appear with a visibly frayed collar, which he wore with New England frugality and pride.

Llewellyn Thompson and Foy Kohler both spoke Russian, as did their wives. Phyllis Kohler, indeed, spoke it so well that she had translated a novel from Russian into French. It had been published in France and sold quite widely. Emily, Jane, Phyllis, and Ruth found one another very congenial traveling companions and were of enormous help where the Russian women were concerned. Throughout the trip, I was very proud of their appearance, good humor, and stamina under some-times trying circumstances.

Also on the train with us was my loyal, hard-working Dep-uty, Clement E. Conger. Clem, who had been in the office of the Chief of Protocol for several years when I took over, was absolutely indispensable to me. The only trouble with him was that he worked too hard; I had to fight constantly to make him leave the office and spend a reasonable amount of time with his three children and his attractive wife Lianne.

One reason for going by rail instead of air was to give Khrushchev a chance to see something of the American countryside, but he did not seem particularly interested. I remember once, when one of us tried to point out a housing development, he growled that he had seen plenty of similar houses in Russia. In all the hours we were to spend together, I never heard any of the Russians express spontaneous admira-tion for anything American, except occasionally the scenery. They would exclaim over a sunset or a waterfall or any other act of God, but not an American building or an American invention—anything created by Americans.

For the most part, as the train sped through the clear Sep-tember sunshine, Khrushchev sat sipping mineral water, talk-ing to members of his entourage or to Henry Cabot Lodge or Llewellyn Thompson or Foy Kohler or myself. All through the trip, contrary to rumor, he was to be quite abstemious when it came to alcohol—a ceremonial glass of champagne or a formal toast or two was the limit of his drinking. Once somebody handed him a Scotch-and-soda and asked how he liked it. Khrushchev wrinkled up his face in distaste. "Spoiled water," he said.

If the welcome Khrushchev had received from the crowds in Washington was cool, in New York it was icy. You could feel the hostility as our limousines moved swiftly along the streets behind a flying wedge of fifty blue-helmeted motorcycle police-men; you could see it in the faces that lined the streets behind the wooden barriers. Our security people were more worried about New York than any other place on our itinerary. Every possible precaution had been taken, but even so it was impossible to keep more than a fraction of Manhattan's restless millions under control or surveillance. I noticed that all the metal trash baskets had been removed from sidewalks along our route —to keep people from throwing them, I supposed. On the tops of the buildings policemen were silhouetted against the deep blue of the sky.

The silence of those crowds must have meant something to Khrushchev. You may be here, the silence seemed to be saying, but we do not like you and we do not trust you. You are a reality that we have to deal with, a menace that we must live with. But don't expect us to welcome you or be glad that you are among us. We'll be glad when you are gone.

By the time we reached the Commodore Hotel, where my friend Mayor Robert Wagner was giving a luncheon for the visitors, all of us were feeling the pressure. And just before the luncheon began, the tension reached an unexpected climax. The national anthems of both countries were played, a standard procedure. As the first notes of "The Star-Spangled Banner" sounded, somewhere in the vast gathering a little man started to sing. People stared at him, amazed, but he went on singing in a reedy, quavering voice. Then, hesitantly, one or two others joined him, then more and more, until the great dining hall was filled with a roar of voices. It was an astounding thing; the emotional impact was tremendous. All the frustration we had been feeling, all the love and pride we felt for our country, all the things we wanted to say and could not, found release and came crashing through in the words of the old song. Some people had tears running down their faces, but everyone was singing. The Russians looked thunderstruck, almost frightened.

Then, suddenly, it was all over. I don't think the press ever reported it adequately, but to me it was unforgettable, one of the great moments of my life.

After lunch, the Khrushchev party moved on to the Waldorf-Astoria, where 842 trunks and suitcases, airlifted from Washington by the Military Air Transport Service, had already been trucked in from Idlewild. Here the much-publicized and inaccurately reported elevator episode occurred. When the Russian leader, myself, and a few others entered the elevator that was to take us to the suite reserved on the thirty-fifth floor, several other elevators were started simultaneously. We rose smoothly enough for twenty-nine floors. Then the circuits became overloaded, and the power automatically cut off. Every newspaper that I saw reported that Khrushchev crawled out of the elevator and climbed the rest of the way to his suite. This was not true. It was embarrassing enough to have Khrushchev immobilized for a few moments, but it would have been a good deal worse to have him squashed like a bug by a capitalistic elevator. Actually, there was no danger; under such circumstances, elevators are always inspected in advance by our security men. We simply waited until power was restored, then rode the rest of the way. But the *New York Post* had us walking "up five flights of steps while security held their breath and searched for the missing Communist chief."

It was obvious that the Russians enjoyed American hotel life, especially room-service where all they had to do was sign the check. Trays full of lobster, filet mignon, strawberries, and other delicacies streamed through the halls at all hours. These were between-meal "snacks," possibly due to the Russians' apprehension over eating meals outside the closely supervised and secured kitchen of the Waldorf. At any rate, the long-suffering American taxpayer picked up the bill.

That night, while Khrushchev spoke at a dinner given by the Economic Club of New York (and again flared up during the question-and-answer period), Mrs. Khrushchev went to a Broadway show, *The Music Man*. She was getting a good reception from the American press. Perhaps it was because her appearance was so disarming; perhaps it was the eternal optimism in the American people that hopefully looks for the best in any situation. In any case, her appearance at the theater caused quite a stir. Since she understood English and could speak it quite well when she chose, she seemed to enjoy the show and stayed almost to the end. Julia and Rada seemed dismayed and bewildered by the whole thing. They wanted to go back to the hotel during the intermission, but their mother finally persuaded them to stay.

The next day, Friday, plans called for Khrushchev to drive to Hyde Park, some eighty miles away, meet Eleanor Roosevelt, and place a wreath on her husband's grave. The Russians themselves had requested this, and Mrs. Roosevelt certainly did her best to cooperate, but the visit was not a success. We had timed everything carefully, but the Russians insisted on leaving late. Since Khrushchev was addressing the United Nations in mid-afternoon, the whole thing became a frantic race against time.

Leaving at 9 o'clock, our motorcade with its escort of fifty motorcycle policemen sped north at speeds up to seventy miles per hour. More than once the thought crossed my mind that Khrushchev was probably in more danger from a blown tire than he had been from assassins in New York. When we arrived, he seemed glum and preoccupied. Mrs. Roosevelt met him, bareheaded in the light drizzle that had started to fall. The only members of her family with her were her son John and his wife Anne.

She tried hard to interest the Russian leader in various items in the old mansion—her husband's stamp collection, letters he had received from Stalin, and so on. But he seemed completely indifferent. "I'm not getting through to him," Mrs. Roosevelt said to me. "He shows no interest . . . none!" I had to agree. Later, a reporter asked Mrs. Roosevelt if her guest had enjoyed his visit. "He enjoyed nothing," said Mrs. Roosevelt tartly. "A Russian behind him kept whispering all the time, 'We have three minutes . . . two minutes . . .'"

At the end of their tour, Mrs. Roosevelt escorted the Russians to her cottage, where a lavish buffet had been prepared. The cottage itself was very simple, with low ceilings, almost austere, and I thought that this might impress Khrushchev. But apparently it didn't. Mrs. Roosevelt made a brave attempt to drink a toast to peace, but Khrushchev took one swallow of champagne and announced that he was leaving. I saw his pudgy hand snatch a roll, which he carried with him to his car. Then his black limousine moved away. Some cars were still arriving. The entire visit had lasted less than an hour.

We roared back to New York even faster than we had come. At one point Gromyko, who was in my car, looked thoughtfully at the landscape flashing past. "Mr. Buchanan," he said, "your country really has excellent roads. You should export some of them." It was the first time I had suspected that the Russian Foreign Minister had a sense of humor.

At the United Nations, knowing that the whole world was his captive audience, Khrushchev made a dramatic plea for "total disarmament." If in the next four years every nation dismantled its armed forces, he said, then war would be abolished and millions of men could turn to peaceful and productive work. The price tag for Russian disarmament, he added, would be withdrawal of American forces from Europe, abolition of American overseas bases, and the recognition of Red China as the legitimate government of that country. He knew perfectly well that these conditions, plus his own country's adamant refusal to accept any workable system of inspection, made his offer worthless. But to anyone who read only the headlines, his speech must have sounded like the dawn of a new era.

One of the things he said, rather proudly, was that the Russians had been proposing total disarmament ever since 1927. I couldn't help remembering the reply that Salvador de Madariaga, the great Spanish statesman and philosopher, had given to Maxim Litvinov, the Soviet spokesman. He reminded him of the fable about the animals' disarmament conference, in which each animal happily proposed the abolition of the weapons he didn't have. The elephant looked at the eagle and suggested that talons be outlawed. The tiger looked at the elephant and demanded the abolition of tusks. The lion wanted horns forbidden; the buffalo was opposed to sharp claws. And so it went until the bear arose, smiling sweetly. "Comrades," he said, "let's abolish everything, everything except the great universal embrace!" It seemed to me that the

Russian bear was still making the same innocent-sounding proposal.

The speech also contained several of the funereal references that were beginning to be almost a Khrushchev trademark. Nationalist China, he said, was a rotting corpse that should be buried. Colonialism was dead, and ready for the graveyard. As someone remarked dryly, all that was lacking was an announcer with an unctuous voice to introduce the speaker: "And now, here is your friendly undertaker, Nikita Khrushchev. . . ."

Next day, the friendly undertaker left for California. We had offered him the choice of his own TU-114 or an American jet, and he had chosen the latter—a Boeing 707. There was more to our offer than mere hospitality, however. We were looking ahead to President Eisenhower's scheduled visit to Russia, and we wanted the same choice to be offered to him. Our security people did not take kindly to the thought of our President being flown around by Russian pilots in a Russian plane. By giving Khrushchev freedom to choose, we were guaranteeing ourselves the same option later on.

At Idlewild airport, the Russian leader made a short speech in which he expressed regret at not having seen more of the working classes while in New York. He understood, he said, that security precautions were necessary because of the objections some people felt to his visit. But the objectors, he added, were very few, a mere "drop in the ocean." Then, having blandly put this astonishing lie into the record, he climbed aboard the plane. A few moments later we were airborne.

Two other jets carrying members of the press took off just behind us. All three airplanes flew west at 31,000 feet. We had this traffic level all to ourselves; no other airliners were cleared for that altitude during our five-and-one-half-hour flight. It was a diamond-clear day. Six miles below us, the great tapestry of America unrolled itself—the checkerboard farms of the Midwest, the Mississippi valley, the great plains ending in the mighty wall of the Rockies. From that height, even the Grand Canyon looked small, a deep gash on the arid face of the earth.

It was somewhere over the Grand Canyon, I think, that the subject of Disneyland came up. During the early discussions of the Khrushchev itinerary, the possibility of a visit to Mr. Disney's fabulous playground had been mentioned, but the Russian Secret Service had ruled it out as too hazardous. Now the idea was revived, and suddenly all the Russians were clamoring to go. Even Gromyko. The thought of that dour-faced functionary soaring away to Never-Never Land on the Peter Pan sky-ride struck me as almost too good to be true, but I knew from bitter experience that such last-minute changes of plans were at best difficult and potentially disastrous from a security standpoint. The Russians knew it, too, of course; that was why they were constantly proposing such changes.

We did make an effort. By radio telephone we got in touch with the police authorities in Los Angeles and at Disneyland. Their reaction, naturally, was that there wasn't time to take the necessary security precautions. The Russians could come if they liked, but the local police could not answer for their safety. As far as I was concerned, this settled the matter: we would stick to the schedule agreed upon. But we were to hear more about Disneyland before the day was over.

We landed at the Los Angeles International Airport just after noon, Pacific Coast Time. On hand to meet us was Mayor Norris Poulson. His greeting to Khrushchev was not exactly effusive. "Welcome to Los Angeles," he said, "the City of Angels, where the impossible always happens." Khrushchev appeared unruffled by this, but I was beginning to realize that he was perfectly capable of masking a grievance until such time as it suited him to release it in a dramatic temper tantrum.

The first event on the official program was a lunch at the Twentieth Century-Fox Studios. We drove there in a thirty-car caravan, heavily guarded by police. Again the attitude of the city was restrained. There were no cheers. Here and there I noticed a few children waving bouquets of flowers, but it was a curious thing—I was to see those same children again in San Francisco, still waving flowers. Obviously they were part of a

staged demonstration. Once an overripe tomato sailed from
the crowd and splattered against the car carrying some of our
Secret Service men. But again, this might have been planned
just so the Russians would have something to complain about.

On the lot, the elite of Hollywood were assembled to welcome the Russians. Frank Sinatra sat on one side of Mrs.
Khrushchev; Bob Hope was on the other. Everyone from
Marilyn Monroe to Gary Cooper seemed to be there. Ruth
found herself sitting with Charlton Heston and the Russian
novelist Sholokhov. When the actor told the writer that he had
read "part of one of your books" and liked it, the Russian replied dryly that he would try to see part of one of Heston's
pictures someday and judge his acting ability from that.

That first day in California nothing went right. At the
luncheon, Khrushchev and Spyros Skouras, president of Twentieth Century-Fox, got into a noisy wrangle over which of them
was the best example of the old Horatio Alger, rags-to-riches
saga. Then, in the middle of his prepared address, the Russian suddenly flew into a tantrum over Disneyland. Why was
he being prevented from seeing it, he demanded; was there a
cholera epidemic? Or secret rocket-launching sites? Or gang-
sters who might destroy him? The movie stars listened in
stunned silence; to them, the outburst came without warning.
But at least one bit of evidence indicated to me that it was
premeditated. Just as the luncheon began, one of the Russian
Secret Service men nudged one of ours. "Wait until you hear
what the Chairman is going to say about Disneyland!" he said.
"He's really going to shake them up today." He did!

After lunch, things went from bad to worse. The Russians
were taken to see a scene from *Can-Can*, the musical then in
production starring Maurice Chevalier and Shirley MacLaine.
It was the worst choice imaginable, a brassy, sexy dance scene
that reached a new low in vulgarity. It was bad enough with
Shirley MacLaine flaunting her legs and sheer black under-
things, but when the male dancer dived under her skirt and
emerged holding what seemed to be her red panties, the Americans in the audience gave an audible gasp of dismay, while

the Russians sat in stolid, disapproving silence. It was hopeless to try to explain to them that much of the sequence would be censored before the movie was released. It was evident that they considered the whole thing a perfect example of capitalist decadence. I could not begin to imagine how the movie moguls had made such a blunder.

Khrushchev's tantrum over Disneyland was mild compared to the explosion that occurred during the formal civic dinner that night. Before we sat down in the crowded Embassy Room of the Ambassador Hotel, Mayor Poulson asked me to look over the speech of introduction that he intended to give. I did, and could see nothing wrong with it. Cabot Lodge also read it. Poulson did say, addressing Khrushchev directly, "We shall not bury you, you shall not bury us." And he did warn him that, "if challenged, we shall fight to the death to preserve our way of life." But these seemed to me to be simple statements of fact that would be supported by any American. Certainly I was not prepared—no one was—for the Russian's reaction.

He gave his prepared speech. Then, suddenly crimson with fury, he lashed out at Poulson and at the whole United States. Given the lack of provocation, his outburst seemed almost insane. "It is a question of war or peace between our countries," he snarled, "a question of life or death!" For the first time during his visit, he rattled his rockets. They stood ready on their launching pads, he roared. He threatened to end his tour and go home. His plane was waiting; it could take him back to Russia in ten hours. And if he left, he shouted, he didn't know when, if ever, a Soviet Prime Minister might visit the United States again.

It was—as he intended it to be—a shocking performance, but I was convinced that that was what it was: a performance. Earlier that day, on the movie lot, a producer watching Khrushchev's Disneyland tirade had murmured, "Somebody here ought to hire him; he's the biggest ham actor in the world today." I agreed completely. Now the man was simply trying to frighten us, to project the image of a fierce and implacable enemy armed with overwhelming power. As for his threat to break off his visit and go home in a fire-breathing huff, I didn't take that seriously for a moment. Khrushchev might be many things, but he was no fool, and he was not going to relinquish the best propaganda platform he had ever dreamed of. As he ranted and raved the thought crossed my mind that it was a good thing for him to show his teeth occasionally—otherwise the American people might have been taken in by his clowning and his constant portrayal of himself as an earnest seeker after peace.

But this was not the general reaction. I believe that Henry Cabot Lodge was more alarmed than I. Some people, like Mayor Poulson, were simply angered. The Mayor hurried to Cabot as soon as Khrushchev sat down and demanded permission to read his introduction again. The Russian, he insisted, had deliberately misinterpreted and distorted what he had said. Cabot was afraid that this might just be throwing gasoline on the fire, and opposed it. So Poulson came to me. I have seldom seen a man so furious. If he weren't allowed to reread the portions of his talk that had set Khrushchev off, he said, the State Department would never again receive any cooperation from him as Mayor of Los Angeles. I told him to go ahead and reread it, if he wanted to—not that I thought it would make much difference. Khrushchev had simply used Poulson's introduction as an excuse to make the coldest and harshest statement of his tour. I was sure that if he hadn't used that pretext, he would have found another one.

The repercussions shook the State Department. Some thought the Russians really might pack up and go home. I felt that wild horses couldn't drag Khrushchev out of the country—and said so in a telephone conversation with Bob Murphy, Under-Secretary of State for Political Affairs, back in Washington. I understand that he quoted me next morning at the staff meeting in the State Department.

Later that evening Gromkyo sought me out. He said stiffly that something had to be done about speeches like the one Poulson had delivered. He said that the Russians could not tolerate such "inflammatory" remarks.

I was exasperated, and showed it. "Mr. Gromyko," I said, "in this country we have something called free speech. The United States government is not in the habit of trying to muzzle its citizens."

Gromyko knew perfectly well that his complaint was unjustified, and that in fact our government did not make a practice of silencing people. But he also descended on Cabot and I suppose on Foy and Llewellyn. The press was soon full of reports that the State Department had urgently requested local authorities in the cities on our itinerary not to disarrange Khrushchev's ruffled feathers any further. But this was not so. Later Jim Hagerty did remind the press of President Eisenhower's appeal to the nation to show good manners and restraint. But no one tried to muzzle anybody.

The next morning, on the train to San Francisco, our visitor at first was all smiles. He should have been—the train was magnificently equipped with a bar and a dining car serving marvelous food at all hours, including caviar that was better than the Russians'. But soon he was complaining again about the restrictions placed on his activities. He was under house arrest, he said; he could not go where he wanted to go. He thought this was supposed to be a free country. Why, in Russia anyone but a criminal could go anywhere he wanted. And so on.

I got more and more fed up with this. Finally, when the train made a brief stop in Santa Barbara, Khrushchev started grumbling to me again, saying that he wanted to get off.

"All right," I said to him. "Let's get off! We've only been thinking about your safety!"

A moment later, peering from his compartment window, Cabot Lodge was astounded to see the Russian leader and myself walking down the platform toward an equally astonished crowd of Californians. I'll never forget the look on Cabot's face. I thought he was going to jump through the window. Actually, he had reason to be concerned. Security men appeared from nowhere and surrounded us, but the crowd was surging through the barricade. It seemed a friendly crowd; even so, we had no way of knowing whether it might contain some fanatic whose intentions were anything but friendly. The Russian Secret Service men were in a tremendous flap; they kept shoving people away from Khrushchev, using a wicked kidney punch when their victim did not move quickly enough. This manhandling of American citizens by Soviet toughs was more than one of our security agents could stand. He whirled an elbow that caught the most obnoxious of the Russians under the chin and almost floored him. Our man was Leo Crampsey, a former Notre Dame football star, and when Leo hits someone, he knows it. In the confusion, Harrison Salisbury of *The New York Times* fell over a barrel while taking a picture and had to be rescued and put back on his feet. For several minutes a kind of mild pandemonium reigned, but Khrushchev seemed to enjoy it. "At last," he kept saying jovially, "I've got some freedom!"

A similar scene, not quite so chaotic, took place at the next stop, which was San Luis Obispo. Actually, Khrushchev's grumbling left us on the horns of a highly uncomfortable dilemma. If we kept him tightly buttoned up, he could complain that he was being treated like a prisoner, not a guest. On the other hand, if we gave him more "freedom," there was a very real chance that a catastrophe might occur. That was why his own security chief had turned thumbs down on the Disneyland visit. In the end, we just had to compromise and pray that the good sense and self-discipline of the American people would prevail.

The trip from Los Angeles to San Francisco took all day. As we passed Vandenberg Air Force Base, Khrushchev got a reminder that he had no monopoly on rockets; two giant missiles were clearly visible on their launching pads less than half a mile away. As the afternoon wore away, some of us took naps. Ruth had found that the best way to keep things going with the Russian women was to let them try to teach her Russian. By now they were quite proud of her progress, although there was much laughter over her mistakes—especially when she confused "I like you" with "I love you."

She was finding Julia the most likable member of the Khrushchev family. Underneath Mrs. Khrushchev's surface amiability, she said, there was a kind of coldness, and Rada remained rather aloof and distant. But Julia, while shy, seemed friendly and sincere.

It seemed ironic to me that San Francisco, in my opinion the most beautiful city in our nation, should give Khrushchev the warmest welcome, but it did. Perhaps to some extent this was organized by Communist elements. Perhaps the people felt that, since Los Angeles had given the Russian a hard time, they should give him an easy one. Anyway, the crowds waiting at the Mark Hopkins were noisily enthusiastic. I remember one well-dressed woman in the lobby clapping her gloved hands as we passed through. Someone must have looked askance at her, because I heard her say angrily, "Yes, I'm applauding—applauding the hope of peace in our time. If that's a crime, then I plead guilty to it!"

I escorted the Khrushchevs to their suite overlooking the city and the bay, one of the most magnificent views in the world. Then I went to set up our usual command post with a secretary and one or two members of my staff. One of our functions was to screen all telephone calls that came in to make sure that the VIPs were not troubled by cranks or publicity seekers. However, the first call that came through for Khrushchev in San Francisco was from the longshoremen's leader, Harry Bridges.

Mr. Bridges entertained Khrushchev at dinner that night. Here the Russian leader had a stormy time with some of the nation's top union officials. No members of our government were there; it was a private affair. George Meany, president of the AFL-CIO, refused to attend; he said he wouldn't be caught dead at a dinner for Khrushchev. But Walter Reuther, president of the United Auto Workers, Karl Feller, president of the United Brewery Workers, and others asked some pointed questions.

Some of them were too hot for Khrushchev to handle. When Feller asked him why so many workers fled from East Germany, the Russian snapped, "Go find the answer to that in your beer!" He became so angry with Reuther that he called him "a capitalistic stooge, a lackey." The Hungarian patriots crushed by Red Army tanks, he insisted, were "hooligans, saboteurs, fascists." Asked why he found it necessary to jam the Voice of America broadcasts or ban American cultural material, Khrushchev brought up the dance scene he had witnessed in Hollywood and performed a grotesque parody of it—surely the first cancan ever danced by a Russian Prime Minister in public. "We don't want that kind of trash in Russia," he shouted. "There should be a law against that sort of thing!" For once, it seemed to me, he had a point.

Twice he threatened to leave, but he didn't. For three and a half hours the rough-and-tumble debate went on. Finally Khrushchev emerged, flushed and sweating, and was taken to the world-famous cocktail lounge on the top of the Mark Hopkins where he could calm down and look at the jeweled panorama of the city by night. It was a view that reminded me of a classic remark I had once heard a visiting Asiatic potentate make when he first looked down from the hotel window at New York by night. "Ah," he said wistfully, "what a city to sack!"

The next day, Monday, September 21, the weather was perfect. Khrushchev went for an early morning walk and admitted that this was the handsomest city he had seen on his tour. Plans called for a morning boat ride around the Bay in a Coast Guard cutter, but on the way to the Navy Yard Khrushchev prevailed upon Cabot to stop by the headquarters of the International Longshore Workers Union. From that point on, security precautions began to fall apart. No one expected Khrushchev at the union hall so early, and only a few tough-looking characters with baling hooks in their belts were on hand. Undaunted, Khrushchev told them he would be back later. He was, too, and a cheering throng of about 500 longshoremen milled around him, giving him a rousing ovation while his security men looked grim. Delighted, the Russian traded his gray felt hat for a white cotton stevedore's cap, and made a short speech punctuated by cheers and applause. Mr. Bridges in particular seemed overjoyed.

Not everyone in San Francisco was so cordial. On our last night in town, as we were leaving the hotel after the civic dinner, a man shouted something in Russian at the Prime Minister. Khrushchev's aides shouted angrily back. I don't know what insults were exchanged, but a few days later I learned that the man, a Hungarian refugee, had been found badly beaten in one of San Francisco's side streets.

Meanwhile, Ruth and Emily Lodge were having their adventures with the distaff side of the Khrushchev family. Mrs. Khrushchev had expressed a desire to go shopping at Sears, Roebuck and Company. This seemed simple enough until the group, consisting of Rada, Julia, Mrs. Khrushchev, Mrs. Gromyko, Emily, and Ruth, arrived at Sears and found that the store didn't open until noon on Mondays. As they stood helplessly on the street corner, Ruth noticed just behind them a beautiful elementary school, brand-new, magnificently equipped. It took only a moment to secure permission to bring the unexpected visitors in and show them around. This impromptu tour was a great success. Mrs. Khrushchev, who had taught school once herself, was fascinated by the schoolbooks and classrooms. The school was completely integrated, white children sitting side by side with Negro or Chinese children. The whole thing was a splendid example of American democracy in action, and even the Russians sensed this. For once the Russians were impressed and admitted it.

From the school they went into Sears, open at last, where Mrs. Khrushchev seemed to thoroughly enjoy shopping for baby clothes, toys, and stockings. Rada and Julia were completely indifferent and obviously anxious for the shopping to end. Ruth was, if anything, more anxious for it to end, for she knew Mrs. Ambrose Diehl, the State Department's valuable and tireless assistant in San Francisco, was waiting patiently at Trader Vic's for the group to join her for luncheon. Finally my wife managed to get the ladies back to their cars; among those in her car was Mrs. Gromyko, who insisted that they should all go to the hotel for lunch. For once my gentle, quiet, and unperturbable wife decided the time had come to be firm. She told Mrs. Gromyko in no uncertain terms that they were now going to Trader Vic's to join Mrs. Diehl, who had already waited one hour for them, and *not* to the hotel.

At Trader Vic's we all went into a private dining room and had a delicious luncheon. The Russian ladies admitted they had more fun here than they had had on the entire trip. Ruth had learned, just as I had, that these people understand force better than politeness and indecision.

After lunch, we were followed by the ever-inquisitive press; so, instead of visiting a supermarket as planned, we settled for a drive across the Golden Gate Bridge and back to the hotel via Chinatown. Afterward, the ladies of the press begged for an interview with Mrs. Khrushchev, but as usual she simply smiled and refused to talk. Ruth was left to face the press and tried to give them an accurate account of the lady's day. What Ruth could never understand was why the press seemed so kind to Mrs. Khrushchev when actually she was one of the least cooperative visitors we ever had.

That night there was a tremendous banquet at the Sheraton-Palace Hotel. I was told that there were more than 1800 people in the main dining room, with 800 or 900 more in other dining rooms, watching the speakers on television. It was, in fact, the greatest turnout in the history of San Francisco. Khrushchev, in mellow mood, drew frequent applause from his audience. He praised California lavishly, comparing its golden sunshine to his own sunny Crimea. He even had a good word for the Scriptures. Universal brotherhood, he said, was a Biblical idea. "We have taken lots of Christ's precepts," he said cheerfully; "love thy neighbor, for instance." At this I wondered why the roof did not fall down on us all, but as a matter of fact Ruth and I had been astonished to note how often this salesman for atheism referred to the Deity. He was forever using such phrases as "God has been good to you" or "as God is my judge."

It was evident, as Khrushchev spoke, that he felt that finally his tour was going well, that at last he was getting a significant degree of acceptance. It seemed to me, ruefully pondering the whole situation, that his calculated rages had been successful; they had forestalled or eliminated certain shafts of criticism—legitimate criticism—that otherwise might have been hurled at him. Now he was playing the game on his own terms —and enjoying it.

The next morning, riding in an open blue convertible instead of a bulletproof limousine, Mr. Khrushchev drove to the airport. Before leaving he ordered a set of artificial fireplace logs like the ones in his hotel suite to be sent to Moscow. Evidently the mechanism that simulated flickering flames had fascinated him. At the airport our faithful Military Air Transport Service jet was waiting. Next stop: Iowa, where the tall corn grows.

We landed at Des Moines on a muggy Midwestern afternoon. Our jet must have come in cross-wind, because it was a rough landing—I didn't realize how rough until I saw it later on television. We bounced about ten feet and nearly hooked one wing into the runway.

Our main purpose in coming to Iowa was to allow Khrushchev to visit the farm of Roswell Garst, a wealthy and somewhat eccentric Iowan who had met the Prime Minister in Russia and had assured him that Iowan corn was the best in the world. Khrushchev rather fancied himself as an agricultural expert, and so plans called for a speech in Des Moines that night and a visit to the Garst farm in Coon Rapids (the name was early-American, all right) next day.

By now we were all getting pretty frazzled. Ruth showed signs of developing a monumental cold, and I could feel my own threshold of irritability getting lower by the minute. Even Khrushchev's boundless energy seemed to be waning a bit, although he was determined not to show it. "Are you tired?" a reporter asked him in Des Moines. "I have no right to be tired," the Russian said. "Life is too short!"

That afternoon we went through a meat-packing plant and an agricultural implement factory. At the packing plant,

Khrushchev was offered his first hot dog (it had been tested for radioactivity with a Geiger counter by an ultra-cautious security man), and seemed to enjoy it. "Capitalist," he boomed at Cabot Lodge, who also had one, "have you finished your sausage?" "Yes," said Cabot bravely, "we capitalists get hungry, too, you know."

We had a bomb scare at cocktail time that night. One of our security men quietly drew us aside and told us that a bomb had been reported in the dining room. The report was false, but we had to wait for our cocktails while the room was searched.

Khrushchev's meeting with Garst at the dinner that night was a photographer's delight. The chunky Russian spotted his friend and advanced upon him in a kind of wrestler's crouch, arms wide, grinning broadly. Garst arose and made a similar approach until finally they met in an embrace that reminded me of a couple of waltzing bears. At Garst's table was Adlai Stevenson, who was also to be a guest at the Garst farm the next day.

That night Khrushchev let his interpreter read his speech in English, making no attempt to deliver it himself in Russian. His interpreter, Oleg Tryanovsky, was a handsome, dark-haired young man who spoke English—including American colloquialisms—so perfectly that some members of our party wondered whether he might not be a renegade American who had assumed a Russian name. I rather doubted this, but was fairly sure that Mr. Tryanovsky was a highly trained espionage agent—in his spare time. My own interpreter, a Russian-speaking American named Akolovsky, was just as good and a great help in letting me know when Tryanovsky departed from what Khrushchev actually said.

Next morning, plans called for a 9 A.M. departure for Coon Rapids, but again, with their usual delight in disrupting schedules, the Russians decided they wanted to leave at 6:30. Henry Cabot Lodge was willing to humor them to the extent of leaving at 8:30, but I wasn't, as I knew that such disruptive changes made a shambles out of our security precautions.

Later on, I heard that the Russian Ambassador, Mikhail Menshikov, complained to some State Department officials that I wasn't accommodating enough. But I took this as a compliment.

In any case, the day began in a state of utter confusion, with Lodge and Khrushchev leaving at 8:30 and the rest of us following the official schedule. Life down on the farm turned out to be a combination picnic and circus. Khrushchev, in expansive mood, joked with Adlai Stevenson, complimented a gate-crasher on his massive midriff, told Garst how corn should be planted (he said Iowan corn stalks were too close together; Garst explained that Iowa had more rainfall than most parts of Russia, and hence could crowd its corn).

At one point, a remarkable dialogue between Khrushchev and Garst ran about as follows:

Khrushchev: "I must admit that you are very intelligent people, but it's also true that God has been very good to you."
Garst: "He's on our side."
Khrushchev: "You think God helps only you. He is helping us, too. God is on our side."
Garst: "We have a saying that God helps those who help themselves."
Khrushchev: "God helps the intelligent."

Listening to this exchange, I was reminded of Napoleon's observation: that, in war, God was on the side of the biggest battalions. At another point, Garst suggested that if the diplomats would just get out of the way, farmers like Khrushchev and himself could soon settle all the world's problems. The Russian nodded, and then noticed me watching them. "Excuse us," he said with an apologetic grin.

The food Garst gave us for lunch was excellent: fried chicken, spare ribs, apple pie. But the stampeding crowds of newsmen finally got on Khrushchev's nerves. He threw corncobs at some, and took an angry poke at a newspaperman. It all began to seem like the Mad Tea Party in *Alice in Won-*

derland, and I was glad when the time came to drive to the airport for our flight to Pittsburgh.

It was on this flight that Khrushchev seemed to abandon his actor's role for a few minutes. We were all relaxed, too tired to be formal. Khrushchev wandered out of the VIP compartment, and I asked him if he had enjoyed his stay in Iowa. Yes, he said, he had enjoyed it very much. Then he added pensively, "You know, I talk a lot about how in seven years we'll surpass your country. But that's not really true. You're far ahead of us. It will take us years to catch up. Years and years."

I was so startled by this admission that I could hardly believe my ears. I was afraid no one would believe me when I reported it, either, and so I beckoned to Jane Thompson, who was nearest to us, to come and listen, too. You had to give the man credit for one thing: he was totally unpredictable—tantrums, smiles, threats, jokes, boasts, lies, and now, for just a moment, an almost childlike candor.

We came over Pittsburgh just at dusk. All the lights of the "Golden Triangle" where the rivers come together had been left on, and we could see the orange fires of the steel mills glowing. It was a magnificent sight, full of the power and purpose of America, and I hoped Khrushchev took a good look at it.

In Pittsburgh, Khrushchev was given the key to the city—the first time this had happened. The next day we raced through another tight schedule that included a visit to the Mesta Machinery Company, lunch at the University of Pittsburgh, and a flight back to Washington barely in time for a crowded reception at the Russian Embassy. Among the 500 guests was Van Cliburn, the towering pianist, who got a big hug and kiss from his roly-poly host. Ruth brought Elsa Maxwell, who followed Van Cliburn through the receiving line. The Nixons arrived about midway through the party, and the Vice-President evidently thought the Russian looked weary. "How's your health?" he asked with some concern. "Fine," said Khrushchev with a smile, "did you think I had succumbed?" "No," said Nixon, "you have too much energy for that." The Premier patted his substantial stomach. "Like an iceberg," he said. "Partly hidden."

It was this "partly hidden" energy that carried him through still another dinner that night, and off to Camp David the next day for his talks with President Eisenhower. Separate plans were made for Mrs. Khrushchev while her husband was gone. Mrs. Nixon gave her a luncheon, Mrs. Herter gave her a dinner, and she gave a luncheon herself for the women who had accompanied her on the trip. She went to see Mount Vernon, and also inspected a dry-cleaning plant. "Dry cleaning doesn't really interest me very much," she said with a sigh. She visited a suburban home in Chevy Chase, and also asked to come to our house for tea.

Upon learning that Mrs. Khrushchev had asked to come to see our home, I immediately thought of what could be a rather sticky situation—this being that our butler was a Hungarian refugee whose wife was our cook and an East German refugee as well. Having a second man in the household and other maids who could pinch-hit, I spoke to the butler and asked him if he had any feelings about being on duty on this occasion. I offered to give him the day off and have the second man in charge. Without a moment's hesitation, he replied that he would be very glad to do whatever was expected of him, that it was just as hard on me as it was on him, and if I could do it, so could he.

"A pretty little house," Mrs. Khrushchev called it, "for a pretty little lady." Ruth was somewhat baffled by the compliment—our house has more than twenty rooms. It was a scorching hot afternoon, so she served iced tea, which apparently is unknown in Russia and which made a big hit. Mrs. Khrushchev drank two glasses. In fact, Julia told us later that her mother said the two American items she would most like to import into Russia were air-conditioned automobiles and iced tea.

For the first time in her life, while her husband was at Camp David, she finally agreed to hold a press conference. She met about twenty female reporters in the living room of the President's Guest House, and ended by revealing more about her private life than the people of Russia probably know. She first met Khrushchev, she said, at Stalino in the early 1920s when she was teaching an adult education class and he was studying mining and engineering. His first wife had died "in a famine," leaving two children: Julia, and a son Leonid, destined to be killed in action during World War II. She married Khrushchev in 1924 and bore him three children, Rada, Sergei, and Yelena, a Moscow University student who did not come along on the trip.

She and her husband lived in a big, state-owned house in Moscow, she said, and they also had a place in the country. They had a cook, a maid, and a waitress—all paid by the state. She didn't like housework (here the reporters applauded sympathetically) but did like gardening. All in all, she managed to convey an impression that had never varied from the moment of her arrival: a retiring, good-natured housewife who kept as far away from politics as possible. I must say, my own impression was that she was a shrewd, cold, hard-core Communist who was also an accomplished actress.

On Sunday night, the fantastic odyssey ended. Eight of us drove to the airport with the Russians: the Lodges, the Thompsons, the Kohlers, and ourselves. Meeting us there were the Nixons, the Herters, and others. Baggage from the Presidential Guest House had gone on ahead—in three Army trucks and three station wagons. All the women had been given bouquets of red roses. There were polite little speeches of farewell. Then the big TU-114 lumbered down to the end of the runway, turned, and hurled itself into the air.

Watching its lights fade into the darkness, I remember I had two distinct and conflicting feelings: one of foreboding, one of relief. The feeling of relief was understandable enough. Khrushchev was gone. He was out of our hands, off our necks. Nobody had assassinated him. Nobody had even tried. There had been no major incidents. This in itself was remarkable—and a great tribute to our security people.

But along with the relief was a chilly premonition that the whole purpose behind the Khrushchev visit was going to be negated. It was evident to me that the invitation to Khrushchev had not been issued because of a wistful hope that such a visit might change his attitude or bring about a thaw in the cold war. It had been issued, as a calculated risk, because we wanted our President to visit Russia. We wanted Ike, with all his honesty and warmth and charm, to be seen and welcomed by the Russians. We believed that if he could appear in Moscow or Stalingrad or Leningrad or anywhere, nothing could prevent him from reaching over the heads of the Communist leaders to the Russian people themselves. We were hoping for genuine demonstrations of admiration, the kind we had seen the President receive in other European capitals. That was what we were counting on. That was what would make all the exasperations and dangers of the Khrushchev tour worthwhile.

But would we get it? Not if the Russians were as clever as I knew them to be. Why should they take such a chance? Why should they permit a situation to arise in which the head of a hated capitalistic government might prove to be embarrassingly popular inside their own boundaries? Khrushchev had had what he wanted: thirteen days in the citadel of freedom, thirteen days of unmatched opportunities for propaganda and psychological warfare. Why should he give anything in return?

The night sky was empty now, except for stars. The other members of the farewell party were heading for their cars. Suddenly I felt very tired. The President's invitation to Moscow still stood. Plans for his visit would go forward. There had even been talk of his taking his grandchildren. But I was convinced that the visit would never take place. Something would come up, something that could be used as an excuse to prevent it. Or if there was no legitimate excuse, the Russians would invent one. . . .

I walked dispiritedly back to my car. I felt, suddenly, like a very small pawn on the great chessboard of international power politics. The United States had made its move on that board; we had proved our willingness to take a calculated risk, to gamble. But a cold voice whispered in my ear, "You are going to lose the gamble. You're going to lose. You're going to lose. . . ."

And in the end, of course, we did lose.

II   Protocol—Oil on Troubled Waters

What does the Chief of Protocol do? What is protocol, anyway? What is this mysterious area of government, and how does it work?

The derivation of the word itself is interesting. It comes from two Greek words: *protos*, meaning "the first," and *kolla*, meaning (of all things) "glue." In ancient Greece, a *protokollon* was a summary of the contents of a roll of papyrus. It was glued to the first leaf of the roll, rather like the title page of a book. So the idea of being "glued on first," or of taking precedence, still survives.

Protocol, to attempt a simple definition, is the method by which nations conduct their affairs with one another in an orderly fashion. And this is highly important. As the late John Foster Dulles once said, years of patient work in diplomacy can be negated by one social blunder, or one unintentional slight based on carelessness or ignorance. Over the centuries, therefore, a body of accepted practices has been evolved, designed to avoid friction and misunderstanding and promote an atmosphere of friendliness and courtesy. As this nation's stature in world affairs has grown, so has the importance of protocol, until today, with a constant stream of world leaders coming to Washington and thousands of foreign officials in our capital, protocol has become a key factor in the conduct of foreign affairs.

This importance is reflected in the fact that the Chief of Protocol, appointed by the White House, has a personal rank of Ambassador and an official rank of Assistant Secretary of

State. He is responsible only to the President, the Vice-President, and the Secretary of State. He is the first person officially to meet every foreign Ambassador accredited to the United States and often becomes that Ambassador's chief point of contact with our government. Chiefs of Protocol frequently find that ambassadors are much more direct and candid in discussing confidential matters with them than with the appropriate Assistant Secretary or even with the Secretary of State himself. This is because the ambassadors feel that every word they say on the official level must be weighed very carefully, while with the Chief of Protocol they can establish a more relaxed and intimate relationship.

When the President of the United States invites another Head of State or Foreign Minister to visit this country, again the first person to greet such people is the Chief of Protocol. He is the individual on whom the visitor relies for every sort of information and guidance. It is his function to attend the VIP during every phase of his visit, travel with him, get him to all meetings, make certain he knows the names and identities of every person he will encounter. The old adage, "You don't know a person until you have traveled with him," certainly applies to the relationship between the Chief of Protocol and these visitors. When you are with a person day after day from 9 in the morning until midnight or later, it stands to reason that you will know more about that person than those who see him only around the conference table or at some official luncheon or dinner. Conversely, the impression that the Chief of Protocol makes on the visitor is equally important.

Most of us in the Protocol Division were always wryly aware that in the minds of a good many people a protocol expert is a semi-comic figure in striped pants who spends his time figuring out who should precede whom through a doorway and where dignitaries sit at dinner. And as a matter of fact, this *was* one of our less-important functions. But most people in government now realize that the Chief of Protocol must be primarily an expert in human relations—and that very often the prestige of the United States depends on how he conducts himself.

In past centuries, protocol concerned itself mainly with the elaborate etiquette of European courts. Traditionally, Americans shy away from official pomp and glitter, and so for the first 125 years of this country's existence, the State Department had no protocol department. There were practically no state visits as they are known today, due to the length of time it took to travel between countries. Generally, when ceremonial officers were needed they were appointed from the Foreign Service ranks and represented the United States at various types of functions. The most noted among them was the late Robert Woods Bliss. As early as 1920 he was our country's official representative during the visit of the Prince of Wales to San Diego. Immediately following this visit, Mr. Bliss became the Chief of the Division of Western European Affairs, but in 1922 Mr. Bliss again assumed the position of Director of Matters relating to Ceremonies and Protocol. In 1923, when he became Ambassador to Sweden, protocol functions were once more assigned on a day-to-day basis.

Then on February 4, 1928, the Division of Protocol was formally established. Those listed below are the officers serving in what is known today as the Chief of Protocol.

Robert Woods Bliss 1920,	1922	Richard Southgate	1935
James C. Dunn	1928	George T. Summerlin	1937
F. Lammot Belin	1930	Stanley Woodward	1946
Warren Delano Robbins	1931	John Farr Simmons	1950
James C. Dunn	1934	Wiley T. Buchanan, Jr.	1957
	Angier Biddle Duke	1961	

When I became Chief of Protocol I found that the organization of my department was quite simple. Below the Chief were two Deputy Chiefs who could represent him when necessary or run the office in his absence. The department, staffed by some forty experts, was divided into five sections, each with a name that indicated its function.

The Visit Section was concerned with matters of ceremony such as dedications, state funerals, presentation of national gifts, greetings for visiting heads of state, and so on.

There was the Ceremonial Section that arranged for the presentation of letters of credence for ambassadors and ministers, acted on matters concerning diplomatic immunity, and arranged social functions for the Secretary of State and other high-ranking department officials.

There was the Courtesies and Privileges Section that arranged for customs courtesies and free-entry privileges for foreign officials, issued diplomatic license plates and handled the visits of foreign naval vessels.

There was the Accreditation Section, which determined the acceptability of personnel in the diplomatic missions in Washington. Once, I remember, we held up the accreditation of an Ambassador from Latin America because there were indications that he was a Communist. It turned out, finally, that he simply had the same name as a well-known Communist in his own country. But until we had this assurance from the FBI, we refused to approve him. This section also prepared various diplomatic lists and maintained custody of awards, gifts, and decorations conferred upon American officials by foreign governments until such time as they were legally entitled to receive them—usually after they had left government service.

Finally there was the Administrative Section, which acted on administrative and fiscal matters. It was also responsible for the operation of the President's Guest House, where distinguished foreign guests were usually housed during their stay in Washington. The Administrative Section had to cope with such touchy matters as the cost of state visits, the endless bills for entertaining of one sort or another, and the always-controversial liquor funds.

Every year I had to appear before the House Appropriations Committee to be questioned about my budget requests. The chairman of this all-important committee was Representative John Rooney of New York. Congressman Rooney was often pictured in the press as a fire-eating dragon where State Department funds were concerned—a dragon who became particularly sulfurous about money spent on liquor. But I must say that whenever I went before Congressman Rooney, which

I did on several occasions, I found him to be extremely fair, reasonable, and courteous in every way.

There are, of course, many stratagems in this business of asking for money and then defending your budget against the assaults of economy-minded Congressmen. Secretary Dulles once told me of the time when he found himself being pressed rather hard on some complicated point. "I had a formidable-looking brief case with me," he said, "and I showed it to my questioners. 'Gentlemen,' I said solemnly, 'if we are going into this matter I think we should do it properly. I have some material in this brief case, and if you will allow me to consult it I think I may be able to explain the matter to your satisfaction but it will take two or three hours.' Of course, the Congressmen did not relish the thought of sitting there all afternoon, so they waived the question. They never knew that all I had in the brief case was a couple of whodunits and a bottle of Listerine!"

As Chief of Protocol, I administered the oath of office to all State Department appointees and other Presidentially appointed delegations. I also had to accompany each new Ambassador to the White House when he presented his credentials to President Eisenhower.

In some countries, the accreditation of a new Ambassador is an occasion of great pomp and circumstance. He may find himself in a gold coach drawn by six or eight horses with liveried footmen standing behind, or in a royal barge being rowed down a river to some palace where the Head of State awaits him. We Americans do it more casually, but—as I must have pointed out five thousand times during my four years as Chief of Protocol—we try to make up in friendliness what we lack in formality.

Soon after a new Ambassador arrived it was my duty to present him to our Secretary of State. This was quite informal; the new Ambassador would usually join me at my office and we would go to see the Secretary, taking with us a copy of the letter of credence that the Ambassador would ultimately hand to President Eisenhower. This was so that an appropriate reply could be prepared by the State Department for the President's signature.

On the appointed day, I would take one of the White House limousines, make sure that it was flying the flag of the Ambassador's country as well as the flag of the United States, drive to the Embassy with a motorcycle escort, and pick up the new envoy. Sometimes this was quite early in the morning. The Ambassador might be in colorful native costume or a plain business suit. With him he always had three large white envelopes. One contained his letter of credence, in which his Head of State in rather high-flown language attested to his worth as a representative of his country. The others contained a letter of recall for his predecessor and a letter of remarks that might contain any message that his government wanted to convey. On more than one occasion, in our country and in others, these envelopes were empty—the harassed envoy having forgotten his credentials in his excitement.

Three corresponding letters, also in white envelopes, would be waiting on the desk of the President's appointment secretary, just outside the President's office. We always arrived about five minutes early. At the appointed time we would be admitted to the President's oval office with its big desk, green rug, and comfortable chairs. I would present the Ambassador to the President, the letters would be formally exchanged, and then the President and the new envoy would talk informally for a few minutes.

Sometimes a new Ambassador would suffer an attack of stage fright and find himself with nothing to say. On one such occasion, I remember, despite the President's valiant efforts, the silences grew longer and longer. Finally I recalled hearing the visitor say that he had met and admired the President's brother, Milton Eisenhower. In desperation, I threw this idea out like a lifeline, and with marvelous results. The President's eyes lit up, the ice was broken, and they proceeded to talk animatedly for perhaps twenty minutes.

Theoretically, no serious business was supposed to be discussed at these initial meetings, but if the conversation progressed beyond pleasantries it was my responsibility to remember what was said and file a report later. Once, I remember, one new Ambassador hurled himself into a complicated and somewhat controversial topic and refused to be stopped. President Eisenhower suggested several times that he take the matter up with the proper people at the State Department, but he went doggedly on. In the end, I practically had to drag him away, still babbling, while over my shoulder I could see the President shaking his head with a look of patient resignation on his face.

American ambassadors presenting their credentials to foreign nations invariably wear full dress—white tie and tails—no matter what the time of day. Years ago, when knee breeches were part of the traditional costume for our Ambassador to wear to Buckingham Palace for the ceremony, our outspoken Ambassador-designate, Charles G. Dawes, caused a mild furor by announcing that he wouldn't wear them—and didn't. I always liked the story of the man at a White House reception who was criticizing Dawes' action rather vehemently to a lady he had just met. Why hadn't Dawes been willing to follow tradition, he wanted to know; such independence was absurd, and so on.

"Sir," said the lady, fixing him with a gimlet eye, "do you know who I am?"

"No."

"I am Mrs. Dawes!"

A moment of startled silence. Then:

"Madam, do you know who I am?"

"No!"

"Thank heaven! Good-by!"

Probably the most hilarious moment I encountered in any accreditation ceremony (there were perhaps fifteen or twenty a year) was one I shared with Tom Stevens, the President's appointment secretary. Even now, I never hear anyone refer to the "emerging" nations of Africa without a secret smile.

On this particular morning I had escorted the brand-new Ambassador of a brand-new African nation to the White House to present his credentials. He was wearing his colorful African robes, and kept rearranging them rather nervously as we waited in the outer office for the President to receive us.

I was not aware of anything amiss until I happened to look at Tom Stevens and saw on his face the most extraordinary expression: amazement, incredulity, almost uncontrollable mirth.

I followed his glance and saw that in his agitation His Excellency had hoisted the rear of his robes until they were almost up to his waist—and that under them he was wearing no more than a Scotsman wears under a kilt!

Mercifully, the robes descended a bit before we were ushered into the President's office, but Tom was still crimson in the face and almost exploded again as we came out. And from then on the mere mention of "emerging" nations was enough to send either of us off. It certainly helped, I might add, to have a man with a sense of humor outside the office where so many grave and serious questions were settled. Tom's successor, Bob Gray, was just as delightful a person as he was. Later he became a very efficient secretary to the Cabinet.

After each of these ceremonies, photographers would descend on us, clamoring for pictures, and newsmen would ask if anything significant had been discussed (we always said no, whether it had or not); then we would drive back to the Embassy and usually celebrate with champagne. Sometimes it would not yet be 9 o'clock, but more than once politeness decreed that I polish off a bottle of champagne with the new Ambassador and then totter off in search of my morning coffee.

The endless parade of ambassadors gave me fascinating glimpses into the complexities and contrasts of our rapidly shrinking world. Early one morning, I remember, I presented the envoy from a new African state to the President and then returned with him to his Embassy for the ceremonial bottle of champagne. The building had been the home of Franklin D. Roosevelt when he served as Secretary of the Navy. I mentioned this to the Ambassador, who was a handsome and attractive man, soft-spoken, with thoughtful, penetrating eyes.

"Yes," he said, "I know. And I'm so proud to have this house that I'd have urged our government to buy it even if it had been falling down." Which, I might add, it almost was!

There was almost no furniture in the place, and he apologized for this, saying that he was in the process of acquiring some.

"You must have beautiful native wood in your country," I said. "Why don't you have your furniture made of that? Or use it to panel some of these rooms? It would be distinctive and appropriate, don't you think?"

He agreed that it would. Then, sipping his champagne reflectively, he began to reminisce about his childhood. His family, he said, lived right at the edge of the jungle. There were so many children that he could slip away for days at a time and never be missed. "I used to love the jungle," he said. "I knew just about every tree in it. Sometimes I'd climb up and spend the night in one of those trees. I wasn't the least bit frightened." He smiled with a flash of white teeth. "It wasn't until I became civilized and lived in England, France, and the United States, and saw some of those jungle movies that I became frightened. Now I'd be afraid to go into the jungle at all!"

I smiled, too, but I couldn't help thinking of the fantastic transition that had brought this man, in one short lifetime, from a jungle treetop to Franklin Roosevelt's former home.

One of the things about Washington that never failed to astonish me was how often you'd find people from very primitive societies or nations dealing with problems of staggering complexity. One night, I remember, a Far Eastern delegate to a top-level monetary conference told me that he had never worn shoes in his life until he came to the United States. He described the little village where he had been born; apparently it had not changed in hundreds of years. He described the house where he grew up, a sort of grass hut on stilts. Yet here was this man influencing the disposition of not just millions, but billions of dollars.

I couldn't resist exposing him to the little visual financial shocker that I sometimes used to impress visitors to Washington. It goes like this:

A million dollars in thousand-dollar bills makes a stack of currency approximately eight inches high.

A *billion* dollars in thousand-dollar bills would make a stack of currency 111 feet higher than the Washington Monument—which is 555 feet high!

It's an effective little dramatization, I've found, for people (including perhaps a few Congressmen) who think that a billion isn't really much more than a million!

Sometimes several weeks might pass without my having to escort a new Ambassador to the White House. Then three or four accreditations might be scheduled close together. The date on which an Ambassador presented his credentials determined his precedence thereafter in all official functions attended by the Washington diplomatic corps—a firm and sensible yardstick that saved a lot of trouble.

There were times, especially in my early days as Chief of Protocol, when I felt that we really ought to make our accreditation ceremony a little more impressive. I also thought that it would be much appreciated if somehow the wives of the new envoys could be presented to Mrs. Eisenhower. This never worked out. I did persuade the White House, for a time, to have one of the President's military aides, resplendent in uniform, greet the new envoy when he came to present his credentials. But in the end even this small gesture was abandoned. The truth was that since our Chief Executive was both Head of Government and Head of State, he simply didn't have the time for elaborate ceremony, whereas in other countries where the two functions are separate, more attention can be paid to such formalities.

Another function of the Protocol Division is to be custodian of the official State Department list of precedence. For years—for centuries, I suppose—it has been the American fashion to poke gentle fun at such rules, partly because there is a democratic instinct in most Americans that balks at the notion of one individual being considered superior to another and treated accordingly. We smile, nowadays, when we read of the Congress of Vienna, attended by several European monarchs, where an equivalent number of doors had to be cut in the grand salon where they met so that all could enter simultaneously.

But precedence is actually a very necessary thing, and we use it all the time. In our society, the problem of who should go through doors first has been settled by awarding this privilege to ladies, and it saves a lot of trouble. A junior Army officer will enter an automobile ahead of a senior one, so that on arrival the ranking officer may emerge first. At the family dinner table the father and the mother usually have established places; so do the children in many homes. In an airplane, the copilot always sits on the right, the pilot on the left. And so on. Nobody has to waste time making decisions about such things; they are already made.

In international diplomacy, precedence becomes a matter of great importance because the dignity and honor not only of individuals but of sovereign nations are involved. An Ambassador from a foreign country represents the Chief of State of that country, and since very ancient times has been accorded extraordinary privileges. He is immune to arrest. He is exempt from local taxes. His communications with his own country may not be tampered with or cut off. Such rights were officially established by the Congress of Vienna in 1815, but they are much older, dating back to the grim days when ambassadors were likely to find themselves beheaded if the actions of their own nation displeased the ruler to whom they were accredited.

An Ambassador, therefore, is a semi-sacred person who holds very high rank on the precedence list of the country which has received him as an envoy. In the United States, an accredited Ambassador from any country is outranked only by our President, the Vice-President, the Speaker of the House of Representatives, and the Chief Justice of the Supreme Court. In the line of guests being presented to some important personage at a formal reception, the Ambassador from, say, Costa Rica would take precedence over an American Cabinet member or an American Senator, although these gentlemen also hold high positions on the list. If there were several ambassadors in the line, they would be ranked (as I have said) according to the date of their accreditation to the United States. First come, first served—as simple as that.

When I took office as Chief of Protocol, there were only three copies of the State Department's precedence list. The White House had one, the Secretary of State had one, and I had one. There were forty-seven categories, beginning with the President and ending with "subordinate government officials." Only the President had authority to make changes. The reason for this semi-secrecy was to avoid the necessity for endless explanation and to discourage people from requesting changes or expressing dissatisfaction with their position on the list.

I say "semi-secrecy," because through the years the substance of the list had leaked out to the press. At one point, before I took office, *The New York Times* published the whole thing. And various social registers have more or less accurate versions.

Thus any worried Washington hostess could call the Protocol Office and find out whether a vice-admiral would take precedence over a Washington bishop (yes, by two categories!). The Chief of Protocol, I found, was ranked in category 25, along with Deputy Under-Secretaries of State and ambassadors of career rank of the United States. I was always faintly startled to find myself taking precedence over four-star generals and admirals (category 27), but that was the rule—according to protocol.

Changes in the order are made from time to time. When the Democratic administration replaced the Republican one in 1960, the Speaker of the House was moved up to Category 3 and Chief Justice was moved down to Category 4. I don't know what the reason was, but I don't imagine the Chief Justice was very happy about it—most dignitaries are quite jealous of their prerogatives. And sometimes the established order does seem a little out of balance. A foreign Ambassador, for example, outranks our own Secretary of State. This seemed so preposterous to President Eisenhower that sometimes he would avoid inviting Secretary Dulles to functions where the foreign ambassadors would take precedence over him.

In Washington, where over 100 chiefs of mission are now in residence, the diplomat with the longest continuous accreditation is known as the Dean of the Diplomatic Corps, a distinction held at present by the Nicaraguan Ambassador, Sr. Guillermo Sevilla-Sacasa, a delightful man with an equally charming wife. The Vice-Dean is Sr. Fernando Berkemeyer, Ambassador from Peru, who with his American wife Clarabel has added much to the Washington scene.

The Chief of Protocol alone does not make changes in the precedence list, but he is the first to feel the pressure for such changes. I remember when Secretary Dulles died, and Christian Herter became Secretary of State, he wanted to make use of the services of Charles E. ("Chip") Bohlen, a well-known authority on Russia. So Mr. Bohlen was appointed special assistant to the Secretary of State.

Special assistants to the President have fairly high rank, but special assistants to a Cabinet member do not. Mr. Bohlen had served as our Ambassador to Russia and to the Philippines, and of course at that time had held very high rank indeed. So Secretary Herter wrote me a penciled note asking if something couldn't be done to improve Mr. Bohlen's order of precedence. I had to reply that there was nothing I could do about it.

Later Mr. Bohlen was made a career Ambassador, which gave him an established rank. But then I got another request from Douglas Dillon, Acting Secretary of State, to have Mr. Bohlen's position improved still more.

This time I passed the request along to General Andrew Goodpaster, one of the President's top advisors, for President Eisenhower's attention and decision. I didn't have to wait long. The answer was a very firm and final "No."

On one other occasion I had a similar but gentler request. Senator Walter George of Georgia, a great Southern statesman much beloved in Washington, finally retired from the Senate but agreed to serve as special assistant to the Secretary of

State. Technically, then, his rank as Senator (category 11) disappeared. One day I had a phone call from Mrs. George. She said that the Senator would be very cross with her if he knew about her call, but that many of their friends were indignant because her husband was still serving the government, but now had practically no rank at all. What, she wanted to know, should she say to them?

I had to tell Mrs. George that the laws of precedence could not be altered to suit individual cases. But I also told her I was sure that almost every member of the government and many members of the diplomatic corps would gladly yield precedence to her distinguished husband on any occasion without even being asked . . . and to tell her friends that I had said so.

As Chief of Protocol, it was my job to know personally every member of the diplomatic corps and be able to introduce them on state occasions to the President or the Secretary of State or the guest of honor, whoever he might be. I would stand in the receiving line and present each individual as he came along in the proper order of precedence, husbands preceding wives, unless the wife was the VIP. Most of the time my memory for names and faces was reasonably good, but once in a while my mind would go totally blank—a horrid feeling. Usually, if the owner of the approaching face was a good diplomat, he would see my distress and supply his name—and then tease me about it later. If he failed to do this, I just had to fall back on a polite but vague, "Mr. Ambassador."

Actually, most people moving along a receiving line don't hear anything anyway; they are too interested in gazing at the celebrity or celebrities they are about to meet. I remember one classic example of this when I was Ambassador to Luxembourg. We were giving a reception at the Embassy, and I was in the receiving line with Ruth on my right, and beyond her General Anthony McAuliffe, the hero of the Battle of the Bulge. In the line of guests was a little man who looked so bewildered that I was sure he had blundered into the reception by mistake. Dan Gaudin, my minister-counselor of the Embassy, a very able Foreign Service officer with a great sense of humor, was introducing the guests to me. Dan obviously didn't know the man and murmured, "Mr. Ambassador, this is Mr. God-knows-who!" I shook this "distinguished guest" warmly by the hand and turned to Ruth. "This," I said, "is Mr. God-knows-who!" She shook his hand and turned to McAuliffe. "General," I heard her say, "this is Mr. God-knows-who!" Mr. God-knows-who vanished down the line, but I'm sure he didn't hear a single word we said and I know he had a fine time at the reception, because he got gloriously squiffed and was the last to leave.

I never knew whether Mr. God-knows-who was a gate-crasher or not. All embassies, to a greater or lesser degree, have this problem. Small functions can be controlled, but at large ones there are always uninvited people who filter in and mingle with the crowd. Sometimes these are uninvited reporters looking for a story, sometimes adventurous souls who simply want to brag about their exploit later.

A few "crashers" are simply odd. There is one woman in Washington who attends practically all Embassy receptions whether invited or not. She invariably makes her way to the refreshments, fills a paper bag with food, and puts it carefully into her handbag. When not so engaged, she chats animatedly with the guests, switching to flawless French or Spanish when necessary. Her conduct might be understandable if she actually needed the food to live on, but at one point she gave a luncheon herself and I was told that it was beautifully prepared and served—quite lavish, in fact, and attended by many ambassadors' wives and dignitaries.

In the past, Washington has seen some blazing feuds over the question of precedence. The most famous, perhaps, was the one between Dolly Gann and Alice Roosevelt Longworth. Dolly Gann was sister of Vice-President Curtis and acted as his hostess. She claimed that this entitled her to precedence over Mrs. Longworth, who was wife of the Speaker of the House of Representatives and, of course, the daughter of a former President. I never understood, myself, how the sister of a dignitary could share his rank at all, and consequently would have ruled—had I been Chief of Protocol and had anyone asked me—in favor of Mrs. Longworth. But most Washington hostesses simply ducked the issue by being careful not to invite the two ladies to the same function.

Mistakes, of course, are made—some by accident, some perhaps by design. Not long ago at a dinner the hostess, more patriotic than polite (since I'm sure she knew better), planned to seat Adlai Stevenson, our Ambassador to the United Nations, above Herve Alphand, the French Ambassador. M. Alphand glanced at the seating plan for the dinner, and announced firmly that unless it was changed to conform with protocol, he would leave. His personal feelings, he said, were not important at all—but the prestige and dignity of France were very important. The seating arrangements were changed. A U.S. Ambassador ranks below a foreign Ambassador to the U.S. in protocol. But this was compounded by the fact that Stevenson was our Ambassador to the UN and France was no great admirer of that institution.

On another occasion, while dining in an American Embassy overseas, I saw someone come up during the first course and whisper to the hostess that she had made a mistake in her seating arrangements. Much flustered, she apologized for her error, and asked the two persons concerned to change places —which they did at the end of the first course. I always thought she would have done better to ignore the situation and apologize afterward. It would have saved embarrassment all around.

Such social crises are mild compared to some of the quarrels over precedence that used to flare up in past centuries. In 1661, for instance, France and Spain nearly went to war because of an incident in England. The British sovereign drove to the docks of London to meet the Swedish Ambassador. As the royal coach left the waterfront, the coach of the French Ambassador tried to take the place directly behind it. The retinue of the Spanish Ambassador took this as an insult, attacked the French party with swords, and took the second place in line. In Paris, Louis XIV was so enraged when he heard about the incident that he ousted the Spanish Ambassador and threatened war unless his envoys were granted precedence at foreign courts.

About a hundred years later, at a court ball in London, the French and Russian ambassadors quarreled so violently over precedence that they drew their swords and the Russian was wounded. It was largely to prevent such incidents and the serious consequences that could result from them that a body of common procedures and practices was developed into a generally accepted system of ceremonial rules.

The Protocol Division has many other functions, one of which is to determine policy and take necessary action regarding cases of diplomatic immunity in the United States. All foreign diplomats, their families, and even their servants are exempt from most taxes and are immune from arrest, unless they agree to waive that immunity. Now and then this causes a furor when some individual breaks a law or behaves badly and seems to be getting away with it. At one point, during my tour of duty as Chief of Protocol, the son of the Irish Ambassador was involved in a traffic fatality. The car he was driving killed a pedestrian, a colored woman. The boy had a record of previous offenses. The Ambassador and the boy attended the funeral, but when I asked the father if he would waive his son's diplomatic immunity, I got a flat refusal. The Ambassador, in fact, seemed highly indignant over the way the police and the press had handled the matter. It was a sticky situation, but there was nothing we could do about it—short of declaring the boy *persona non grata*, which we were reluctant to do in such a case. Fortunately, within a few weeks the Ambassador and his wife returned to Ireland for a visit and took their son with them. The boy did not return to the United States.

Once, I remember, my office got word that a murder had taken place in the Iraqi Embassy. Two domestics had gotten into a quarrel, and one had killed the other. Here again, the Washington police had no jurisdiction; the Embassy was technically foreign soil. So no action was taken; the Iraqi handled the matter themselves.

On another occasion in New York, a Polish diplomat was found with a .38-caliber pistol in his possession for which he had no permit. An American citizen would have been fined or perhaps even sent to jail, but since the man was covered by diplomatic immunity, the police simply issued him a permit. Illegal parking is an offense that is quite common, the traffic tickets simply being sent to the State Department to be "fixed" —which they always are. Incidentally, if an American is injured by a foreign diplomat's car, he cannot sue for damages unless the diplomat happens to be insured and is willing for the insurance company to pay. There have been such cases where the diplomat ordered his insurance company not to pay—and there was nothing the victim could do about it.

Occasionally there are incidents in which foreign diplomats become drunk or disorderly—and get away with it. On one such occasion, a pair of envoys from behind the Iron Curtain were jailed by an irate Midwestern sheriff. When the State Department told him to release them, he refused—until informed that Title 22 of the United States Code (which dates back to 1790) makes any officer or individual liable to a three-year jail term if he dares to "imprison or offer violence" to persons with diplomatic status. There was a similar case in New Jersey when the seventeen-year-old son of the Pakistani Ambassador refused to appear in court on a charge of reckless driving. In this case the Chief of Police threatened to march on the Ambassador's summer home and drag the boy into court —but Title 22 stopped him.

Of course, this sort of protection works both ways. There was an American Ambassador in a European country who, hearing a noise on a shed outside his Embassy window, fired three shots at the "prowler" and killed the son of a prominent labor leader. The boy was paying a romantic visit to one of the Embassy maids. Feeling ran high, and things might have gone hard with our Ambassador had he not been protected by diplomatic immunity.

There are probably some 5000 persons in Washington and another 2000 or 3000 assigned to the United Nations in New

York who enjoy diplomatic immunity. Occasionally it is suggested that full immunity be limited only to top-ranking envoys and withdrawn from their families or servants. But the State Department usually opposes such proposals. Laws and punishments vary from country to country; penalties in other countries for minor crimes can be much more severe than ours, and we do not want any of our people at the mercy of judicial systems that may differ greatly from our own.

Of course, a great deal of spying goes on under the cloak of diplomatic immunity—and a good deal of smuggling, too. But if this becomes too blatant, the culprit can be declared *persona non grata*—or a quiet word to his government may lead to his recall. This happened in the case of Guy Burgess, who finally defected to the Russians. At one point, he was secretary to the British Embassy in Washington, but he was recalled to London in 1951 after we passed along to the British complaints about his reckless driving.

Diplomatic immunity at times may seem to protect the guilty, but it is a two-way street, and since the United States has more diplomatic personnel abroad than any other nation with the possible exception of Russia, we probably gain more than we lose.

Any nation, of course, may declare a foreign diplomat *persona non grata*—highly undesirable and unwelcome—and have him recalled. But sometimes just the threat of this is sufficient. I remember one Ambassador from behind the Iron Curtain who made insistent and unreasonable demands about a certain matter, and kept on making them after our State Department considered the matter closed. President Eisenhower told me in rather picturesque language that his patience was running low, and to convey this to the Ambassador. So I informed His Excellency that our official position was clear and final, and that if he did not subside, drastic action would have to be taken. I didn't spell out what the "drastic action" would be, but he got the message and gave us no more trouble.

All governments, of course, have various ways of indicating their regard, or lack of it, for another government. As Chief of Protocol, I always had to attend the receptions given by the various embassies on their National Day (we have such receptions ourselves, at our embassies all over the world, on the Fourth of July). But the State Department would also send other representatives, and the higher the rank of this representative, the more cordial the attitude of our government was judged to be. If relations were very good, the representative might be the wife of the Secretary of State, or an Under-Secretary of State or his wife. If they were very cool, we might send some very minor member of the department. This sort of diplomatic signaling goes on all the time.

It was the policy of Secretary Dulles, and of Secretary Herter after him, not to attend these national-day functions. There were just too many of them, and the Secretary of State is too busy. However, in every instance that I can remember, Janet Dulles and "Mac" Herter faithfully attended every gathering where they were supposed to represent their distinguished husbands. Equally faithful was Phyllis Dillon, wife of Under-Secretary of State Douglas Dillon and one of the most attractive women in Washington. The Senate had diligent representatives in Mrs. John Sherman Cooper and Mrs. William Fulbright. Lorraine and Betty were always on hand, rain or shine.

Sometimes the women would make three or four such appearances in an afternoon, always with the greatest good humor and charm. If Ruth and I met them, they would say, "Well, have you done such-and-such a national day yet?" These wives were always beautifully dressed, with lovely and appropriate jewelry, and I wish more people realized how hard such women work in the service of their country.

Sometimes relations with a given country could become very chilly indeed. Once, I remember, the chief security officer of another nation actually threatened our chief security officer. If anything happened to his Chief of State while visiting the U.S.A., he declared, he would see to it that some American throats were cut. When this insolence was relayed to our State Department, Bob Murphy—our Under-Secretary of State for Political Affairs—called the Ambassador of that country into his office, gave him a tongue-lashing, and received an apology. I was glad to see us get tough, since sometimes I felt that our good humor and tolerance were interpreted, not as a willingness to cooperate, but as a sign of weakness.

The most publicized function of the Protocol Division, of course, is to welcome and arrange for the entertainment of distinguished foreign guests. During his eight years in office, President Eisenhower received visits from 128 kings, queens, presidents, and prime ministers—quite a change from the placid days of 1937 when there was exactly one state visitor, Lord Tweedsmuir, who was Governor General of Canada.

The amount of work that goes into preparations for these visits is staggering. My staff used to slave twelve or fourteen hours a day, weekends included, when such visits came close together, or actually overlapped, as they sometimes did. Every detail had to be anticipated. Who should meet the arriving guest? Where should he stand? Would the welcoming band be sufficiently rehearsed in the visitor's national anthem? Has the red carpet been returned from the cleaners? What about security precautions? What about the visitor's preferences or taboos where food and drink were concerned (no alcoholic beverages, at least theoretically, for Moslem guests; no beef for Hindus; no web-footed fowl for Coptic Christians like the Emperor of Abyssinia)? Would His Excellency prefer a hard or a soft bed? Would the Prime Minister prefer his toast thick or thin? What sort of flowers would Her Majesty like? Were photographs of the less prominent members of the visiting party available so that our own officials would be able to recognize them readily? And so on, far into the night.

Much of this information, of course, is supplied by our Embassy in the visitor's country or by the visitor's Embassy in Washington. This exchange of information usually begins months in advance. Thus, about ten weeks before the arrival of Queen Elizabeth and Prince Philip in 1957, my department was able to issue a guidance sheet with such pertinent facts as follows:

The Queen and Prince Philip prefer short, simple meals.

The Queen likes Rhine wine, sherry, Canada Dry ginger ale.

Prince Philip prefers Scotch-and-soda or gin-and-tonic.

Neutral water (distilled water containing no minerals) must be served at all events.

Neither smokes.

Although the Queen has no strong feeling about it, she prefers ladies to wear gloves. Whatever is chosen, it is well to stick to this and not try to put on or take off gloves just before being presented.

The reason for the distilled water (the Queen brought her own) was to avoid the possibility of gastric disturbances sometimes caused by a change of drinking water. The preference for gloves was to protect the Queen's hand from flesh contact and ease somewhat the pressure of a handshake—an important matter to anyone who must shake hundreds of hands in a day.

Sometimes these preliminaries called for a good deal of tact. In 1960, when the King and Queen of Thailand were about to visit the United States, our envoy in Bangkok, Alexis Johnson, informed us that the Queen's fondness for Paris creations might cause mutterings at home, where she was already being criticized for not wearing the beautiful silks of Thailand. So one of my staff suggested gently to the Thai Embassy in Washington that the American public would probably prefer to see the lovely Queen in native costume as much as possible. As a result, she did wear native dress on all formal occasions, even though her Paris wardrobe was so fabulous that she appeared the following year on the list of The Ten Best-Dressed Women in the World.

Now and then a crisis would arise for which there was no precedent whatever. I'll never forget the time when the Chief of an African state arrived in Washington with an entourage that included his lawful wedded wife. It also included a shapely secretary-typist who seemed to be a "very good friend" of the President of her country.

The usual formalities had been arranged, including a state dinner at the White House. But about thirty minutes before the dinner was to start, the Ambassador of the country in question came to me in great agitation. The shapely secretary-typist, he said, was not on the list of dinner guests.

I said that this was true, but that since the White House was rather small, such lists had to be restricted to VIPs, usually of Cabinet rank. It certainly wasn't possible, I added, to invite clerks or secretaries to state dinners.

The Ambassador looked extremely glum, and asked if I would speak to his President. So we had a hasty three-cornered conference in which I said the same things all over again. The President, if possible, looked glummer than the Ambassador. If the shapely secretary weren't included, he announced with an air of finality, he wouldn't go himself—not under any circumstances.

I pointed out to the President that our own President was expecting him and his wife, that if he suddenly withdrew the press would want to know why, and everyone would be greatly embarrassed.

There was a grim silence, but suddenly a great light dawned in the President's face. "You said Cabinet rank?" he cried. "Why, that's easy! I hereby appoint her Secretary of State right now!"

And he did. And she went. But of course she sat at the foot of the table.

Such bizarre episodes, I am happy to report, were few and far between. Virtually all state visits go very smoothly; there are few mistakes precisely because it is the job of the Protocol Division to see that no such mistakes are made. To avoid them, every step of an important visit is rehearsed in advance and every move committed to writing. For the reception of Queen Elizabeth and Prince Philip at the Washington National Airport we prepared a fourteen-page memorandum complete with names and titles of the arriving party, names and titles of the

welcoming committee, maps, diagrams, the order in which hands
would be shaken and bouquets presented, the time allotted
for photographs and for reviewing the guard of honor, the order
in which the dignitaries should move toward their assigned
automobiles—each limousine being indicated on the diagram.
Absolutely nothing was left to chance. There was always an
alternative plan, equally detailed, in case of inclement weather.

Some of the jobs in the Protocol Division were highly spe-
cialized. One long-time member of the staff, Mrs. Lois Wil-
liams, was our seating expert; for years she had been advising
harassed hostesses on the correct placement of dinner guests
according to precedence. Another specialist was Charles Hatton,
our "engrosser," whose talented pen could fill in the name of
a guest on an engraved invitation so beautifully that his letter-
ing was barely distinguishable from the engraving itself. Like
everyone in the office, Charlie was sorely overworked at times;
occasionally we had to hire a part-time assistant to help him.
In case anyone wonders what an engrosser does in his spare
time, I can offer some enlightenment—at least where Charlie
was concerned. He loved to take dancing lessons. He subscribed
to a $5000 lifetime course of lessons—and they paid off, too.
It was at a dance studio that he met the girl he eventually
married. He died recently and is greatly missed—a skilled prac-
titioner of a vanishing art.

Having described the function of a Chief of Protocol, I might
now say something about how one is chosen. He may be a
career diplomat or he may be—as I was—a Presidential appointee. The controversy over which is better is an ancient one,
and I might be tempted to take part in it except for one thing—
I think it is futile and childish. There are good appointees and
bad ones; there are also bad career men and good ones. It
seems to me that in government service a man should be
judged on the way he does his job, not on how he got it.

You can argue the question both ways. A professional diplomat, a man who has made government service a life-long
career, is bound to be more experienced than a political ap-

pointee. In his early years he may have made real sacrifices: poor pay, hardship posts, boredom, monotony, perhaps even physical danger. It must be trying for such a man to see a post that he desires—and feels he has earned—handed to someone who has not "come up the hard way."

On the other hand, a Presidential appointee very often has special qualifications for the job. He may speak the language fluently, or have valuable business or social connections in the country to which he is being sent. A notable example of this was the appointment of Sir David Ormsby-Gore as British Ambassador in Washington. Sir David was not a professional diplomat, but he was a close friend of the late President Kennedy when the Kennedys lived in London, and has been a splendid Ambassador in every way. Since the prime objective of every Ambassador is to establish the most intimate possible contact with the head of the state to which he is accredited, the value of such a friendship is obvious.

An American decision of equal brilliance, in my opinion, was to send Clare Boothe Luce to Italy as United States Ambassador. The situation in Italy at the time was very touchy; there was danger of a complete Communist take-over. We needed a person of great personal charm and magnetism, and we got one. She proved herself an excellent administrator, especially where the allocation of American aid to Italy was concerned. She achieved a settlement of the extremely touchy Trieste question. She filled the Villa Taverna, the official Embassy residence, with her own personal art treasures. When she finally ended her tour of duty, she left countless admirers behind her. I am quite sure that no career diplomat, however able, could have brought the same unique qualities to a very difficult task.

Another point in favor of an appointed diplomat is that sometimes he may be more in touch with current trends and happenings at home than the career man, who often spends so much time overseas that he becomes almost a foreigner. Furthermore, since his appointment is only temporary, and his whole livelihood is not usually involved, the appointee may be less afraid to make hard decisions when necessary—decisions that might affect a career man's future career, or might not be popular with the next administration. Another thing should be kept in mind: a political appointee to an Ambassadorship must be approved by the Senate, which is a valuable safeguard. The Senate is certainly not going to put its stamp of approval on anyone grossly unqualified.

So there is much to be said on both sides.

One myth that has come to be widely believed—and ought to be dispelled—is that a great personal fortune is necessary if a man is to be a successful Ambassador in any one of the more important posts. This simply is not true. Our present Ambassador in Paris, "Chip" Bohlen, is not a man of wealth—neither was his predecessor, General James Gavin. Neither Frederick Reinhardt, now in Rome, nor Douglas MacArthur, formerly in Tokyo and now in Brussels, is a man of great means. Yet all of these men represent the United States admirably.

Actually, a private fortune is not necessary because all our embassies are well equipped and well maintained, with ample funds provided for reasonable needs. I have heard it said that the "great fortune" myth was propaganda deliberately spread by career diplomats to discourage private citizens from accepting appointments. Whether this is true or not I cannot say. What I do know is that there are untold millions of dollars in Presidential funds that can be used for almost any purpose and accounted for privately. There are also such funds in the State Department. How much any Embassy receives depends, in part, on how well "wired in" the Ambassador is with the people controlling the purse-strings at home.

Actually, I think the dangers involved in unlimited funds are worse than the hardships that might result from a tight budget, because of the tendency in human nature to go overboard and overdo things when expense is no consideration.

It is true that most ambassadors with private means do "pick up the tab" occasionally and wind up considerably out of pocket—I did this myself during my tour of duty. No one in the State Department ever complains about this for the rather obvious reason that the more the man of means spends out of his own income, the more government funds will be left for others to use.

Many are the maneuvers and tricks that go into the complicated chess game of Embassy financing. The government's fiscal year ends on June 30. If any funds remain as that date draws near, then is the time to request—say—a new automobile for the Embassy. Nothing troubles a bureaucrat quite so much as the prospect of appropriated but unspent funds!

I must say, for all the jealousy and resentment that are said to exist between career men and appointees at lower levels in government service, I never had anything but the most cordial relations with career diplomats in the State Department. I recall especially brilliant young career men like Charles Whitehouse, now on the African desk in the State Department, and other young men in the Foreign Service—Robert Anderson, Arch Calhoun, Robert Corrigan, Robert C. Creel, James D. Hurd, John Wesley Jones, Roger Kirk, Matthew J. Looram, Francis T. Meloy, Jr., George Renchard, and William Tyler in particular. I think the department should use the best men it can get—career men and any qualified non-career man who is willing to serve.

The scope of protocol is far broader than the assigned functions of the office. As one of my able precedessors, Stanley Woodward, put it: "Protocol is the rule-book by which international relations are conducted. Any organization, any society, must, if it is to thrive, operate under certain rules if for no other reason than to prevent chaos."

And his successor, John Simmons, wrote: "'To ignore these practices brings trouble, undoubted confusion, and even conflict."

Four years of standing in their shoes convinced me that both of them were eminently right.

III   The Parade Begins

For the first four years of the Eisenhower administration, I served as United States Ambassador to the Grand Duchy of Luxembourg. It was a colorful and fascinating assignment, and every member of our family enjoyed it. During those years we kept our Washington home open, even down to cigarettes in the cigarette boxes, so that our three children would not feel that my European assignment had uprooted them. They loved Luxembourg with its fairy-tale castles and friendly people, but all three of them were as American as baseball, and we wanted to keep them that way.

It is customary for all chiefs of foreign missions—and for all resident appointments as well—to tender their resignations automatically at the end of each Presidential term. So in the fall of 1956 my wife and myself and the children and our staff of servants and our dogs and several cars plus seventy-two pieces of hand luggage and a score of trunks began our final trek back to the States. It was a good deal like moving a small army, and (although nobody listened) I said more than once in loud tones that if somehow I managed to get home and back to private life I was never going to stir hand or foot again. Had I known that in the next four years I was to travel some 400,000 miles—the equivalent of going round the world sixteen times—I probably would have jumped right off the boat.

On arrival in Washington, I went through the usual debriefing process in the State Department, and was given a couple of assignments to keep me busy until January 20 when President Eisenhower was to be inaugurated for his second term. The children were back in school, we were settled once more at "Underoak," our Washington house on Nebraska Avenue, and I was looking forward to returning to my business affairs.

During the early days of my return, I heard rumors that my good friend Jack Simmons, who was Chief of Protocol, had reached the age of retirement. As a matter of fact, he had passed it, but had agreed to serve an extra year or so. One day I had a phone call from Phyllis Bernau, Mr. Dulles' efficient Girl Friday. She said that the Secretary would like to see me. I had a very brief interview, in which the Secretary merely asked whether or not I was available for reappointment to some job for the second term of the administration. I said that I would certainly give serious thought to serving in any capacity in which I could be of use.

Shortly thereafter I flew down to Texas to see my mother, who lives in Dallas. While I was there, Secretary Dulles came to speak to the Dallas Council on World Affairs. After the dinner and the speech, he and Mrs. Dulles attended a small reception at my mother's home. Here he drew me aside and told me that he had spoken to the President about my taking over the job of Chief of Protocol, and that the President had given his approval. This conversation was also brief, because that day the Hungarian Revolution had broken out, and the Secretary was receiving a stream of frantic phone calls from Washington. But the suggestion appealed to me. I liked people. I was interested in international affairs. I would be able to live—part of the time, at least—in my own home. Furthermore, for a Washington assignment, this job offered considerable freedom from frustration, and latitude in making decisions. I would be directly responsible to only two people, the President of the United States and the Secretary of State, both of whom I admired greatly. Also I would have considerable contact with my friend Dick Nixon. A few days later, in Washington, I had one more conversation with Secretary Dulles, and the wheels were set in motion. Shortly thereafter, I had word that the White House had approved my appointment.

As the January days flashed past, Jack Simmons and his charming wife Caroline somehow found time (His Majesty Saud ibn Abd al-Aziz Al-Saud, King of Saudi Arabia, was very much in town) to brief Ruth and me on some details of the job. He told us that it was the custom, after the ceremonies on Inauguration Day, for the Chief of Protocol to give a luncheon for all Washington diplomats at the President's Guest House. They asked us to stand with them in the receiving line. This, Jack explained, would mark the beginning of our tour of duty—though unofficially, since I was not sworn in until a few days later.

At that time, my wife and I knew personally more than thirty ambassadors out of the eighty or so in Washington, many of them on a first-name basis. Thus, from the start, what might have seemed like work to another person was pleasure for me because I was dealing with my friends.

I was also very fortunate in my State Department associates. My three main contacts, aside from Secretary Dulles and later Secretary Herter, were Robert Murphy, the able and popular Under-Secretary for Political Affairs, Loy Henderson, Under-Secretary for Administration, who was such an encyclopedia of knowledge that he was known as "Mr. Foreign Service," and Livingston Merchant, Assistant Secretary of State for Western Europe. All three were unfailingly considerate and helpful, and often went out of their way to help me in every possible manner.

Another valued colleague was Carl McCardle, who in many ways was Foster Dulles' closest and most confidential advisor, so close that some people resented the influence he had. Carl McCardle was the first Assistant Secretary of State for Public Affairs to believe that the American people are entitled to know what is going on in their country's foreign policy—within security limitations and restrictions necessarily imposed when publicity might jeopardize delicate negotiations. When he was in the State Department, I believe that the American Secretary of State and American foreign policy were better known all over the world than they have ever been before or since.

Phyllis Bernau, Foster Dulles' private secretary, was also outstanding in her devotion, and always had a smile for everybody. One the White House side, Ann Whitman, President Eisenhower's private secretary, was an absolutely fantastic organizer, as well as being highly intelligent, attractive, and a tremendous help always. Equally remarkable was Mrs. Eisenhower's social secretary, Mary Jane McCaffery. I shall never understand how it was possible for Mary Jane and her small staff to accomplish so much.

President Eisenhower's second term began on January 20, 1957. Just fifteen days after his inauguration, on February 4, I was sworn in as Chief of Protocol. Mr. Dulles made it a pleasant occasion by saying some kind things about Ruth and me. President Eisenhower had already told me, with his famous grin, that he expected to be seeing a lot of me during the next four years. Jack Simmons had briefed me as thoroughly as he could on the requirements of the job. I had also received plenty of unsolicited advice. One earnest well-wisher, I remember, urged me to be sure and keep a black necktie in my office drawer so as to be ready for unexpected occasions when I had to attend funerals, pay condolence calls, or display a proper degree of mourning!

After the swearing-in ceremony, I went back to the office to meet those members of the staff whom I didn't already know. I assured them that I planned no drastic shake-up or personnel changes, and that my door would be open to any of them at any time. I added that I hoped they would continue to take everything about their jobs seriously except themselves. I thought it possible, I said, for people constantly dealing with important personages to become a bit overimpressed with their part in the proceedings, but that—as my father used to say when I was a boy—all men have to put their trousers on one leg at a time, and I thought all of us should keep that undeniable fact in mind. I have admired many people in my lifetime, but have never been awed by any of them.

During the four years that followed, I could not have asked for a better or more devoted staff. My office in the State De-

partment building was a very pleasant one; in government, as
in the Army, rank has its privileges. All Assistant Secretaries of
State—the Chief of Protocol has this rank—have identical
offices. The suite included a reception room, an office for my
two secretaries, and a conference room for staff meetings that
adjoined my Deputy's office. My own office, large and well
appointed, also had an adjoining dressing room and bath—
very useful for the quick changes of costume that were often
necessary.

I had my desk situated strategically near the window so that
I could see the main entrance and observe the arrival of cars
containing ambassadors or other VIPs and be ready for them—
or sometimes go to meet them. One of my telephones was a
direct line to the White House. During the next four years I
was to be constantly impressed by the efficiency and intelligence of the White House operators; they always seemed to
recognize one's voice and always had the answer to almost any
question.

I was fortunate in my secretaries, too. Both were blonde,
attractive, married—and willing to work like slaves. Ruth
Donaldson kept track of my appointments; Martha Newton
handled my correspondence. Both were extremely adept at
coping with almost any situation and taking the initiative when
necessary. Well-dressed, neat, intelligent, they were a credit to
the government in every way.

On a desk in this outer office was a big rotary file that contained the correct form of address for every dignitary in the
world. Should one address the Shah of Iran as "Your Majesty"
or "Your Highness"? A glance at the file would set you straight
(correct answer: "Your Imperial Highness").

With a dedicated staff and good friends inside the State Department, I felt prepared to face the headaches that go with
any new job. Actually, there was one all ready and waiting for
me. "East is east," wrote Kipling, "and west is west, and never
the twain shall meet." But they had already met with a loud
bang, and were still meeting, at the President's Guest House,
usually known as the Blair House, where King Saud of Arabia

and his entourage were completing a state visit. From what I could gather, the Guest House was just about a wreck, and so was Mrs. Victoria Geaney, the housekeeper whose fierce possessiveness where the house was concerned was something that the whole State Department had to reckon with.

The old Blair mansion and the adjoining Lee mansion diagonally across Pennsylvania Avenue from the White House had been acquired for official use shortly after World War II. The negotiations were handled by Stanley Woodward, Chief of Protocol during the Truman administration. When Mr. Gist Blair died, this handsome residence, complete with its furnishings, was sold to the government at a very reasonable price— I believe it was $125,000. The price might have been even lower had not the fact come to light, during the negotiations, that the government had paid a considerably higher price for the Lee residence next door. The Lee House was about the same size, but it was not so impressive architecturally, nor did it come with any furnishings.

In any case, the two old mansions were extensively renovated, joined together, and turned into a sort of double guest house for distinguished visitors. The location was very convenient, but there were drawbacks. Pennsylvania Avenue can be very noisy at times. The garden was small and inadequate. In summer this garden could be stiflingly hot; in fact, with a canopy over it, it could be worse than a circus tent. The furnishings of the Guest House were luxurious and attractive and included some splendid early-American furniture, original Chippendale pieces, period rugs, and a large collection of Lowestoft china and Revere silver. Most state visitors were charmed with it. But it would sleep only ten or twelve persons comfortably, and consequently was much too small.

It was rich in history, though. From its earliest days it had played an important part in the nation's history because of the continuing friendship between the Blairs and most of the occupants of the White House. On the right, as you enter the building, is a small room known as the Lincoln Room, where Abraham Lincoln is said to have offered a Cabinet post to one of the Blairs. On the left are twin drawing rooms, with a large doorway cut through into the adjoining Lee House. Originally these two rooms had a handsome pair of matching eighteenth-century Aubusson rugs on the floors, but Mrs. Geaney had decreed that they be moved upstairs to one of the bedrooms where they would not receive so much wear.

For almost four years, during the restoration of the White House, President and Mrs. Truman lived in the Blair-Lee House. President Truman had his office in a study on the west side of the Lee House, and the President's flag and the American flag that he used are still in that study. Mrs. Geaney often told me how much Mrs. Truman preferred the Blair House to the White House. Even after the attempt to assassinate President Truman, which could not have occurred so easily in the White House with its high, guarded fence and extensive grounds, Mrs. Truman never wavered in her devotion to the Blair House and to Mrs. Geaney.

There is an elevator in the back hall of the Blair House that stops on split levels between floors, leaving the visitor with a few steps to mount or descend. On the second floor is a handsome library with comfortable furniture and a color television set. There is also a large table in case the visitors want to hold meetings or conferences. Adjoining the library is a bedroom with a dark maple four-poster bed and matching highboy; this is usually used by the ranking male guest. In the back of the house is a very feminine suite that contains the matching Aubusson rugs sent upstairs by Mrs. Geaney; this is known as "the Queen's room," and many queens have slept there.

During the next four years I was to become very fond of Mrs. Geaney, who had been housekeeper for the Blair family for more than a quarter of a century before the house was sold. She was a spry, energetic woman with short, curly gray hair and glasses. She had a happy, friendly disposition, and her one aim in life was to please the guests who came into "her" residence. I have seen her dragging a large suitcase with a royal monogram to her own automobile on her way to have some impatient monarch's broken lock repaired. I have seen her leaping into a taxi, when time was short, to buy a dress shirt for a visiting potentate or to pick up rented formal clothes for persons who came ill prepared or whose luggage had been delayed. I have seen her with needle and thread repairing the gowns of visiting dignitaries' wives, or shortening a skirt as the wearer literally walked out of the front door. No task was too much trouble if it involved the hospitality of Blair House.

From a housekeeping standpoint, Mrs. Geaney's main problem—which she shared with most Washington hostesses—was keeping an adequate chef. Periodically, during my four years in the State Department, I would get an urgent phone call from Mrs. Geaney pleading for an instant appointment or begging me to stop by as soon as possible. Whenever I got one of these calls, I knew there was trouble in the Blair House kitchen. My solution invariably was to send two very competent members of my staff, Mrs. Katherine Laird and Mrs. Mary Wilroy, to offer Mrs. Geaney aid, comfort, and moral support. Among them, the three ladies always ironed out the problem.

Aside from the chef and Mrs. Geaney herself, there were three or four faithful retainers who made up the permanent staff of the Guest House. There was a houseman who was responsible for handling the luggage, housemaids for cleaning, and personal maids for feminine visitors. We also had a list of butlers, footmen, parlormaids, and so on, all cleared by security, who gave our needs at Blair House top priority, although they were not employed full time. This system of hiring a part-time staff only when needed helped to keep operating costs down, but even so, maintenance on the President's Guest House ran above $40,000 a year.

In my first official contacts with Mrs. Geaney, her normally sunny disposition was somewhat clouded by the presence in her beloved mansion of King Saud of Arabia and his merry men. The King had brought with him a retinue of some seventy persons (most state visitors brought only ten or twelve), and eighteen of these were officially assigned to the Guest House. Actually, since Saudi-Arabians consider it a great honor to sleep near their king, they were taking turns in rotation from nearby hotels. Food-tasters were haunting the kitchens. Incense burned in the halls. Bodyguards with naked scimitars were sleeping on the floor outside the King's bedroom. Attendants (some of our people were convinced they were slaves) were constantly brewing thick, sirupy coffee in braziers full of glowing coals that they propped casually on brocaded chairs (one chair burst into flames and the fire department had to be summoned). Everyone munched dates. They got rid of date seeds and coffee grounds by tossing them into a corner, a method of disposal that brought Mrs. Geaney close to apoplexy. They didn't understand the draw-pulls of the draperies, so they simply tied knots in the fabrics that had cost $25.00 a yard. Rumors flourished that they were also keeping live sheep on the premises to be slaughtered whenever the King called for shish kebab. This was not true, but I got the distinct impression that Mrs. Geaney would just as soon have had the sheep as the Saudis.

In the end, repairs after their visit came to more than $5000. The King no doubt would have been glad to pay such a trifling sum—his minions were constantly handing out Swiss watches (not very good ones) and jeweled daggers to anyone who pleased him, and the bill for flowers alone at one of his receptions was said to be over $10,000. But, reasonable or not, our government always paid for such wear and tear.

In any case, the Saudis were certainly enjoying themselves. We supplied them with ten limousines (at $50.00 apiece per day), and they did not let them stand idle. One Cadillac, I remember, was in use twenty-three hours out of twenty-four. They knew their time in our fair country was short, and they were making the most of it.

I must say, some of these people from lands that we consider primitive are quite psychic. Years ago, at a dinner given at the Mayflower Hotel in Washington for Prince Feisal of Saudi Arabia, Ruth found herself sitting beside an emir, one of the King's sheiks. Quite often at such dinners guests sign menus for one another as souvenirs. When the time came for the emir to sign the menu for Ruth, he smiled and said, "I will write you a little message in Arabic."

This he did, but of course Ruth couldn't read it. When she asked the emir what it meant, he blushed a bit and said that he really couldn't tell her.

Ruth thought it was probably some mildly amorous message. A friend of ours who spoke Arabic was sitting nearby, so she asked him to read it. He also demurred, but she insisted, and so finally he translated the message: "You are in a condition created by God. You have the congratulations of my king and my country." Ruth was astounded. She was about two months pregnant with our second child. No one at the dinner—outside of ourselves—could possibly have known it, but the emir did.

The Saudis finally departed, and Mrs. Geaney's frayed nerves began to mend, but almost at once I threw her into a new tizzy by deciding that the Blair-Lee House needed considerable renovation. One of the first things I did after the Saudis left was to go through the house with Mrs. Geaney and some of my staff on an inspection tour. The kitchen equipment struck me as totally inadequate. In both the Lee House and the Blair House the kitchens were in the basement, where they remain today, and during a state visit both were in continuous use, with meals often going on simultaneously in both dining rooms. In addition, the bathrooms were old-fashioned and badly lighted—there wasn't a shower in the place. As I made notes on such things, Mrs. Geaney viewed my note-taking with increasing concern. Just as I was about to leave, she pulled me into the Lincoln Room with a look of despair. "Now, you're not going to tear up these kitchens and bathrooms, are you?" she demanded. "This old house won't stand that kind of remodeling!"

I listened to her pleas, and sympathized with her feelings, but insisted that much had to be done. She fought us all like a small gray-haired tigress, but in the end Secretary Dulles approved the changes and they were duly made.

Mrs. Geaney worked year after year without ever taking a vacation. She was absolutely convinced that Blair House could not function without her, and although she owned a pleasant cottage in Virginia, she lived with her dog in the housekeeper's apartment in the basement of Blair House until her dying day.

She was very fond of Boston bull terriers. On one occasion, I remember, she acquired two Boston bull puppies and installed them in her rooms. A Prime Minister was arriving with his wife for a state visit, and when I stopped by Blair House to do some last-minute checking I heard this incessant yelping coming from the basement. When I asked what it was, Mrs. Geaney brought the pups upstairs and proudly showed them to me. They were very cute, but the last thing we needed to greet a Prime Minister, so I suggested that she farm them out temporarily.

She agreed to do this, but the next day as I ushered the distinguished guests into the Guest House, with Mrs. Geaney waiting to greet them, out from behind her rushed the two puppies, yelping deliriously and piddling all over the back hall.

Mrs. Geaney looked as if she wanted to sink through the floor, but with a cry of delight the Prime Minister's wife ran forward, picked up one of the puppies, and began to tell me enthusiastically how much she and her husband loved dogs, and what a charming surprise this was. The look of relief on Mrs. Geaney's face was something to behold. I never mentioned the incident to her, but it was a long time before I saw the puppies again, and when I did they were quiet and well-housebroken dogs.

When Mrs. Geaney died in February, 1961, the government lost one of its most dedicated and hard-working employees. Even in death, her devotion to Blair House was apparent. We found that she was actually well over the age of retirement, but—womanlike—had deducted about a decade on all her government records so that nothing could interfere with her reign at the Guest House.

I don't think Mrs. Geaney was ever aware of one particular deception that was put over on her—with my sanction, I blush to admit. A very important state visitor was arriving—a Queen, in fact—and Mrs. Geaney decided that the so-called Queen's-suite dressing room and bathroom in the Blair House needed new carpeting. The pattern chosen for the dressing room was attractive, but the same could not be said for the wall-to-wall carpeting in the bathroom. It was really horrible! There the pattern was so bold and startling that some of us felt the Queen would be amazed, not to say aghast.

The question then arose: who would tell Mrs. Geaney that her taste in carpeting left much to be desired? There wasn't much time to bell the cat, either; the Queen was arriving within forty-eight hours. I was wrestling with this thorny problem when some member of my staff had a brilliant idea: why not have a piece of plain white carpeting cut, exactly the same size as the bathroom, and at the last split second lay it like gentle camouflage over Mrs. Geaney's monstrosity?

This solution seemed to save face all round, but the awful possibility loomed: would Mrs. Geaney inspect the bathroom at any point after the Queen arrived? I held a staff meeting with myself and decided that the risk would have to be run. We had the carpet cut—top-secretly. It was rolled up and hidden under the bed in the Queen's room. Just before Her Majesty arrived, an agitated member of my staff sneaked in and placed it in position. There was a moment of dreadful suspense when Mrs. Geaney showed the Queen to her apartment, but courage and daring paid off—she didn't look in the bathroom. When the royal visitor left, we whisked the white carpet away. Mrs. Geaney never knew—and neither did the Queen—that Her Majesty had been given the white-carpet treatment. Shortly after the Queen's departure we did re-cover the floor in spite of Mrs. Geaney's protestations.

The Blair-Lee House still continues to function as the President's Guest House. Improvements are constantly being made; central air conditioning is now being installed instead of the unsightly window air-conditioning units. But accessible and attractive though the Guest House is, it remains much too small for the constant stream of visitors that we have in this country today.

During my tour of duty, it was always my hope—and it still

is—that the government might acquire one of the more spacious Washington estates for an official guest residence. The most desirable property that might have been acquired during my term of office was "Tregaron," the estate of Mrs. Herbert May who was then Mrs. Joseph Davies. After Mr. Davies died, this property was available for purchase, as Mrs. May had moved to "Hillwood," truly the most magnificent estate in Washington. But it was left with very restrictive covenants; in Mr. Davies' will there were many heirs, and apparently no satisfactory arrangement could be worked out.

"Tregaron" is surrounded by more than twenty acres of some of the most beautiful gardens in America. It is not more than ten minutes from the White House, has ample room for a large staff, and offers every type of facility that any guest could desire. There is even a small golf course on the estate.

The purchase and refurbishing of "Tregaron" would have cost perhaps a million dollars, but I think it would have been well worth the money. It is very important to influence favorably people who may become our friends and allies in this troubled world. I believed when I was Chief of Protocol, and I believe now, that such an expenditure would be a far better investment than some of the hundreds of millions of dollars that we seem to delight in giving to Communist-Bloc nations.

The first official visitor I had to greet in my new job was His Royal Highness, Amir Abdul Ilah, Crown Prince of Iraq. I remember him vividly, not only because he was my first "client," but because my impression of him as a quiet, civilized person was in such violent contrast with the barbaric death that ultimately befell him.

When I met the Crown Prince at the railroad station in Washington, no one had briefed me on exactly what to do or say, but my experience with greeting VIPs in Luxembourg came to my aid and everything went smoothly. The Prince, I observed, was quite a natty dresser. His hat was made by Gelot, a French hatter on the Place Vendôme, his shoes were hand-made in England, and he wore a ring set with a ruby that was very similar to one I happened to be wearing. He noticed

this immediately and commented on it. His English was somewhat hesitant; he was more relaxed speaking French.

His visit, which was a short one, went according to plan
except for one rather amusing episode at a Press Club luncheon. It is the custom there for the guest of honor to make a
speech, followed by a question-and-answer period. The Crown
Prince made a few preliminary remarks, saying that he was
glad to be in the United States. But, he added, he was not used
to making speeches. At home he made only one a year—to open
Parliament. He then turned abruptly to the Iraq Ambassador,
who was sitting at the head table, and said, "I command you
to read my speech."

The Ambassador looked stunned. Finally he stammered,
"Your Royal Highness, I don't have my glasses and can't see to
read anything."

The Crown Prince frowned. The Ambassador, looking
around wildly, then ordered some lesser member of the Embassy to read the royal speech. While the audience tittered,
the designated individual came forward calmly and read the
speech in faultless English.

I was afraid that the press notices next day might poke fun
at the Crown Prince for this buck-passing, but they were quite
friendly. The press notices that did give me a shock came a few
years later, when a revolution in Iraq overthrew the government. I was horrified one morning to see in the newspaper a
photograph of the Crown Prince's naked body hanging by the
feet. He had been murdered, along with some other members
of the palace guard. It made me realize how thin the veneer
of civilization is, and how dangerous life can be in some of
these primitive countries, whether you wear French hats and
English shoes or not.

It didn't take me long to discover that my job had all sorts
of lively sidelines. When the Saudi Arabians departed, for
example, various government officials turned in to me gifts,
including $6000 in cash, fifteen or so wrist watches, and sev-
eral ornate Arab robes which King Saud had given them.
Actually, one of the robes was given to me, although I had

had little to do with this visit. I turned it in with the rest, to be held until my departure from government service. Ruth took a rather dim view of this; she said the King would probably be very unhappy if he knew that his gifts had to be buried in a government vault.

By now Ruth was keeping a diary which was to be an invaluable record for us both. One of her early entries ran as follows:

> The funniest thing happened yesterday. We were to dine at a South American embassy in the evening. In the morning, Wiley had an angry note from one of our military men who complained that a certain official in this particular embassy was annoying his wife by making persistent advances to her. He wanted Wiley to speak to the Ambassador or to "this gentleman" and put an end to these unwelcome attentions.
>
> Of all things, when we were seated for dinner at the embassy, this "gentleman" turned out to be my dinner partner! I purposely asked him about his family, to see what might be causing him to chase an American officer's wife. The reason was plain enough; his wife is an invalid back in South America and he is stationed here with their small children. How to stop him from chasing another man's wife I'm sure I don't know. Neither does the Protocol Office!

Actually, the Protocol Office did know. A discreet word to the Ambassador was all that was necessary. The lonely Romeo was told to quench his ardor forthwith—or else he would be sent back to his ailing wife.

Our next visitor was an amiable gentleman from Paris, Guy Mollet. M. Mollet was President of the Council of Ministers of the French Republic, which was equivalent to being Prime Minister. I had met him in France and in Luxembourg and knew that he was pleasant and easy to deal with. He was a short, cheerful man with auburn hair and freckles who dressed very simply and wore horn-rimmed glasses.

I met him in New York and rode back to Washington with him on the Presidential airplane, the *Columbine*. Vice-President Nixon and Secretary Dulles were at the airport to meet us. So was Ruth. I spotted her in the crowd and even managed to wink at her. Colonel Draper, the President's pilot, always took great pride in having the plane touch down exactly at the appointed moment. When it had taxied up to the waiting dignitaries, my job was to descend first, make sure that everything was ready, then give a hand signal to one of the crew members still on board. Waiting at the door, the visiting dignitary would then descend, and I would introduce him to the VIPs who were waiting to meet him. Then other members of the visitor's official party would descend in order of rank, each individual being followed by his wife, if ladies were included in the party.

Since Guy Mollet was not a Chief of State, there was no official dinner for him at the White House, but Secretary Dulles was host at a dinner in the Pan American Union. We used this handsome building frequently in those days because at that time the State Department had no official dining room. Unfortunately, it had almost no kitchen facilities. Whenever we gave a large dinner, we had to put up screens in the halls and set up temporary kitchens in the men's and ladies' rooms. We also used Anderson House, the magnificent French residence of the late Larz Anderson, which had become the property of the Cincinnati Society. The Anderson House contained a superb dining room with a ceiling forty feet high that could seat as many as eighty people.

Ruth and I were very anxious for this dinner to be a success, because it was the first one in which she had been asked by Mrs. Dulles to do the flower arrangements, and there were certain changes in procedure that I had discussed with Secretary Dulles. All of us felt that state dinners had a dismal tendency to be stiff, formal, and boring. There were always floral arrangements, but, as Ruth said, these were usually "just flowers." We felt that frequently the lighting was too harsh and bright; by using candlelight or subdued lighting we might obtain a more relaxed and intimate atmosphere. Also the music was often too stereotyped. I remember being very favorably impressed by certain restaurants in Paris where the violinists strolled among the diners and serenaded them between courses. We thought that if we introduced this innovation, Guy Mollet might be pleasantly reminded of home.

Ruth had always been interested in flower arrangements and had won several prizes in various exhibits. The day of the dinner she went down to the Pan American Union and spent several hours working with the florist. She also brought some of our own candelabra, and—with Mrs. Dulles' approval—gave orders that the lights in the big overhead chandeliers be dimmed. Meantime my office arranged for a group of Air Force musicians known as "The Singing Strings" to be on hand and play during the course of the dinner. Everyone seemed pleased with the results. The guest of honor complimented the Dulleses, and the Dulleses complimented Ruth. Next day, Betty Beale, the Washington columnist, wrote a glowing description as follows:

> It was like a spring garden in bloom yesterday in the grand ballroom of the Pan American Union as the Secretary of State and Mrs. John Foster Dulles entertained at a state dinner in honor of the visiting French Premier Guy Mollet.
>
> Nearly 100 French and American dignitaries, seated at one tremendous horseshoe table, looked onto a beautiful center arrangement of 2 large pink azalea trees banked with pink and white azalea and gardenia plants.
>
> The floral arrangements, which were largely the brainchild of Mrs. Wiley Buchanan, wife of the new Chief of Protocol, included a trellis behind the Dulleses and their guests of honor. This was decorated with smilax and forsythia, and on either side were two large vases of pink peach blossoms and white cherry blossoms.
>
> At the head of the table were silver vases filled with baby orchids of lavender and green and down each side were

Wiley Buchanan leaving his office for an appointment

Captain William Drap
Presidential pilot, with
back to camera, the
thor, and President Eis
hower awaiting arrival
Khrushchev at Andre
Air Force Base

Left to right: General Nathan Twining, the author, Foreig
Minister Gromyko, Henry Cabot Lodge, Soviet Ambassado
Menshikov, Secretary of State Herter, Eisenhower, an
Khrushchev

The Khrushchev family leaving Blair House to go to White House dinner

The author huddles with security officers to discuss
security arrangements and program

Welcome in New York Harbor for Queen Elizabeth

Wiley Buchanan greeting Queen Elizabeth and Prince Philip
on behalf of President Eisenhower at Williamsburg, Virginia.
Governor Stanley of Virginia at left waiting to be introduced

Mrs. Eisenhower welcoming Queen Elizabeth at White House

Secretary of State and Mrs. Dulles welcoming Queen to dinner at Pan American Union. Mrs. Victoria Geaney, housekeeper at Blair House, stands behind the author

Dinner given at American Embassy, London, by Vice-Presi dent and Mrs. Nixon in honor of Queen Elizabeth. Seat clockwise: Mr. Heathcoat Amory, Countess Mountbat U.S. Ambassador Whitney, the Queen, Mr. Nixon, L Macmillan, the author, Duchess of Devonshire, Gen Lauris Norstad, Dowager Marchioness of Reading, Selwyn Lloyd, Mrs. Whitney, Mr. Harold Macmillan, N Nixon, Earl Mountbatten, Mrs. Buchanan

Queen Elizabeth, the author, and Mayor Daley of
Chicago in parade through city

Queen Elizabeth speaking before the United Nations

Mrs. Buchanan and Chief of Protocol, dressed for formal dinner, sit with their children (left to right: Dede, Buck, and Bonnie) while they eat

Mrs. Buchanan giving last-minute touches to flo[r] arrangements at State Department dinner for Pre[si] dent Frondizi of Argentina in Anderson Hou[se]

low vases of assorted spring flowers—tulips, jonquils and iris. These arrangements were connected with greens and mimosa.

Silver candelabra were used and the table gleamed with an impressive silver service. The chandeliers and indirect lighting overhead were turned low instead of the usual bright glare. Strolling violinists wandered among the guests.

Guy Mollet's visit was a short business visit with a minimum of social frills. He was followed by the Foreign Minister of Germany, Dr. Heinrich von Brentano. The Germans were entertained with a small dinner at Blair House. This time Ruth brought some of our own Meissen china for the table, and the Germans admired it greatly. She and Mrs. Geaney, now fast friends and co-conspirators, decided to keep the ownership of the Meissen a dark secret, and it was reported in the papers as some hitherto unknown and undiscovered Blair heirloom. Eventually, of course, the secret leaked out, but Mrs. Dulles seemed to approve and all was well.

The Chief of Protocol is supposed to know all members of the diplomatic corps in Washington. I have a fairly good memory for names and faces, and thought I was doing pretty well, but I made one resounding mistake at the Washington airport. Vice-President Nixon and Mrs. Nixon were taking off for Africa to represent the United States at the ceremonies celebrating the independence of Ghana. Quite a few diplomats were at the airport to see them off. I was busy lining them up in proper order of precedence when I discovered that one of the representatives from Ghana was missing. Take-off time was approaching; the Vice-President was ready to say good-by. Still no sign of the missing diplomat. Suddenly I spotted a large, cheerful-looking colored gentleman walking down the airport corridor. He had on a blue suit with bright tan shoes, which I thought a rather unusual combination for a diplomat, but anyway I rushed up to him and said, "We've been waiting for you!

Where have you been?" He gave me such a blank stare that I continued, "Aren't you from the Ghana Embassy?" "Lawd, no, man," he cried, "I'm just here to fix the Coca-Cola machine!" Fortunately the missing diplomat did appear shortly and took his proper place in the line. But after that I was less inclined to jump to conclusions.

The first Chief of State that I had to greet was His Excellency Ngo Dinh Diem, then President of the Republic of Vietnam. To meet him I flew all the way to Hawaii, and Ruth went with me. The weather was cold and rainy—not at all what we expected—but we enjoyed our stay at the Royal Hawaiian Hotel with its magnificent view of the surf riders and outrigger canoes and catamarans with their colorful striped sails.

President Diem, whose regime ended with his violent death in November, 1963, was a very interesting man. A bachelor and a Roman Catholic, he had been in exile from his country and during that time had lived in a monastery in the United States. He had great natural dignity, and like many people of the Far East had a very youthful skin; there was not a wrinkle in his face. In all my dealings with Orientals, I found it very difficult to judge their age. Madam Chiang Kai-shek also has this porcelain skin and quality of agelessness.

President Diem arrived wearing a business suit and remained in Western clothes until the night of the state dinner for him at the White House. Then, when I went to Blair House to pick him up for dinner I was quite startled by the change in his appearance. On his head was a little turban with gold braid around it. He was wearing an elaborate robe of velvet brocade over white trousers and a white tunic that fell just below the knee. It made him look like the Far Eastern potentate that he was supposed to be.

He seemed to enjoy himself at the White House, and the President and Mrs. Eisenhower liked him. The last night of his visit he gave a small dinner for the President at his Embassy. The Ambassador of Vietnam to the United States was a charming, able diplomat named Tran Van Chong. He had a lovely wife with skin like porcelain, and in her native costume she looked like an oriental doll. They were the parents of the later famous Madame Nhu, who was married to President Diem's brother and served as the President's official hostess.

I remember the dinner very well, because I sat next to Field Marshal Montgomery, who was visiting President Eisenhower at the White House at the time. To my knowledge, this was the only time that a private visitor of the President ever attended one of these state functions. I found it fascinating to discuss with the Field Marshal various aspects of his wartime association with President Eisenhower. I knew that since the war he had made some rather critical remarks about the President, but I also knew that in spite of these an autographed picture of the Field Marshal stood on a table in the main hall of the President's private living quarters in the White House and remained there throughout his administration. The Field Marshal had a reputation for extreme bluntness, and—I had been told—did not necessarily wait for an invitation to the White House or anywhere else. His practice in visiting anyone was simply to write and announce that he was coming on a certain day. This evening, however, he seemed to be in a good humor and made a pleasant dinner companion.

I remember we talked about General Al Gruenther, who was head of NATO when I was in Luxembourg. I told the Field Marshal of visiting General Gruenther in Paris and how, when the time came to sign the guest book, our five-year-old Bucky laboriously scrawled his first name, then looked at me worriedly and said, "What's my last name, Daddy?" I also told him of Mrs. Gruenther's fondness for shopping in the Flea Market in Paris and how she always made a point of identifying herself as Mrs. Green so that the Flea Market merchants wouldn't take advantage of her position and raise their prices. One day when she was haggling over some picture frames two American officers appeared with an urgent message from her husband. "Mrs. Gruenther," they said, "you'll have to come home right away. The General is leaving on a trip in half an hour and wants you to join him." Mrs. Gruenther was furious to have her disguise removed, but as she left the little salesman pulled one of the soldiers back and said in perfectly good English, "Don't be upset, friend. I've known it was Mrs. Gruenther all along."

Another guest at the Vietnam Embassy that night was Francis Cardinal Spellman. Ruth and the Cardinal got along famously—so well, in fact, that I said jokingly to His Eminence that if I weren't aware of the vows he had taken I would be quite jealous of him. "Ah," said the Cardinal, with a twinkle, "that's the finest compliment I have heard in a long time." I was also interested to hear the Cardinal say to Mrs. Dulles, as we were all taking our leave, "Thank you for giving us your son." This, of course, was in reference to the boy's recent conversion to Catholicism. I couldn't help wondering how Secretary Dulles felt about this, considering his position as one of the leading Protestant laymen in the country.

President Diem was here for more than two weeks. We took him to Fort Belvoir to see some troops being specially trained in guerrilla warfare. This interested him greatly, since the primary purpose of his visit was to obtain military aid against Communist infiltration—a problem just as acute then in Vietnam as it is today. We also took him down to Tennessee to show him the spectacular job the Tennessee Valley Authority had done. Once a backward and poverty-stricken area, it has been redeemed and revitalized by cheap electric power. In addition it is now a prosperous yachting, fishing, and boating resort area.

We took the President and his party to a typical farmhouse not far from the dam. We had told the farmer that we were coming, but had made no other preparations. I was never more pleased in my life. The young man and his wife were completely natural and at ease. He was wearing a sport shirt and slacks and his wife had on a spotless housedress. They showed us around their place with great pride, and told President Diem what it meant to them to have cheap electricity. The milking machines and freezer equipment interested the President, but he was more impressed by the fact that the young man had just built a room on his house for his mother. She was an elderly woman who had known a much harder life; her hands looked as if she had spent many years working in the fields. But the natural dignity of these people was deeply impressive.

The officer who showed us around was Brigadier General Herbert D. Vogle. When we were alone for a moment he said to me, "You don't know me nearly as well as I feel I know you."

I said, "Well, General, I know you by reputation and by the wonderful work that you have been doing here."

"Oh, no," he said, "it's much more personal than that. Do you remember when you were Ambassador in Luxembourg that one night very late your doorbell rang? When your sleepy butler came to the door he found a frantic young Army officer. That young officer was my son and, as you may recall, his wife was having a baby. They had two other small children, the baby was arriving early, and they had no one to leave their children with while the wife went to the hospital. You woke up your wife and got some of the Embassy staff together and made arrangements for the children to be looked after and for the wife to come to the hospital in Luxembourg. Until now I never had a chance to meet you, but if you will look back in your files you will find a letter from me thanking you for the help you gave this boy."

It was just a minor episode, and this is a trite observation, but it made me realize once more how small a place the world really is.

The last few days of President Diem's visit were spent in New York, where Cardinal Spellman gave a dinner in his honor. This was the first time I had been in the Cardinal's residence and I was very interested to see how he entertained. The whole atmosphere is what one would expect to find in a very comfortable private home. Later I learned that the Cardinal always was delighted to give such dinners to honor some visiting Catholic Head of State. Often he would say a special Mass for them in his own residence. There was a handsome chapel on the top floor, and sometimes there would be an early morning Mass with a Communion breakfast. I am not a Catholic myself, but many of my security men were, and I always tried to give them an opportunity to be greeted by the Cardinal. He was very warm and gracious about this, and I think it meant a lot to them.

For President Diem, the highlight of his whole trip was a visit to the monastery where he had lived during his period of exile. This was up the Hudson not very far from the magnificent estate of the John D. Rockefellers at Pocantico Hills. The Rockefellers had asked President Diem to have Sunday lunch with them, and I drove up with the official party that morning. Ruth somehow missed connections with our cavalcade at the Waldorf-Astoria and was left behind. She persuaded a taxi driver to follow us, but then discovered that she had no money. The driver was quite understanding—once he found out where she was going. "If you're having lunch with the Rockefellers," he said serenely, "I guess somebody there will be able to pay for the ride." Actually, I became quite worried about her and had alerted the security men. She finally arrived, just in time for lunch.

After lunch we drove over to the monastery. Up to this point President Diem had always been rather formal and reserved, but as we drove into the courtyard of the monastery a group of fine-looking young monks gave him a hearty cheer. Instantly he became an entirely different person, full of gaiety and enthusiasm. He took me to see the room where he had lived; it was very bare and austere—little more than a monastic cell. We went down to the kitchen, where he had taken his turn at washing and drying dishes. It was obvious that he was deeply moved by the whole experience, and I have thought of this episode many times while reading about the strife between the Catholics and Buddhists in Vietnam.

President Diem left Los Angeles on May 18 and six days later Dr. Konrad Adenauer, the Chancellor of Germany, came to town. This remarkable man was already eighty-one years old, but he was as erect and alert as a person half his age. There was, I thought, something almost Oriental about his high cheekbones and hooded eyes. His mind was razor sharp;

his memory for names and faces was phenomenal. Although his political enemies depicted him as austere and unyielding, I found him to be an extremely warmhearted person, devoted to his family (he brought his son and daughter with him) and full of humor.

Plans called for the German Chancellor to meet President Eisenhower at his Gettysburg farm, and so on the appointed day—it was a Sunday—I took off in an Aero Commander (a small twin-engine aircraft) with Colonel Draper acting as pilot. We flew up to an airfield near Greenwich, Connecticut, where Dr. Adenauer was spending the weekend with friends, Mr. and Mrs. Daniel Heinemann. It struck me as interesting that just a dozen years after the fall of the Third Reich, the leader of the German nation should be visiting a Jewish family. But, of course, Adenauer had never accepted the Nazis or their twisted ideas. It was, in fact, his refusal to substitute the swastika for the German flag that had resulted in his being taken into custody by Hitler's men. Our troops found him at the end of the war calmly working in his garden and waiting—rather like De Gaulle—for Destiny to place him at the head of his people.

After some difficulty I was able to find the Heinemann home, pick up the Chancellor and his interpreter, Heinz Weber, and fly them back to Gettysburg. Herr Weber was one of the most remarkable interpreters I ever met. He was not only very accurate and very fast and took very few notes, but he was able to catch and reflect the very intonations and gestures of the speaker.

We had a pleasant flight to Gettysburg and landed on the grass runway near the farmhouse where the President was waiting in slacks, tweed jacket, and wide-brimmed hat. His son John, then a major in the Army, was with him. John is well-informed and articulate, but always defers in military fashion when in his father's presence. This day I rarely heard him speak at all, except in answer to direct questions, as the Chancellor and the President covered many topics.

By now it was almost lunchtime, and we walked up to the famous farmhouse. It is an attractive, white-painted brick colonial house with an entrance hall down the center, a large living room on the left, the President's study and a dining room on the right. Across the back of the house is a spacious screened porch with a fine view of the rolling Pennsylvania countryside. I remember hearing President Eisenhower say that as a young man, after graduating from West Point, he was stationed at Gettysburg, and he would sometimes drive over to the Gettysburg battlefield in an old Dodge car that he had, sit there on Sunday afternoons, and go over the details of the great battle in his mind. He said that this made an impression on him that never faded and finally was one of the factors that brought him back there to live.

Our lunch on this particular day was an American-style meal that seemed to intrigue Chancellor Adenauer. It was actually a rather elaborate version of a TV dinner—frozen food heated and served on the tray itself. As I recall, we had tuna fish with a sauce, carrots and peas, and potatoes, served to us by Filipino house boys and enhanced with a good German white wine.

After lunch the President took the Chancellor on a tour of the farm. This was the first time that the press had been allowed to be present, and it seemed to me that the President became a little irritated with reporters swarming at his heels and climbing on the fences. Adenauer showed a great interest in American farming methods and particularly in a three-year-old prize bull that tipped the scales at 1650 pounds.

After the inspection the President and the Chancellor climbed into an Aero Commander with Colonel Draper and a security man (at this time the Aero Commander was the only small plane approved for the Presidential flights). I got into another one with John Eisenhower and General Snyder, the President's physician. The flight to Washington from Gettysburg takes only a few minutes, but the air was rough and we bumped around considerably. When we landed, Foster Dulles, who was on hand to meet us, remarked to Chancellor Adenauer that it was a bit alarming to see two such important persons flying on such a windy day in such a small plane. "Three important persons," said the Chancellor with a twinkle. "The pilot was more important than either of us."

Adenauer stayed at the Blair House for four days. I became quite fond of his son George, who had a passion for jazz music. I like it myself, and so one night we went to a Washington night club and listened to Dixieland music until about 3 in the morning. We both must have looked a little seedy the next day, because the Chancellor glanced at us and said dryly, "When you're my age, your sleep will become more important to you than any amount of jazz."

Often, when a distinguished foreign statesman left this country, I would be asked by the Secretary of State or some of my other colleagues in the State Department for my impressions of the visitor. Did he seem genuinely friendly toward the United States? Did he mention any particular aspects of our policy that seemed to displease him? In the case of Chancellor Adenauer I felt sure that his friendship for our country and people was completely genuine, and that we were fortunate to have a man of such firmness and ability at the head of a nation destined to play such a critical role in world history.

Less than a month after Adenauer's departure, Prime Minister Nobusuke Kishi of Japan arrived. Curiously enough, I had a few qualms about playing host to a Japanese. I was used to the Germans, because I had seen a lot of them as Ambassador in Luxembourg. In the case of Chancellor Adenauer I knew that he had been strongly anti-Nazi and was now strongly pro-American. But I remembered vividly the day of the attack on Pearl Harbor and seeing the smoke rising from the courtyard of the Japanese Embassy in Washington as their secret documents and files were being burned. After all, we had defeated these people, made them lose face. Could they really be as friendly as they seemed?

Fortunately, the Japanese Ambassador in Washington was a most able and attractive man. His name was Koichiro Asakai but everyone called him "Ko." He had short-cropped hair and a very winning smile. He was an excellent tennis player. His wife, a member of a distinguished Japanese family, had gone to school in Washington and was a very attractive woman, especially when she wore her Japanese dress, as she did sometimes at official functions. She and her husband spoke fluent English, were members of the Chevy Chase Club, and were as popular a diplomatic pair as we had in Washington.

My friendship with the Ambassador was very helpful in planning the Prime Minister's visit, because if you are on a first-name basis you can speak frankly about what the visitor wants to do or what the State Department wants him to do, and in the end get much more satisfactory results. I learned, for example, that Mr. Kishi loved golf and baseball and so was able to arrange a golf game for him with President Eisenhower and a visit to Yankee Stadium that included lunch with the inimitable Casey Stengel.

Mr. Kishi had a beaming smile, and since he also had rather protruding teeth he was affectionately dubbed "Bugs Bunny" by the press. A photograph of him in a Yankee baseball cap was so widely circulated that on one occasion, when we were driving from one appointment to another in New York and were held up in traffic, a truck driver stuck his head out of his cab and yelled, "Hey, Kishi, where's your baseball cap?"

As I grew to know him, I became convinced that Kishi really did admire Americans and desire their friendship. Proof of this came later on, in Japan, when he was stabbed by a Japanese youth who considered him too pro-Western. Fortunately he recovered, and was very kind to Ruth and me when we saw him in Japan on a round-the-world trip that we made after my retirement from office.

In terms of energy and personality, our next visitor was in a class by himself. This was Pakistan's Prime Minister Huseyn Shaheed Suhrawardy. I liked this man from the moment I met him. He was very short and bulky, almost as wide as he was tall—Mr. Five-by-Five, some of us called him. He had a rather dark skin, a flashing smile, and a sense of humor that was as sharp as a stiletto. Educated at Oxford, he spoke perfect English and was one of the most impressive orators that ever came to the United States. His command of our language was almost

Churchillian. Shortly after his visit here a change of government forced him to resign as Prime Minister, and he has been
out of office ever since. This baffles me, since in my opinion he
did an excellent job for his country while in office and I cannot understand why a man of his talents is not being used
today.

The first thing I noticed about the Prime Minister was that
he was a fanatical camera addict. When he arrived at the airport, and American photographers began taking pictures, he
seized a camera and started taking pictures of them. He did
this so often during his visit that he became known as a VIP
shutter-bug.

Prime Minister Suhrawardy was a man of fantastic energy.
He hated to go to bed. Time and again, when some official
function ended at 11 or 11:30 in the evening, he would ask
Ruth and me to join him at Blair House. There we would talk
or listen to music until 2 or 3 in the morning, and he would
protest volubly when we tried to leave. He never drank anything but orange juice and consumed gallons of this. He loved
to dance, and like many heavy people was marvelously light
on his feet.

His official conversations in Washington dealt mainly with
the touchy question of Kashmir, the disputed area that lies
between Pakistan and India. He made frequent references to
this in his speeches, although our State Department—not wanting to offend India—was trying to play the matter down.

When these conversations were ended, we took the Prime
Minister on a cross-country tour. He wanted to see Pikes Peak,
the Grand Canyon, Hollywood, and Las Vegas, so we included
all of these points in our itinerary. In Colorado Springs we
stayed at the Broadmoor Hotel, where we had beautiful rooms
looking out over the swimming pool and gardens to the snow-
covered peaks of the Rockies. We had planned a dinner for
the official party at a wonderful restaurant called the Garden
of the Gods, owned by some friends of mine, Mr. and Mrs. Al
Hill, of Dallas, Texas. Just before dinner I was astounded to
get a telephone call from Jim Curry, formerly my air attaché

at our Embassy in Luxembourg. He said that he had read of my arrival in the paper and that he hoped we could get together. He added that another friend of ours was in town and wanted to see me. This was Peter Townsend, famous for his romance with Princess Margaret Rose.

Townsend had served as air attaché to the British Ambassador in Luxembourg while I was there, and we had gotten to know him quite well. This was at the height of the furor over whether or not a divorced man would be allowed to marry a British Princess. Townsend was always rather reserved about the matter, but we would discuss it occasionally. I felt that he was a little bitter about the decision that was finally made, but I also felt that the Princess was more infatuated than anything else and that eventually she would make a happy marriage—which, of course, she did.

Peter happened to be in Colorado Springs because he was writing a series of articles about North America for some British periodical. He was traveling in an elaborately equipped Land Rover, with every conceivable attachment and gadget, and was on his way from Canada down to Mexico.

I suggested to Prime Minister Suhrawardy that we invite the Currys and Peter Townsend to our dinner, and with his permission they were included in our rather small group. The evening turned out to be a very pleasant one, and the Prime Minister seemed to enjoy himself enormously. He laughingly made the comment to me that he was particularly interested to meet Peter Townsend because during his own career he had had a few collisions with the British Crown himself, and he knew how formidable such opposition could be.

The Prime Minister continued to drink only fruit juice, but not all of his Moslem followers were such abstainers. Now and then one would sidle up to me and say very quietly, "Don't you think a little gin would help this orange juice?" And on some occasions the official cars in our cavalcade filled with these nondrinking Moslems had a very alcoholic aroma. This never bothered me; if our visitors wanted to drink, it was perfectly all right with me. After all, it was their religion, not mine.

None of them overdid it, and if an occasional drink made their trip more enjoyable I certainly had no objections.

The next day the Prime Minister was determined to drive to the top of Pikes Peak. We rented a couple of cars with drivers, and set off with the Prime Minister in very good spirits. With us was the Pakistani Ambassador, Mohammed Ali. I was a bit worried about the Ambassador because I knew he had a heart condition. Pikes Peak is over 14,000 feet high, the oxygen content of the air at the top of the mountain is quite low, and I felt sure that Mr. Ali's doctor would not want him to make the trip. I suggested that he stay behind, but the Prime Minister was one of those people who has so much health and vitality that he thinks everyone else must be the same. He kept teasing his Ambassador about being a sissy, with the result that in the end Mohammed Ali came with us.

About halfway up the mountain I noticed that the Ambassador was getting very pale and was beginning to gasp for breath. There is a roadside filling station and soft-drink place about halfway to the top of Pikes Peak. I suggested that we stop there and stretch our legs. While the Prime Minister was drinking Coca-Cola with two of his Cabinet members, I quietly bundled Mohammed Ali into the second car that had been following us and sent him back to Colorado Springs. Suhrawardy thought that Mohammed Ali was still with us, but when we got to the top of the mountain and two of his Cabinet ministers passed out, he became very worried and started blaming himself for having persuaded his Ambassador to come. He was much relieved when I told him that Mohammed Ali was on his way back to the hotel where a doctor could take care of him. "I see now," he said, "why they call you Wiley. You're a wily fellow, Wiley!"

At the top of the mountain the Prime Minister enjoyed the view and had a fine time snapping pictures. He even took photographs of what he called "my fainted Cabinet." He seemed totally unaffected by the altitude, but I felt a bit light-headed and noticed that even one of our indestructible American security men was looking rather pale and unhappy. We finally drove back down, and everyone revived. The doctor at the hotel, however, ordered Mohammed Ali to bed and told me that he really might not have survived a trip to the top of the mountain. The Ambassador did, in fact, die of a heart attack a few months ago, which ended a useful and colorful career.

After showing the Prime Minister the Air Force Academy at Colorado Springs, we took off for our next stop which was to be the Grand Canyon. It is impossible to land a big airplane very near the canyon, so we landed at Winslow, Arizona, and made the rest of the trip by bus. At Winslow the Governor of Arizona was on hand to meet the Prime Minister with various dignitaries, including an Indian chief leading a delegation of Indians. Suhrawardy was constantly amazed at the warmth and friendliness of the American people. He could not understand why the citizens of a big, powerful country should be so attentive to the leader of a small, new one. When he thanked the Governor he said, "I am ashamed to have all of this happen to me." Everything about Arizona delighted him. He was particularly amused by the fact that in one small town the sheriff was a woman. He kept saying that he was going to import some women sheriffs into Pakistan, where they could certainly use some.

Our bus ride up to the Grand Canyon was a memorable one. The Prime Minister had the first seat just inside the door, I sat across the aisle, and the rest of the bus was filled with members of our party and some of the Arizonians who had met us at Winslow. The Prime Minister decided that the best way to pass the time would be for all of us to sing songs. He started teaching us songs he had sung when he was a student at Oxford, songs from Pakistan and India, and some of his favorite dance tunes. Those of us who had hoped to get a cat-nap during the ride were sadly mistaken. The Prime Minister would turn around and point a finger at someone and cry, "You're not singing! I order you to sing. I have been made an honorary sheriff by the Governor of this state and anyone who doesn't sing will have to go to jail." In between songs he would become ecstatic about the scenery. He would nudge me and say, "Oh, Wiley, look at that, isn't it magnificent! Are you sure it isn't painted? Could I really go out and touch it?"

The Grand Canyon made a profound impression on Suhrawardy, as it does on everyone. Accommodations there are rather limited. The furniture in my own room looked as if it were older than the canyon itself. The room was very small, and I was brooding about my primitive quarters when there was a knock at the door. It was one of our security men who told me that, as a result of some mix-up, he and one of the military aides for the Prime Minister had no accommodations at all. As a result, two cots were brought into my room, which made it so crowded that we couldn't even close the door. But we were all so tired from our singing bus trip that we slept well anyway.

The next day we flew on to California, where the Prime Minister was to address the Los Angeles Council of World Affairs. The speech that he gave after dinner at the Ambassador Hotel was a real spellbinder. He gave a most lucid and illuminating account of the situation in Pakistan and India and —somewhat to the dismay of the State Department, I suppose— spoke very forcibly about the importance of settling the Kashmir dispute.

On our second night in Los Angeles the Prime Minister was entertained by a group of motion picture producers, including Cecil B. De Mille. Again the Prime Minister's talk was so effective that Mr. De Mille leaned over to me and whispered, "This man ought to be in the movies!" De Mille also told me that he once had asked Suhrawardy whether or not he should make his famous motion picture *The Ten Commandments*, to which the Moslem Suhrawardy replied, "There are two forces at work in the universe, one that builds up and one that tears down. Let nothing stop you from making such a picture. The world needs it."

After dinner, a good friend of ours gave a private party for the Prime Minister. This was Cobina Wright, who, of course, is very much at home all over the world and certainly knows everyone in Hollywood. Cobina's house is charming, with beautiful French furniture and one of the most spectacular views in California. The Prime Minister was fascinated by Cobina herself and the story of how, after the stock market crash, she had had to earn money for her family and so had taken up writing as a career. Cobina told me how impressed she had been by our security men, some of whom she had met that night. I suggested that she mention them in one of her columns, which she did. I am sure that the superiors of Frank Madden, Joseph Rosetti, and Hibbard Lambkin were startled to read in Cobina Wright's column about their boys being out on the town with the Hollywood "Jet Set."

Another highlight of our stay in Los Angeles was a party given for the Prime Minister by Mary Pickford. Suhrawardy had looked forward with great anticipation to this evening at "Pickfair," and so had I. I remembered riding around in Beverly Hills as a small boy and seeing "Pickfair," where Miss Pickford and her husband Douglas Fairbanks lived. For this occasion the gardens had been lighted and the house was a mass of flowers. Many members of the movie colony were there, and Suhrawardy distinguished himself on the dance floor. By 2 o'clock many of the guests had left, and our own cars were waiting at the front door, but now Mary Pickford led us downstairs into a small room with a long bar across one end and heavy oaken tables and chairs, rather like an English tavern. The walls were covered with pictures of scenes from motion pictures in which the mistress of "Pickfair" had starred. Sitting on the bar was a young man with a guitar who turned out to be an accomplished folk singer. He played for us until about 3:30. By this time I was more than ready for bed, but when we got back to the Ambassador Hotel Suhrawardy insisted that I have sandwiches and orange juice with him in the VIP cottage. The man was incredible; he seemed able to function with no sleep at all.

I had a little fun with him the next morning, though. At about 10:15 I went to the VIP cottage and found Suhrawardy eating breakfast. He was dressed in white silk pajamas and a silk robe and was joking with some members of his entourage about the party the night before. They were teasing him about his dancing and saying that it was just as well that the people back in Pakistan had not seen him cavorting with Hollywood starlets. "Yes," said Suhrawardy, munching his toast, "I'm glad there were no photographers. Sometimes such pictures can be very misleading."

I happened to have the morning paper under my arm. "Oh," I said, unfolding it, "but there are pictures! There's a large photograph here of you dancing with one of those little blonde actresses. I'm sure it'll be picked up in Pakistan." He turned as pale as his complexion would permit and snatched the paper. "Where is it?" he cried, feverishly turning the pages. "This is terrible, horrible, a disaster!"

I let him look for a few seconds before admitting that I was just teasing him. "Oh," he said, "there goes that Wiley again. I swear you've got the right name!"

From California we went to Las Vegas, Nevada. The reason was not just to inspect the night life and gambling. The Prime Minister wanted to visit the Hoover Dam, and Las Vegas was the nearest place with adequate hotel accommodations. The dam was of great interest to Mr. Suhrawardy, because he felt that such hydroelectric plants were badly needed in his own country. At the dam itself, which is certainly one of the most impressive man-made objects in the world, engineers explained every phase of the operation to us.

After this briefing we went back to Las Vegas, where we were guests at Wilbur Clark's Desert Inn. Very much aware of the fact that official visitors live in a constant glare of publicity, I had arranged with Ambassador Mohammed Ali for each member of our group—both Pakistani and American—to pay his own hotel bill. The Pakistani were just as eager for this to be a matter of record as we were. The Prime Minister did not gamble himself, but he was astounded by the number of people at the gambling tables and the pleasure they seemed to derive from losing their money. He was also amazed when somebody told him that none of the doors had any locks on them—none being needed because the buildings remain open twenty-four hours a day.

We had a fine dinner at the Desert Inn, then went over to Stardust directly across the street, where again we were guests of the Clarks. When the time came for us to leave the next morning the Pakistanis were astonished to find that their only expense had been the cost of their rooms and their breakfast. Everything else had been taken care of by the generosity of the Clarks. "Why do they do it?" one puzzled Pakistani said to me. "Most of us will never come back here again, so they'll never get their money back through our gambling!" I tried to explain that Wilbur and Toni Clark were simply generous Americans who wanted to offer hospitality to the guests of their nation.

If I have emphasized the social aspect of this trip rather than formal functions and civic dinners, it is probably because Suhrawardy was a man of such refreshing vitality and enthusiasm that when I think of him it is more in terms of gaiety than duty. He certainly made a great many friends in the United States.

The Prime Minister left for home on July 27, but I had no chance to relax. Already my division was working day and night on plans for the most important visit of the year, and Washington was beginning to work itself into a social dither. In October, England's Queen and her Prince Consort were coming to town.

IV
Her Majesty the Queen

In the spring of the year 1607, a handful of sea-weary settlers in three cockleshell ships made a landing on the coast of what is now Virginia, planted a flag in the presence of some startled Indians, and took possession of the land in the name of the British Crown.

Three hundred and fifty years later, the royal possessor of that same crown made a landing at almost the same spot. She came by air, not by sea, and she planted no flags. But in the next six days she conquered the land and its inhabitants all over again.

The state visit in October, 1957, of Her Majesty, Queen Elizabeth II, and His Royal Highness, Prince Philip, Duke of Edinburgh, required months of the most intensive preparation. Their itinerary sounded deceptively simple. They would fly from Canada to Williamsburg, Virginia, spend one night at that handsomely restored capital of the Old Dominion, stay briefly at the White House in Washington as guests of President and Mrs. Eisenhower, visit New York, and then fly home.

But the Queen of England doesn't just drop in on the President of the United States or anyone else. For one thing, her engagements are planned as far as two years in advance, and the amount of free time that she has is more precious than rubies. For another, she is not only the living symbol of the British Empire, she is its proudest possession. France may have the Mona Lisa and Italy the Sistine Chapel, but England has the Queen, and when she goes abroad, centuries of pomp and circumstance go with her.

For weeks, I had had almost daily conferences with Sir Harold Caccia, the able British Ambassador in Washington, and my office had been in the closest consultation with the other Commonwealth embassies involved. Her Majesty was coming not just as the Queen of England but as the Head of the British Commonwealth of Nations, and so the envoys of each of these nations were actively concerned. The six days allotted for the visit had been timed down to the last split second. We had walked over literally every inch of ground, stop watches in hand, with a stand-in whose feminine stride (we hoped) matched the Queen's, and with carefully calculated time allowances for Prince Philip's incurable habit of dropping behind. Ten thousand questions had been asked and answered, ranging from crucial matters affecting the Queen's safety to the amount of time she would need to change her clothes and her preferences where almost everything was concerned: Did she really like her bed with its head to the wall? (yes) Would she bring her own feather pillows? (yes) Was she really allergic to shellfish? (yes)

An avalanche of invitations had descended upon us. Every organization in the United States, it seemed to me, wanted the honor of entertaining the Queen. A blizzard of mail had arrived from people giving frantic and ingenious reasons why they should be invited to meet Her Majesty face to face. When they were politely turned down, as in most cases they had to be, they were likely to write outraged letters demanding to know who *was* being invited, and why. This always reminded me of the remark attributed to Sir Ronald Lindsay, who was the British envoy in 1939 when King George VI and his Queen paid us a visit. "It's just like heaven," Sir Ronald said serenely, "some are taken and some are not!"

Some of the letter-writers, clearly, were more interested in the Prince than in the Queen. We had had requests for locks of his hair, buttons from his uniforms, endless pleas for his autograph. One woman even begged plaintively for one of his socks. It was evident to me that in the last eighteen decades or so, attitudes in this country had undergone considerable change. Instead of wanting to get rid of royalty and all that it stood for, most Americans now wanted to get as close to it as possible!

Certainly Virginia was in a great state of excitement. Williamsburg was scrubbed and polished. Patrick Henry Airport, where the Queen's plane would shortly land, had been manicured down to the last blade of grass. There were name-tapes fastened to the runway showing everyone in the receiving party where to stand. President Eisenhower would not be there; the Chief Executive does not leave the capital to greet state visitors —the Chief of Protocol represents him. But Governor Thomas B. Stanley of Virginia was on hand; so were about ten thousand other pageant-hungry natives of the Old Dominion. Six hundred photographers waited with cameras poised. Every radio and television network was represented. Flags whipped in the bright sunlight; there was an electric expectancy in the air. As Ruth said, preparations had been so feverish and had gone on for so long that the last few moments of waiting felt like the night before Christmas when you were a small child.

As I stood there in my dark suit with my black homburg in hand, my mind was a jumble of last-minute question marks. Some of them were faintly ridiculous: would they remember to give tranquilizers to the horses that would pull the royal couple's coach through the streets of Williamsburg? Others were serious: would the Queen have the stamina to endure the rigorous program that had been laid out for her? Her personal advisors had assured me that she would. I had spent much time with the Queen's press secretary, Commander Richard Colville, and her assistant private secretary, Lieutenant Colonel Martin Charteris, a tall Briton who fascinated everyone by languidly taking a pinch of snuff now and then from an elegant silver snuffbox. Both these gentlemen had approved all our arrangements. Indeed, it seemed to me that they had an astonishing amount of authority; they could say yes or no to anything with far less fuss and red tape than we sometimes had to endure. They traveled everywhere with Her Majesty, and certainly were in a position to know what she could or couldn't do. But her visit was going to be something of an ordeal just the same.

The Queen herself was reported to have said that she wished to see—and be seen by—as many Americans as possible. The six-day schedule (or shedge-yule, as our British friends pronounced it) had been planned with this in mind. It was so tight that if we lost even half an hour anywhere along the line I was sure that we would never make it up.

The official timetable for the first few hours that the Queen would spend on American soil contained twenty-six separate arrivals and departures—some at five-minute intervals. And this was just the first half day. Succeeding days in Washington and New York were just as crowded. I was tired already—responsibility can be more fatiguing than anything else—but I was counting on the excitement and drama of the occasion to give me all the strength I needed. Actually, I felt as if I might be coming down with a cold. But I was determined to attribute my sniffles, if any, to hay fever. The royal couple were taking no chances with contagion; they had been given shots for Asiatic flu before leaving England, and had left one of the Queen's ladies-in-waiting in Canada when she developed a heavy cold. We had matched these precautions by having the staff at the Williamsburg Inn given flu shots also, one of the endless details my department had handled.

It was hard to say which side of the Atlantic had seen the most strenuous preparations. Months, of course, had gone into the planning and creation of the Queen's wardrobe. Protocol decreed that if she wore a dress in one country, she could not wear it in another, and so she was said to be bringing at least fifty changes of costume. Her designers, Norman Hartnell and Hardy Amies, had to be sure that every outfit was impeccable in fit and taste. Moreover, they had to work within a rigid framework of rules. No tight skirts: too tricky when it came to getting out of automobiles. No garish colors, but enough so that the royal figure would stand out in a crowd. Small hats, so that the monarch's face could easily be seen. I knew that the Queen sometimes wore broad-brimmed hats at garden parties or in the Royal Enclosure at Ascot, but this was the exception to the rule—and even then the big hats were likely to have lacy or transparent brims. The hat, I was told, was held in place by a pair of spring clips so that the Queen would never be seen in the awkward position of having to hold her hat. It was also said that her skirts were weighted to keep them from blowing in a sudden breeze, but as a mere man I could not say whether or not this was true.

Her Majesty, I knew, would wear white gloves almost constantly, so that every wave of her hand could be seen. Her clothes would have no frills or bows that might catch on projections. Her handbags would have straps or handles to slip over her arm, leaving her hands free for receiving bouquets or the endless handshaking. Such pocketbooks would contain no money; royal ladies do not carry anything so mundane. A lady-in-waiting would supply currency if the Queen decided to buy anything. A lady-in-waiting would also have extra stockings and shoes in a handbag in case Her Majesty snagged a stocking or lost the heel of a shoe. I doubted whether the royal handbag would contain a lipstick, either; the Queen does not repair her face in public. The perfection and durability of her make-up were really amazing. I had been told that on her world tour shortly after her coronation, her beauty advisor had preceded her everywhere, taking notes on temperature, humidity, sunlight, and any other factor that might influence the Queen's choice of cosmetics. I could well believe it.

I knew that the Queen was not tall—five feet four at the most—and that her designers would have been concerned with giving her height and dignity. She would be wearing fairly high heels, and had a preference for open-toed shoes—more comfortable for standing interminably as she often had to do. Sometimes, it was said, the royal toes would be seen to wiggle— a trick she had learned from her own Guardsmen who used it to lessen the fatigue of standing at rigid attention.

With the royal party, I knew, would be Miss Margaret ("Bo-bo") MacDonald, who had attended the Queen ever since Her Majesty was a small baby. As the Queen's personal

dresser, Miss MacDonald was responsible for the royal wardrobe and supervised the packing and unpacking of dresses,
coats, suits, evening gowns, and accessories. Each costume
would be catalogued and assigned a number. If a suit, for example, was Number 15, then the hat, belt, gloves, and shoes to
be worn with it would also be so numbered, and each outfit
would be packed in its own black leather case bearing the
Queen's monogram.

As we stood there, watching the sky, I was sure that Miss
MacDonald would be hovering over the Queen's dressing table
in the big Royal Canadian Air Force plane, checking the light
floral scents that she used, supervising make-up and hair-styl-
ing, and generally putting the final touches on her royal mistress. To help her there would also be a hairdresser, an assistant
dresser, and a couple of maids. Her Majesty had changed her
hair-style lately from a center part to a slightly bouffant arrangement that was more attractive and better suited to the
magnificent tiaras she would be wearing in the evening.

All in all, it seemed to me that the Queen's designers were
a pair of lucky men: they were given almost unlimited funds
to create fabulous clothes for a lovely young woman with an
admirable figure and magnificent jewels. Dame Edith Sitwell's
sour observation that the average Englishwoman dressed "as
if she had been a mouse in a former incarnation, or expected
to be one in the next" certainly did not apply to the most important Englishwoman of all.

No one knew in advance, of course, what the Queen would
wear. From the moment Hartnell and Amies brought their first
sketches to the Palace for her approval to the moment when
she finally appeared in public wearing their creations, this was
a closely guarded secret. The Queen's preference for pastel
colors was well known; also her distaste for green and black.
But that was all. This had led to some feverish speculation
among the ladies in our party who would meet the Queen and
be seen with her: would their costumes be in harmony with
the one Her Majesty had chosen? My own wife had made a
special trip to Rome, where her favorite Italian designer—

Fontana Sisters—had created four evening gowns and several other items for her. So she was well prepared, but as late as that morning she had still been worrying about whether or not her beige suit was "the right thing to wear." From the way she looked, I was sure it was.

Another question that apparently was rocking the nation to its foundations was whether or not American women should curtsy to the Queen. For weeks in Washington, it seemed to me, the ladies had talked of little else. The British Embassy had let it be known that such a gesture, while not required, would be appreciated as an act of courtesy. My own position was that while this might be proper on British territory, American citizens owed allegiance to no foreign sovereign, and therefore should follow the custom of their own country and simply shake hands. This, I knew, was what Ruth was going to do, but I was also sure that there were a good many ladies who had been practicing curtsies for weeks and had no intention of being robbed of the one chance they might have to display their skill.

How to address the Queen was also a topic of much discussion. Here the recommendation of our department was to follow European custom, which was to address the sovereign for the first time as "Your Majesty," and after that be content with a simple "ma'am." With Philip it would be "Your Royal Highness" the first time, and thereafter simply "sir."

A murmur went through the great crowd as a speck appeared in the northern sky. In the last few moments of her flight, I felt sure, the Queen would be going through her card trick—memorizing names and key facts about the people she was about to meet. These were written down on cards for her to study. She was said to practice this every morning at breakfast, and to have become highly skilled at it.

On came the big white, red-trimmed plane—an RCAF 1000, similar to a DC-6. It touched down and taxied toward us. For the first time in history, a reigning British Queen was on American soil.

The crowd grew silent as the landing ramp was pushed forward. Then the door of the plane opened and the Queen stepped out. She wore a slightly flared coat of peacock-blue silk shantung with black velvet collar and cuffs, and a matching afternoon dress. Her hat was of pheasant feathers bordered with black velvet.* For a moment I thought she looked tense and uncertain, but as she came down the ramp in the bright sunlight my chief impression—as it had been on other occasions when I had seen her—was that she was far more regal and radiant in person than in her photographs. No camera could catch the perfection of her complexion or the direct glance of her blue eyes.

The tension I had thought I noticed disappeared almost at once; her manner was formal, but gracious and self-possessed. When I welcomed her to the United States on behalf of President Eisenhower, she smiled and said, "Thank you, Ambassador Buchanan; it's a great pleasure to be here."

Behind her came Prince Philip, tall and handsome, blond hair glinting in the sun. He was wearing a gray flannel suit and carrying a brown, snap-brim hat in his hand. I had just such a brown Locke hat that was a great favorite of mine. Ruth had sternly forbidden me to wear it—much too informal, she said. Now here was His Royal Highness carrying an identical hat.

The scarlet-coated Marine Band played "God Save the Queen." The cannon boomed. I presented the waiting dignitaries to the Queen. We proceeded to the battery of microphones mounted on a specially constructed platform where she made a short but gracious reply to my words of welcome and those of Governor Stanley. Then we walked to the limousines that were waiting to take us to Jamestown, twenty-two miles away, for the opening of the festival that was to commemorate the founding of the first permanent English-speaking settlement in the new world.

The Queen, Governor Stanley, and I rode in the first car, President Eisenhower's bubble-topped Lincoln (the Queen

---

* For these and other fashion notes I am indebted to my wife's diary.

liked it better than the one she had had in Ottawa the previous day, which she said was "too bubbly"). The Prince and Ruth were in the second car with Mrs. Stanley. In this separation of the royal couple we were following the rules of protocol: the Queen outranks the Prince. Also, it gave the spectators a double glimpse of royalty, so to speak. As we rode through the excited crowds, sometimes six-deep along our route, I observed to Her Majesty that I had never seen so many happy faces. "Faces?" said the Queen with a smile. "I don't see any faces. All I see is cameras." This was true; I had never felt so photographed in my life. In the car behind us, Philip remarked on it also. "This," he said to Ruth, "is one of those times when I wish I had some stock in the Kodak company."

The role that Philip set himself on such occasions was that of breezy ice-breaker and humanizer of what might otherwise turn into a stiff or sticky situation. The Queen could not unbend beyond a certain point, but her Consort could. He had a quick and lively sense of humor, and used it constantly in little quips and sallies. When Ruth presented him, in the car, with a formidable-looking leather-bound list of the events that were facing him in the next six days, he raised his eyebrows in mock dismay. "What," he said, "no memorial service at the end?"

He was said to have a quick and lively temper, too—perhaps a legacy from his mother who, so the story went, became so annoyed with the Czar of Russia at her wedding (he kept throwing rice at her despite her protests) that she took off her slipper and whacked him over the head with it. Philip's pet aversion was the intrusive press, especially photographers who crowded or annoyed the Queen. He once said, "I am completely stoic; I read about myself as if I were an animal at the zoo." But this was wishful thinking. The newspapers said he had glared at one cameraman in Canada the day before. I knew he would be on his best behavior with us, but still I hoped nothing would happen to annoy him.

Certainly among the female spectators there was as much interest in Philip as in the Queen. Over and over, as they drove along, Ruth could hear a high-pitched, ecstatic squeal: "There he *is;* there he IS!" How any man could endure such constant adulation without either feeling silly or having his head completely turned I could not imagine, but no doubt Philip was used to it.

As for the Queen, she was amazing. Here was a young woman with two children, a personal income of over a million dollars a year, nominal ruler of more than 600 million people scattered all over the planet. She lived in a kind of royal fish bowl where privacy was virtually impossible, where thousands stared, copied her mannerisms, criticized her clothes, objected to the sports she enjoyed, even complained about the way she read her speeches. She could not afford to make a single mistake. If a crease appeared in her dress, some London newspaper was likely to run a picture (one did) with the disapproving caption: "The rumpled Queen." Dining in public, she could eat almost nothing, for fear a photographer might catch her with her mouth open. She could never allow herself to become ruffled or upset or even tired . . . or show it if she did.

No matter what she did—and she did everything almost perfectly—somebody would find fault. Her American visit had already aroused criticism from snipers in England, where grumbling about the monarchy is a well-established literary pastime. As far back as the 1920s, H. G. Wells was complaining that the British court was "alien and uninspiring." ("I may be uninspiring," growled Elizabeth's grandfather, George V, "but I'm damned if I'm alien!") Now Malcolm Muggeridge, former editor of *Punch*, was likening the Queen's visit to "a soap opera" and criticizing adulation of the monarchy as "unhealthy." As a result, I had noticed, he was dropped from a scheduled television appearance on the BBC, as was Lord Altrincham, a publicity-minded young peer who had asserted that his sovereign's technique in delivering a speech was "a pain in the neck."

The Queen not only had managed to endure all this, but had somehow contrived to remain a good-humored, pleasant, warmhearted human being. I noticed, on that first long drive, as I was to notice throughout the trip, that she never failed to acknowledge a salutation. Even if one lone individual along the way waved or bowed, she replied with a gesture or a smile. She must have felt at times as if that smile were pasted to her face, but somehow she managed to keep it bright and genuine.

Ruth and I had been at the Queen's coronation, and so had our children, who of course were thrilled. Bonnie, our oldest, who was then about twelve, wrote a glowing description of everything for one of the Washington newspapers. The high point of her narrative came when the Queen, "looking like a Fairy Princess, stepped back into her royal coach to hold hands with the Prince she loved." I told the Queen about this as we drove along. "But of course," I added, "if Your Majesty had the scepter in one hand, and the orb in the other, I don't see how you could have done much hand-holding." "Oh," said the Queen demurely, "there are stands for those things inside the coach!" So I was left to draw my own conclusions as to the hand-holding.

As we drove along, I became more and more impressed with the range of the Queen's knowledge, and the intensity with which she had done her homework before meeting Americans. She knew all about the Buchanans in Scotland, and who was the present Head of the Clan. The talk veered around to antique furniture, which is a hobby of mine. She was interested when I told her that in London I had been able to buy a Louis XV desk that had once belonged to her grandparents. It came on the market after the death of Queen Mary when some of her possessions were taken from Marlborough House and sold. Following the ancient tradition that if a sovereign admires any of your possessions you must offer it as a gift, I smilingly suggested that I return the desk to her. She refused, of course, but she said she was glad to know where it was.

Our first stop was on Jamestown Island, where the Queen and the Prince attended a brief service in the old church whose ivy-clad tower dates back to the early seventeenth century. Afterward, in the churchyard, they heard the old colored sexton tell the story of the "mother-in-law tree," a sycamore that grew up to separate the tombs of the Rev. James Blair, founder of the college of William and Mary, and his wife Sarah. According to the legend, Sarah's mother-in-law did her best to separate her from her husband while they were alive, and, failing in this, planted the sycamore to accomplish it after they were dead.

At Jamestown Festival Park, an honor guard of halberdiers and pikemen in seventeenth-century costume saluted the Queen. She and Philip seemed fascinated by the restoration of old Fort James. They saw "prisoners" seated in the stocks. ("Does it hurt?" asked the Queen. "Anyone thrown rotten eggs at you?" asked the Prince.) They watched an Indian maiden named Sparkling Eyes grind maize in a primitive mortar. At one point Philip lagged behind to talk to three costumed citizens, a man and two women, outside one of the crude dwellings. The man explained that he was supposed to represent a typical settler. "With two wives?" asked the Prince cheerily. The "settler" was too startled to attempt a reply.

Ruth, meantime, torn between remaining with Philip and keeping up with the Queen, finally joined us. "Your Majesty," she said, "I'm afraid I've lost Prince Philip." "Well," said the Queen resignedly, "you'll have to get used to that!"

When we walked down to see the replicas of the three ships that had brought the colonists to this spot three and a half centuries ago, all of us were amazed at their size. They seemed incapable of crossing Chesapeake Bay, let alone the Atlantic. The Queen wanted to step aboard the 100-ton *Susan Constant*, and she did, while costumed mariners stared from the forty-ton *Godspeed* and the equally small *Discovery*. Some eager spectator sang out, "Be careful, Queen!" as she walked down the gangplank, and Elizabeth flashed him a friendly smile. I had the feeling that all traces of constraint were gone, and that she was really enjoying herself.

Our inexorable schedule drew us on like a strong ebb tide: to William and Mary College where the royal pair had tea with the president, Alvin Duke Chandler, and his wife (time allotted: twenty-five minutes); then to the building designed by Sir Christopher Wren, where the Queen spoke briefly from the balcony, and praised the leaders of the American Revolution, a gesture that must have startled the ghost of Patrick Henry—and the ghost of George III even more.

Next a handsome horse-drawn phaeton appeared, with a Negro coachman in Colonial livery on the box and two Negro footmen standing behind. With Mr. and Mrs. Winthrop Rockefeller, the Queen and Prince were driven at a sedate clip-clop to the Governor's Palace, where a reception was being given in their honor by the proud and happy Virginians.

With their strong sense of family, Virginians had extra reason to be proud. Some genealogical wizard back in England had solemnly reported that Elizabeth was George Washington's second cousin, nine times removed. Not only that, she was also Robert E. Lee's distant relative. So the guests could justifiably regard the Queen as a long-lost cousin.

Now and then, as she moved through the crowd of some 1500 people in the gardens of the Governor's Palace, I would single out someone to present to her. She was always most gracious about this, never refusing, and it was fun to watch the incredulity and delight of the lucky one. Both the Queen and the Prince could become a bit frosty, though, if anyone tried to monopolize them or take more than a fair share of their limited time. Later in the trip, when a well-known socialite was first introduced to her, the Queen was her charming self. But when the same person approached us again, and I mentioned her name, the Queen said coolly, "Oh, yes, I've already spoken to her," and directed her attention elsewhere.

After the garden party with its string orchestra playing English waltzes and its waiters in knee breeches, Mr. and Mrs. Rockefeller showed us through the Governor's Palace. Next came the Capitol, where Patrick Henry had uttered his impassioned plea for liberty or death. Mrs. A. W. Snead, a Williamsburg lady, led the way, resplendent in a billowing cerise gown that she called a farthingale. By now it was almost dark. Two Negro footmen, elegant in knee-length maroon coats, held eighteenth-century copper lanterns so that Elizabeth could find her way along the brick path.

In the old building, Philip seemed much amused by the famed Williamsburg Bible and its misprints which substitute "vinegar" for "vineyards" and "printers" for "princes." When he saw the phrase "printers [instead of princes] have persecuted me without cause," he laughed ruefully and observed: "Very true words," an echo, no doubt, of his distaste for gossip columnists and newspaper critics of the Queen.

From the Capitol, still on rigid schedule, we were driven to the Williamsburg Inn. Here the Queen and Prince had an unpretentious but attractive suite of rooms, the same ones that were occupied by the Queen's mother in 1939. Ruth and I had rooms directly underneath them, and I must say, we never had quieter overhead neighbors—not a sound came through the ceiling.

Not much more than an hour was allowed for dressing for the black-tie dinner given that night at the Inn. Just above us, I knew, the Queen's hairdresser and personal dressers would be working with quiet efficiency to prepare Her Majesty. Lady Caccia, the British Ambassador's wife, had also brought her personal maid. Ruth had left hers behind in Washington—on such trips there was always a shortage of accommodations, plane seats, and so on—but managed to look stunning anyway in her champagne *peau de soie* dress with gold and topaz embroidery.

Actually, Ruth did such an efficient job of packing that it amazed me. Every outfit was in its proper sequence with its proper accessories. I am the world's worst packer; for me the high point of any trip comes when I get home and am able to throw everything into the laundry hamper. Usually I managed to have my suits pressed by the valet service, but Messrs. Anderson and Sheppard, my London tailors, would have been aghast if they could have seen how their masterpieces were sometimes treated.

The Queen that night wore a full-skirted gown of heavy white satin, sparkling with imitation moonstones, pearls, diamonds, and sapphires. Real jewels are never used on royal evening gowns, but Norman Hartnell boasts that never in all his years of designing clothes for the Queen has one of his hand-sewn beads come loose. Her Majesty's tiara was of diamonds and pearls, and she wore a two-strand pearl necklace. Ruth and I both noticed that her long white gloves were made of cloth, not kid—perhaps to enable her to slip her hands out of them more easily. She ate very little of the five-course dinner, of which the main course was boneless breast of fried chicken with Smithfield ham. I knew that our security men had supervised the preparation of the meal in the Inn's kitchen. Another precaution was the locking of the doors of the main dining room during the meal. There had been a few crank letters threatening the Queen, and we were taking no chances.

In her short speech after dinner, the Queen told the guests that she had had "a fascinating day following in the steps of your forefathers and my countrymen." She looked so happy, and her audience so genuinely pleased with her, that I couldn't help thinking that if the underlying political reason for her visit was to heal the rift in Anglo-American relations caused by the Suez incident, the planners of her visit must be congratulating themselves already.

Early the next morning we left the Williamsburg Inn and drove to Patrick Henry Airport where President Eisenhower's plane, the *Columbine III*, was waiting. The *Columbine* herself had been involved in the careful dress rehearsals that had preceded the Queen's arrival—and it was just as well, because on her trial run to Williamsburg she had gotten stuck in some sand and had had to be pulled out ignominiously . . . just the sort of unforeseen mishap that the rehearsals were designed to avoid.

Ruth rode to the airport with the Queen, and the conversation turned to dogs. Ruth confessed to having five dogs in our house. "That's nothing," said the Queen. "I have nine, so many that Philip sometimes threatens to leave home, and the children accuse me of caring more about my dogs than I do about them!" "Oh," said Ruth, "Wiley says the same thing!" We assumed that palace dogs would be beautifully behaved and housebroken, but when we mentioned this later to one of the

Queen's ladies-in-waiting, she rolled up her eyes in an expressive gesture. "That's what the Queen thinks!" she said. Evidently the royal ladies-in-waiting sometimes had to wait on the royal dogs.

On board the *Columbine*, the royal couple relaxed like any married pair. Philip read newspapers. Elizabeth wrote post cards to the children. To do this, she used a handsome leather writing case with her monogram on it, which she opened with a tiny gold key. I couldn't help thinking of all the royal writing cases I had seen in dusty museums: this was the first I had ever seen in actual use. One of our party had a small camera, and was tempted to take a picture of the Queen as she wrote, but one of her attendants objected politely. The Queen, she said, did not like to be photographed in moments of privacy.

The dialogue between the royal couple had a kind of casual hominess that I found quite delightful.

"Philip?" the Queen said in her clipped British accent.

No answer; the Prince, like a typical husband, was buried in the sports section.

"Philip!" (It sounded almost like "Phiddip!")

A startled look from His Royal Highness. "Yes?"

"Which engines do they start first on a big plane like this: the inboard or the outboard?"

A puzzled expression crossed Philip's face, quickly followed by the realization that as an outdoor, masculine fellow he should readily have the answer to this.

"Come on, now," the Queen said laughing, "don't wait until they actually *start* them, Philip!"

So Philip hazarded a guess—fortunately the right one. I was impressed, all over again, with what an extraordinarily handsome man he was: it was easy to understand why the Queen had fallen in love with him. His hands are square and blunt, a sportsman's hands; his feet are quite short and broad for so tall and rangy a body. His eyes are a brilliant, intense blue. His blond hair is thinning a bit now, but he can joke about this. At a meeting in England of the manufacturers of "man-made fibers," he patted himself ruefully on the head. "I'm not very good at producing man-made fibers myself," he said—a typical Philipian quip that brought the house down.

At the Washington airport, according to protocol, I was supposed to leave the airplane first and present the Queen to the President (all other individuals would be presented to her), but I never really had a chance. The Chief Executive was waiting with outstretched hand and the famed Eisenhower grin. I had seen him greet many visiting dignitaries, but never with more genuine warmth and pleasure. "Your Majesty," he said, "you are *most* welcome; indeed you are!"

And indeed, blasé Washington had turned itself inside out to prove it. At the airport, where photographers swarmed, the President gestured wryly at the cameramen. "These," he said to the Queen, "are the nearest thing to a dictatorship that we have in this country!" Sixteen bands were waiting to escort the royal pair as they rode through the streets with the President. Government employees had been given time off to cheer and wave flags; it was estimated later that a million Washingtonians watched the motorcade. Householders had been exhorted to spruce up their property. The grass around the Lincoln Memorial was a bit sunburned, so it had been sprayed with a green dye that made it almost as verdant as an English lawn.

As we moved slowly through the crowds, I could hear the same ecstatic feminine squeals greeting Philip that we had heard the previous day in Virginia. And once, as the car carrying the ladies-in-waiting went by, a goggle-eyed spectator was heard to confide to a companion: "Look! Them's the Queen's maids!" In a way, she was right, but it was an amusing term to apply to those high-born ladies.

At the White House, Mrs. Eisenhower was waiting with her grandchildren to welcome the Queen. She had also given permission for the whole White House staff and their families to line the driveway and thus get a close look at Her Majesty.

Prince Philip was to have the Lincoln Room, where the Great Emancipator had signed the document that freed the slaves, and where his ghost was occasionally said to be seen, sitting on the great eight-foot four-poster bed. The bedroom assigned to the Queen, the Rose Room, had been newly done over in pink, Mrs. Eisenhower's favorite color.

During my four years as Chief of Protocol, Queen Elizabeth and Prince Philip were the only state visitors to stay in the White House. President and Mrs. Eisenhower, who had been guests at Buckingham Palace, wanted very much to return the Queen's hospitality. If Blair House had been functioning at the time, there might have been some awkwardness with other heads of state asking why the British royal couple received special treatment. Fortunately, the Guest House was undergoing extensive renovation at the time, and could not be used. This gave us a valid excuse for extending the White House invitation to the Queen and the Prince. As a matter of fact, fortuitously the renovations were not completed until many weeks after the end of the royal visit.

A regal gift was awaiting the Queen in Washington. It is the policy of the royal family not to accept presents from individuals, but this rule does not necessarily apply to organizations. We had had many requests for permission to make such presentations, but the most spectacular was a $15,000 mink coat designed by Leo Ritter of the Mutation Mink Breeders Association. The Queen graciously accepted it (as what woman wouldn't) and wore it two days later to her first American football game.

The Eisenhowers and their guests posed for more photographs on the North Portico of the White House, to the usual chorus of uninhibited instructions from the cameramen ("Look this way, Queen!" "Move a little closer, Duke!"); then the four of them disappeared for a private lunch in the White House. That afternoon, still wearing the electric-blue traveling costume in which she had arrived in Washington, the Queen placed a wreath on the tomb of the Unknown Soldier at Arlington Cemetery. Then, changing to a pale blue faille dress with full skirt, embroidered bodice, and matching hat, she attended a reception given by more than 1500 members of the Washing-

Diagram of reception committee for Queen Elizabeth

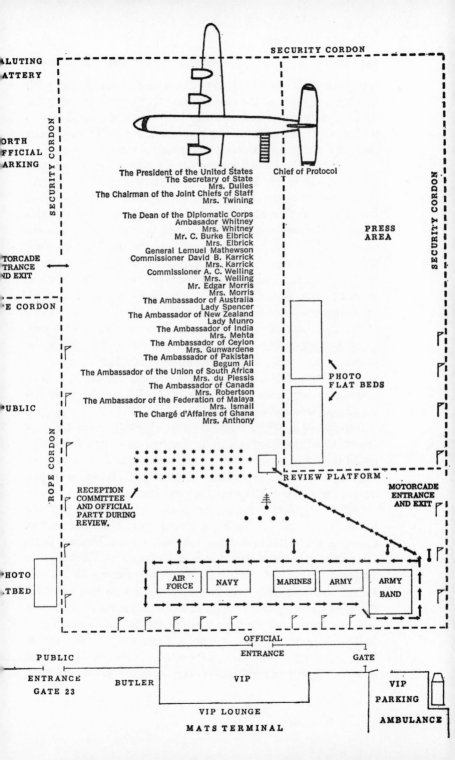

ton press corps at the Statler Hotel and shook hands with hundreds of them at the rate of some thirty hands per minute. There were smiles when one lady limped past the royal couple with her foot in a cast, but she was not daunted. "I'd have been there if the cast had been up to my neck," she said later.

That night the Eisenhowers gave a brilliant dinner for their guests at the White House. The Queen was radiant (our reporter friends claimed they were getting sick of the word, but it was the one that fitted best) in a magnificent Hardy Amies gown of blue-gray satin embroidered in a design of autumn leaves and berries in gold thread and pearls. Her diamond tiara was one that had been presented to her great-grandmother, Queen Alexandra, in 1888. Over her left shoulder she wore the blue sash of the Order of the Garter, held in place by a diamond brooch left to her by her grandmother, Queen Mary. President Eisenhower wore the rare Order of Merit, given him by the Queen's father. Philip wore the Star of the Order of the Garter and other medals. Only Mrs. Eisenhower was not bemedaled, but she looked regal herself in a pink *coup de velour* gown by designer Nettie Rosenstein, with diamond necklace and earrings.

Ruth wore a white *point d'esprit* Fontana dress and her emerald and diamond necklace. She had an emerald and diamond tiara, too, which worried her because she felt it was too elaborate, and she found herself pressing it down in a vain attempt to make it disappear into her hair.

Invitations to the dinner had been much prized, and the State Dining Room was filled to capacity. Sherman Adams, the Assistant to the President, was there—one of the few times I saw him at a White House social function. Jock Whitney, our Ambassador to the Court of St. James, was there with his wife Betsy. Betsy was the only person present who had attended the state dinner given in 1939 in this same room by President and Mrs. Roosevelt for the Queen's parents. Cabot and Emily Lodge were there; Mrs. Nicholas Longworth (the beloved "Princess Alice," daughter of President Theodore Roosevelt); our good friend and my predecessor as envoy to Luxembourg,

Perle Mesta; General Lucius Clay and his wife; Mrs. Floyd Odlum, better known as Jackie Cochrane; the John Eisenhowers; Milton Eisenhower, and many other celebrities.

At the last moment, two guests had dropped out because of illness. I was of the opinion that the resulting vacancies should be filled from Republican ranks, since there were many eager and worthy candidates. But political considerations were ignored and the invitations went to a former Democratic Secretary of War, Kenneth C. Royall, and his wife. The Royalls were charming and distinguished people, but the decision led to a lot of backstage grumbling among indignant members of the GOP.

After dinner, another 200 guests or so were invited to the East Room for forty-five minutes of musical entertainment by Fred Waring and his Pennsylvanians. At the end of the program, when the singers started to take their bows, the President interrupted suddenly. "Haven't you forgotten something?" he asked. "There's supposed to be another number—'The Battle Hymn of the Republic.' It's here on the program."

While the guests listened in amusement and some amazement, the bandleader explained that the song was indeed scheduled, but had not been rehearsed. "We'll sing it, though," he said, "if you'll all sing with us." And so after one false start, which Waring interrupted to complain good-humoredly that "You all sing terribly—let's try again!" the roomful of dignitaries sang the stirring Civil War anthem, and—tapping her foot merrily—the Queen joined in, too.

The next morning, for the first time, the Queen and the Prince went separate ways. Philip, having received The National Geographic Society Medal from the President at the White House, went to the National Academy of Sciences. The Queen went first to the National Gallery of Art, where she impressed everyone with the scope of her knowledge of painting, and then on to the Children's Hospital. It was here that I was struck once more by the Queen's remarkable ability to concentrate on a single individual, and for a few moments make that person feel that she was interested in nothing else in the world. The children gave her a doll for Princess Anne and a football for Prince Charles. The football was presented by five-year-old Butch Perry, a polio victim hobbling on crutches but scrubbed and shining in a blue suit with long pants. Someone asked him later what the Queen had said to him. "She said, 'My, ain't you cute!'" Butch reported happily.

Like Cinderella, the Queen had to leave at the stroke of 12, because the Vice-President and Mrs. Nixon were giving a lunch for her and the Prince at 12:45. We had thought, since the French government had entertained the Queen at the Louvre in Paris earlier in the year, that it might be interesting to have the Vice-President's luncheon at our own National Gallery. But when we took it up with the Gallery's board of governors we got a polite but firm refusal. Apparently during the affair at the Louvre some lighthearted guest, seated beside a priceless piece of sculpture, had used the statue's foot as an ash tray, and the National Gallery preferred not to risk such a disaster. We then thought of having the luncheon beneath the dome of the Capitol itself, but this turned out to be displeasing to the Speaker of the House, Sam Rayburn. "Mr. Sam" said "No!" and so in the end the luncheon was held in the old Supreme Court chambers in the Capitol building.

The Nixons gave the royal couple a splendid lunch: cranshaw melon, breast of guinea hen with mushrooms on Kentucky ham and wild rice, avocado salad, and almond blancmange. Ruth regarded her guinea hen with resignation—it was forever turning up on such occasions. The caterers who handled state luncheons and dinners tried desperately to vary their menus, but sometimes their best efforts failed. Again a host of celebrities was there, including many of the nation's leading publishers. But the guests of honor had to leave promptly at 3 and return to the White House to change for the huge reception being given them by the heads of mission of the Commonwealth Nations at the British Embassy.

I had always admired British organization and flair when it came to staging spectacular ceremonies, but this time they outdid themselves. Their Embassy on Massachusetts Avenue is a handsome Georgian mansion set in a park of some five acres, with peacocks stalking disdainfully through the shrubbery.

Twenty-seven hundred people had been invited, but traffic was handled smoothly and the long line of guests moved steadily past the royal pair who shook—it was said—2000 hands. Among those presented to Her Majesty was our sixteen-year-old daughter Bonnie, whom Sir Harold Caccia, the British Ambassador, had been kind enough to invite. Bonnie was starry-eyed after meeting her "Fairy Princess" in person.

Outside on the terrace a marvelous marquee imported from London had been erected. Two scarlet-coated Canadian "mounties" stood at the entrance. Inside, the tent was draped with white fiberglass, shining like silk, and the floor was completely covered by an enormous royal-blue carpet. Delicate French furniture, chairs and sofas, had been placed near the tent walls, and there were countless baskets of multicolored flowers. Many of the men were in uniform, but some of the Commonwealth's Asian family chose to wear native costumes: the Indian Ambassador in a brown tunic over white jodhpurs, the chargé d'affaires from Ghana in striking yellow, black, and orange robes, and the Ambassador from Malaya in green silk.

Everyone who was anyone in Washington seemed to be there. Among the "chosen" were Alice Longworth; Marjorie Post, now Marjorie May; Ambassador and Mrs. Robert Woods Bliss. Ambassador Bliss, Ambassador Caccia, and myself, I believe, were the only ones in formal morning attire: pearl gray tailcoat, double-breasted gray waistcoat, gray trousers, matching gray tie. I was not trying to set the style; I simply had had mine made for visits to the Royal Enclosure at Ascot, and was glad to have a chance to get more use out of them.

The Queen herself, in gold lamé with gold jewelry and black gloves, went through her handshaking ordeal without any signs of boredom or fatigue, although twice she and the Prince retired into a small adjoining room for a twenty-minute "breather." When I thought of the strenuous day she had already put in, and the formal dinner being given by Secretary Dulles that still lay ahead of her, my admiration for this remarkable young woman increased even more. Some disgruntled Socialists in England might complain about the size of the Queen's allowance, but it seemed to me she earned every penny of it—and Philip did, too. On one occasion in England, someone told me, when the Prince was feeling ill and exhausted, one of his staff tried to dissuade him from going to yet another function. Philip gave him a level glance. "Of course I'm going," he said. "That's what they pay us for, isn't it?" And he went.

This afternoon, though, he seemed in rare form. He asked Leslie Carpenter, a Washington newspaperman, where he was born. Les said he was from Texas. "Ah," said the Prince, "a foreign correspondent!" I had to smile at this awareness of Texas psychology.

The Queen made a little speech which was well received. The whole attitude of the press corps, probably the most cynical and sophisticated group in Washington, seemed to be one of protective affection. A lot of people felt that the Queen should not have been subjected to such a handshaking marathon. "Ridiculous!" they said. "And she's such a little thing, too!" But I noticed that the objectors went through the receiving line as eagerly as anyone else.

One story going the rounds at the party concerned the Queen's visit to the National Gallery that morning. Among the art treasures that she saw were some drawings by William Blake, the great eighteenth-century English painter, poet, and mystic. Some of these water colors actually belonged to the Queen, and had been loaned by her to the Gallery. The day before her visit an official of the U.S. Information Agency telephoned the Gallery's Director, John Walker.

"Is the Gallery showing the Queen anything special?" he wanted to know.

"Why, yes," said Walker, "we're having a special exhibit of the drawings of William Blake."

"Oh, how nice," exclaimed the Information expert. "And will the artist be there, too?"

Another story concerned the breathless lady who allegedly called up the British Embassy, announced she was going out to buy a new dress for the reception, and wanted to know how tight it should be. Back unhesitatingly came the imperturbable reply: "Tight enough to show you're a woman, Madam, and loose enough to show you're a lady!"

The Secretary of State's dinner for the Queen and Prince at the Pan American Union that night was another sumptuous affair. Ruth always took charge of the flower arrangements for the State Department dinners, and her floral decorations were really outstanding. Actually, as she pointed out, everyone was interested to some degree in flowers, and they often provided a useful conversational gambit when all else failed. On this occasion, her tall crystal vases of red, white, and blue flowers alternating with trees of red, white, and blue vigil lights were even more dramatic than usual, but she was worried for fear that she might have run over the State Department's flower-budget—and, as a matter of fact, she had.

Abandoning her full-skirted, wide-swirling ball gowns for once, the Queen wore a sheath of aquamarine romaine embroidered all over with matching crystals. Again I was struck by her remarkable memory. John Haynes, aide to Secretary Dulles, had asked me if his sister, Mrs. Henry T. McKnight, might be invited, since she once had bought a horse from the Queen. Her Majesty not only recognized her name instantly, but thanked her for sending her a photograph of the horse.

The after-dinner entertainment was provided by the well-known team of dancers, Marge and Gower Champion. I had suggested to Secretary Dulles that Fred Astaire might be willing to perform, especially since his sister Adele had married into the English nobility. As a result, the Secretary put in a call to Mr. Astaire. The actor was not available, nor did he call back, so after two or three days another attempt was made. This time the actor made it quite clear that he was not interested in entertaining the Queen, so the invitation was extended to the Champions. They danced so enthusiastically that the shoulder straps of Marge Champion's dress broke, and she had to curtail her performance. Philip was amused and wrote her a note of sympathy the next day.

The next day—Saturday—the grueling pace continued. In the

morning, while Philip paid a visit to the Marine Barracks, the Queen took part in a ceremony of laying the cornerstone of a new office building at the British Embassy. It was a frigid morning, and somehow the men in our party became separated from their topcoats. My cold had been getting steadily worse, and now I felt it progressing by leaps and bounds. The Queen had no coat either, but she looked perfectly comfortable in her wool suit.

At 1:15 we were all supposed to leave the White House and drive to the University of Maryland's football stadium ten miles away. Ruth had not been present at the morning ceremonies; she was busy getting the children off to the football game in our own car. She had expected to take a taxi and arrive at the White House in plenty of time, but the city was so crowded and taxis so scarce that she couldn't find one. Fortunately, she spotted a motorcycle policeman who knew us. He invited her to jump into his sidecar, so she climbed in and arrived—a bit wind-blown but on time—in this unorthodox conveyance.

The best thing to be said about the football game, probably, was that 43,000 people got a look at the Queen. Before the game, she was driven slowly around the cinder track that circled the playing field. Then she and the Prince took their seats in the royal box that had been set up at the fifty-yard line on the south side of the field. The Queen sat between Maryland's Governor Theodore R. McKeldrin and Dr. Wilson H. Elkins, president of the University of Maryland. She showed polite interest in the game, the intricacies of which must have baffled her, and between the halves applauded the University of Maryland band as it formed the initials E-R, topped by the royal crown. Ruth marveled at the way she faced the biting wind without ever repairing her make-up and without having a single hair blow out of place. As for me, I envied Her Majesty the warmth of her new mink coat. Maryland won the game, and everyone seemed happy, but I was glad when it was over.

On the way back to Washington, we made an unscheduled

stop at a supermarket. The manager, hastily summoned by phone, refused to believe that the Queen of England was in his store; he was convinced it was all a practical joke. But the assistant manager came through nobly, and explained everything to the royal couple who seemed genuinely interested. It was just as well that the visit was unannounced; if the public had known about it they would have been on hand in such numbers that they might have wrecked the place.

That night the Queen and the Prince gave a dinner at the British Embassy in honor of President and Mrs. Eisenhower. Often I've had people say to me, "But don't these big formal dinners get terribly dull? Aren't they all alike? Don't you get horribly bored?" The answer to all three questions, so far as I'm concerned, is no. The backgrounds change constantly; so do the people; so do the women's clothes and jewels; so does the conversation. And almost always there's some little unexpected incident that sticks in your memory. That night, for example, just as the royal party was about to enter the elevator in the Embassy, it turned out to be occupied—by a mouse. Poor Lady Caccia, who had redecorated the whole mansion in honor of her sovereign, must have been momentarily aghast. But the guests were highly amused at the thought of the enterprising American mouse who had gone to such lengths for a glimpse of England's Queen. One of the equerries—I think it was Captain the Lord Plunket (grandson of the American actress Fanny Ward)—gallantly marched into the elevator and shooed the mouse away.

The next day, Sunday, my cold was so much worse that I began to wonder if I would survive the royal visit—or indeed survive at all. Fortunately, after church I did not have to be on call until the special train left for New York late that evening, and so I spent most of the afternoon in bed, pouring brandy into myself and sniffling morosely.

The Queen and Prince had a full day, though. In the morning, before church, President Eisenhower presented Her Majesty with a rare historical treasure, the Carleton collection of "Headquarter Papers of the British Army in America," a day-by-day account of the American War for Independence from Bunker Hill to Yorktown as seen through British eyes. The collection, containing over 10,000 items including sixty-nine letters in George Washington's own hand, was said to be worth half a million dollars. It had been purchased by the Rockefellers, who were presenting it as a gift to the British people from the people of the United States. One of the most interesting letters, I thought, was from the turncoat Benedict Arnold, complaining that "when I joined the British army, I sacrificed a handsome fortune and very flattering prospects, to what I esteemed my duty, and I am sorry to say my present prospects are far from being so . . ." the familiar and ancient lament of a man who has backed the wrong horse.

Where church was concerned that morning, there was a little backstage tug of war. The British Embassy wanted the Queen to attend services at the Washington Cathedral, partly because the Episcopal Church is closest of all American denominations to the Church of England, partly because the War Memorial Chapel, a gift of the British people, was being dedicated that morning. President Eisenhower, on the other hand, wanted the Queen to accompany him and Mrs. Eisenhower to the National Presbyterian Church where they usually worshipped. The British reminded our State Department that the Queen Mother had made some needlepoint covers for the "kneelers" in the Episcopal chapel, and that the Queen wanted to see these. President Eisenhower replied with some asperity that when he had been in England, he had gone to the Queen's church—now she should go to his. In the end, a compromise was reached that involved going to both churches, much to the delight of both congregations.

After lunch at the British Embassy, the Queen and the Prince drove to the Middleburg Training Center at Middleburg, Virginia, where they had a glimpse of Virginia's "horse country" before returning to dress for dinner at the Australian Embassy, given by the Commonwealth ambassadors, of whom the Australian envoy was the dean.

The Eisenhowers did not go to this dinner, but said good-by

to their guests afterward on the North Portico of the White House. Their parting was warm and informal: the royal pair said that they had had a wonderful time, their hosts said they were sorry to see them go. By now there was no doubt that the royal visit was a resounding success; even cities that had had no glimpse of the Queen were entranced. According to the *Denver Post*, she was "a honey." The *Chicago Daily News* proclaimed her "a living doll." Some reporters were getting a little numb. Dorothy Kilgallen moaned: "I simply can't write 'radiant' or 'sumptuous' or 'beaming' one more time!" But the rivers of ink continued to flow.

Three thousand people were at the station to see them off, including many children who should have been in bed. In the royal luggage were gifts from the Eisenhowers: a ceramic figure of the Prince playing polo and a portrait of Prince Charles that the President had painted for the Queen. The visitors' gifts to the Eisenhowers were a pair of life-size porcelain birds, parula warblers made by the Royal Worcester Company, and a coffee table made of English walnut, calfskin, and glass, inlaid with a map of the Normandy invasion.

Problems of protocol come up where you least expect them. Prior to the Queen's departure from Washington there had been quite a hubbub going on in the press about Her Majesty's accommodations at the Waldorf. Some reporters—either through ignorance or an irresponsible urge to make headlines out of nothing—jumped to the conclusion that while in New York the royal couple would find themselves occupying the same suite of rooms in the Waldorf Towers that the Duke and Duchess of Windsor used on their visits to Manhattan. There was no truth in this report, but I had to waste a good deal of valuable time denying it. During my term of office, we used the Waldorf on many occasions for state visitors because it was very comfortable and conveniently located, and also because the manager of the Towers, Mr. Delagnese, was a splendid host, a talented linguist, and a past master at making VIPs feel at home. That was why we arranged for the Queen and the Prince to use it as headquarters during their last day in this country.

The last day of the royal visit was the most crowded, exciting, and exhausting of all. At a few minutes after 10 o'clock, the royal train arrived at Staten Island where we were met by my friend Dick Patterson, Commissioner of the Department of Commerce and Public Events for the City of New York. Dick's job, like mine, was to see that all went smoothly for the royal visitors through a day that was to include a ferryboat ride across the harbor, the traditional ticker-tape parade from the Battery to City Hall, a luncheon given by Mayor Wagner at the Waldorf-Astoria, visits to the UN and the Empire State Building, and a final grand dinner and farewell ball. One newspaper reported slyly that in checking the menus for one of these events, Commissioner Patterson had observed to his consternation that the dessert planned by the enthusiastic French chef was "tartelette royale." This was hastily renamed, before anyone could raise an eyebrow or even murmur "Honi soit qui mal y pense!"

The plan calling for a ferryboat approach to Manhattan was a brilliant one, because the view of the downtown skyscrapers was breathtaking—it looked as if the city were standing up to greet the Queen. The sky was a cloudless, autumnal blue—a sparkling day. Ship whistles bellowed; fireboats flung plumes of water high in the air. Overhead were Army planes, Navy blimps, and police helicopters. Our route took us past the Statue of Liberty, which never fails to give me a thrill. Another British visitor, the replica of the Mayflower, was anchored not far away. The Queen was wearing a coat of bright, copper-colored velvet with a collar of snowy mink and small matching hat. The Prince was in a dark suit. Standing behind the glass screen designed to shield them from the spray, they looked as thrilled as any tourists visiting New York for the first time. In fact, a photograph taken of them standing together on the ferryboat deck with the Mayflower in the background is one of the most charming and relaxed pictures of a happy couple that I have ever seen.

The ride up Broadway was an exciting kind of bedlam. The streets were jammed with people waving British and American flags. Thousands more dangled out of windows, tossing down a storm of ticker tape and torn-up telephone books. The chimes of Trinity Church rang out "God Save The Queen." It was, as someone said, a remarkable outpouring of affection and enthusiasm from a city sometimes accused of having no heart.

After the welcoming ceremonies at City Hall, the motorcade continued to the Waldorf-Astoria, Governor Harriman on one side of the Queen in the now-familiar bubble-top Lincoln, the Mayor on the other. At the luncheon, former President Hoover sat beside Her Majesty. Just behind her on the dais was Mrs. Roosevelt. Interviewed by the press as someone who had entertained royalty, she had offered some rather sound advice where the Queen and the Prince were concerned: let them have as much time alone as possible. But, like most good advice, it had gone unheeded in the rush of events.

After the luncheon we drove to the United Nations building, where the Queen spoke briefly to the General Assembly. Then we sped crosstown to the Empire State Building, a visit the Queen had asked particularly to be allowed to make. The building's owner, Colonel Henry Crown, had rented 265 yards of red carpeting for his royal guests to walk on, and had banked the doorway to the observation tower with yellow chrysanthemums. Several thousand people waited patiently behind police barricades in the street; there were, in fact, so many patrolmen that Philip remarked that it looked like Police Headquarters.

We all took the ear-popping elevator ride to the 86th floor, where photographers and reporters were lying in ambush, and then proceeded to the observation deck on the 102nd floor, from which the press was barred. The view was somewhat limited by haze, but even so the Queen was impressed. "It's beautiful," she kept saying, "just beautiful!" And indeed it was, with the setting sun burning a reflection on the Hudson, and the lakes and reservoirs in Central Park shining like steel mirrors. The Prince looked hopefully for the *Queen Elizabeth* among the liners berthed on the west side of the island, but she wasn't there. His own Queen observed, a bit sadly, that "a visit to New York for a day is really just a teaser," and the thought crossed my mind—not for the first time—that for all the glitter and glamour of their lives, there weren't many times when the royal pair could relax and do as they pleased.

From the Empire State Building, after a cup of tea for the Queen and a Scotch-and-soda for the Prince, Philip went on alone to the American Institute of Physics, where he was to make a speech. Ordinarily on such occasions the speaker merely made polite noises, but sometimes Philip spoke his mind plainly. Once, addressing the British Association for the Advancement of Science, he startled his audience by saying bluntly, "It's no good shutting your eyes and saying 'British is best' three times a day after meals and expecting it to be so." But today he was affable and tactful, saying merely that he "would like to see the day when scientists from everywhere work together . . . for no other reason than the advancement of knowledge and the benefit of mankind."

Philip's departure left me with the pleasant task of escorting the Queen back to the Waldorf, where she was to dress for dinner in the suite reserved for her by our State Department. Plans called for us to drive up Park Avenue, but I knew that all the great stores on Fifth Avenue were decorated in the Queen's honor, and so I asked her if she would like to see one of the most famous shopping thoroughfares in the world. She said that she would, and so we made the necessary change of plans—to the pleasure of sidewalk crowds on Fifth Avenue, and I suppose the disappointment of those on Park.

It's amazing how clearly you can hear sidewalk comments in an open car; most spectators don't realize this. "Hiya, Liz," cried one excited onlooker at one point. "Hiya, yourself," promptly replied the Queen of England. Her reaction was so spontaneous and so democratic that I couldn't help remembering a story I had once heard in England. When the Queen was a little girl, it seems, her grandmother, Queen Mary, took her shopping. The flustered shopkeeper looked down and said,

"And what would this little lady like to see?" Elizabeth tilted her royal nose. "I'm a princess," she said icily, "not a lady!" But Queen Mary was equal to the occasion. "Yes," she said serenely, "my granddaughter was born a princess. But we're hoping she'll grow up to be a lady!" Sitting beside her now, I knew that her grandmother would be very proud of her.

The dinner given that evening at the Waldorf by the Officers and Directors of The Pilgrims of the United States and the English-Speaking Union of the United States was a fantastically elaborate affair. Seventeen hundred guests had been at the Mayor's luncheon—which seemed like quite a lot—but 4500 had been invited to the dinner. Womanlike, the Queen had saved her most fabulous gown for her last appearance—a slender dress of multicolored lace in palest pastels, re-embroidered in iridescent shades with faint pink, green, and blue paillettes and tinted brilliants. From the low waistline in back flowed a fantail train of silk tulle in all the colors of the rainbow. I was told that the designer, Norman Hartnell, had telephoned from London to make sure she was wearing it, and I could see why. With it she wore a tiara three inches high of solid diamonds, a diamond necklace, bracelet, and a white mink stole. Over her shoulder, once again, was the blue ribbon of the Order of the Garter. "She's just a dream," people kept saying, and she was.

Forty-five hundred people, of course, could not be accommodated in one room. They were scattered throughout the hotel in various dining rooms, with television cameras relaying the proceedings in the main ballroom. But most of the guests got at least a glimpse of the Queen. After a private reception in the Palm Court, the Queen and the Prince visited the Starlight Roof, then entered the west foyer of the ballroom preceded by kilted pipers of the Canadian Black Watch with bagpipes skirling. Then, following eight gold ribbons stretched overhead, the procession passed through every room surrounding the main ballroom so that all the guests could see the fairytale Queen and her handsome Prince.

Ruth, I remember, was escorted by Jock Whitney. Actually,

as Chief of Protocol, I outranked Jock as an Ambassador-not-in-residence, and should have preceded him in the procession, but he gaily seized upon Ruth and sailed off with her. Actually, I was glad that he did, because by so doing he took care of a situation that had always bothered me—namely, the down-grading of our ambassadors when they return to the United States during a state visit of the ruler or head of government of the country to which they are accredited. The theory, of course, is that our Ambassador cannot represent our own Head of State when the President is acting as host to some foreign visitor—and therefore the Ambassador drops down to a relatively low order of precedence. But this, I am sure, must confuse the foreigners themselves, who are accustomed to ac-cording our ambassadors very high rank indeed. To some Oriental observers, I know, it looks as if our Ambassador is being forced to lose face. I think myself that it would be much better if an Ambassador who returns to this country escorting a Head of State, or a Prime Minister of the country to which he is accredited, should be allowed to retain a very high order of precedence—somewhere near our own Secretary of State. In any case, by escorting Ruth, Jock cleverly and expeditiously took care of the situation. Betsy Whitney and I followed Jock and Ruth. Also in the procession, I remember, were our former Ambassador to the Court of St. James, Winthrop Aldrich, and his charming wife Harriet, both great friends and favorites of the Queen as well as of Ruth and myself.

At 10:30 the royal pair returned to their suite for about twenty minutes before leaving for the Commonwealth Ball at the Seventh Regiment Armory, farther up Park Avenue. It was at this point that they gave Ruth and me signed photographs of themselves in blue leather frames bearing the crest of each. We were all getting desperately tired; at dinner I had even seen the Queen rest her tiara'd head momentarily on her hand. But we had one more lap to go.

More than 4000 people had been invited to the Common-wealth Ball. The Armory, a vast place, was decked with flags and candles and flowers of red, white, and blue. Guy Lombardo furnished the music. First official guests to arrive were the Commonwealth ambassadors and their wives. They were escorted to the dais where they were to await the Queen. When she did arrive, military honor guards and groups of British war veterans were standing at attention on either side of the long carpet. All of us had to stand, of course, until the Queen was seated, and it seemed to me that the minutes stretched into years. All I wanted to do was sit down and lean back and rest my aching bones. When at last the Queen did sit down, I collapsed as if I had been shot. But before my weary spine could touch the back of my chair, I noticed the Queen. She was just as tired as I was—probably more—but she was sitting erect, straight as a ruler, not even touching the back of her chair, and it was obvious that she intended to sit that way as long as necessary. Well, Buchanan, I said to myself, if that girl can do it, you had better try. So I did.

The ceremonies and presentations lasted for perhaps forty-five minutes. Then the Queen and the Prince began slowly to make their way to the limousine that was to take them to Idlewild Airport. Frequently, on her way out, the Queen stopped and spoke to war veterans, often singling out those who had been wounded. In one wheel chair, immaculate in dinner jacket, was a blinded flier of World War I. It was touching to see the thin, frail man struggle to lift himself to his feet in the presence of his sovereign. She put a gentle hand on his shoulder and told him that he should not rise. She spoke to him for several moments, then moved on, and Prince Philip took her place.

We were almost an hour behind schedule when we reached the car, but by now nobody cared. I took my place with the Queen and the Prince, hoping I did not look as exhausted as I felt. Near the floor of the limousine, behind the driver's seat, was a light that could be directed upward. This was turned on, and as its glow fell on the Queen's sparkling dress and gleaming tiara she was a splendid sight.

As we sped through Manhattan and out through Queens, the streets were jammed with people waiting up to see the Queen.

By now it was 1 o'clock in the morning, and many of the spectators seemed to have gotten out of bed. The Queen was astonished by this. "Philip," she said, "look at all those people in their nightclothes. *I* certainly wouldn't come out in *my* nightclothes to see anyone drive by, no matter who it was!"

At Idlewild, their BOAC DC-7 was waiting; the royal pair, actually, were going to be the first passengers to leave from the newly completed airport. Philip looked around at the modernistic buildings gleaming in the darkness. "Where are we?" he wanted to know. "In the land of Oz?"

The final good-bys were said. "It's been fabulous," the Queen kept saying, "just fabulous." "Well," said the Prince, giving me a strong handclasp, "you were the first and the last."

The door of the big plane closed, the great propellers whirled, it moved away. We watched it go with real regret. I think that every one of us felt that it was carrying away from us a woman who was magnificent not only in appearance and bearing, but in heart and duty—a woman who was every inch a Queen.

V   Money, Morals, and Moroccans

There are two questions that I am asked quite frequently when these state visits are being discussed. The first is, how much do they cost? And the second, is it worth it?

The final cost of a state visit depends, obviously, on its duration, the number of people in the official visiting party, the personal habits and desires of the visiting dignitary, and other variables. The exact figures are never publicized. Comparisons, as the saying goes, are odious, and the State Department has no wish to offend anyone. But the prices paid for the main items are a matter of record and available to anyone sufficiently interested to dig them out.

My experience was that an "average" state visit, one in which an official party of twelve persons spent a week in this country, cost our government about $11,000 in direct outlays. If the visitors spent three days in New York and four in Washington, the breakdown was about as follows:

Air travel	$1400
Expenses plane crew	150
Hotels	1900
Travel expenses of U.S. officials	1150
Entertainment	4000
Miscellaneous expenses at the Guest House	900
Automobile rental	1750
Total	$11,250

Of course, some visits were far more expensive than this. The visit of King Saud, which was just ending when I took over my job, cost our government at least $30,000—not counting the damage to the Guest House already mentioned. For one thing, King Saud brought far more people than anyone expected. Only eighteen were in his official party, but there were about fifty others. These, technically, were the financial responsibility of the Saudi Arabian Embassy, and were quartered in Washington hotels, but they were always drifting in or out of Blair House, eating meals, or using the official cars.

And there were other expenses. As a sworn enemy of Israel, for example, Saud was not—to put it mildly—among friends in New York, with its large Jewish population. We never had less than a dozen security men guarding him. Again, when plans called for him to go down to Virginia and stay in a hotel, he announced that he liked the President's Guest House just fine, and saw no reason to move. Nor did he. This was a blow, because it costs the State Department more to keep a visitor in Washington than "on the road," where sometimes state or civic governments help with the expense.

One of the major items in a state visit is usually air travel. We figured it costs about $300 an hour to keep the *Columbine* flying. Protocol demands that a visiting Chief of State be furnished with transportation from the point where he first touches American soil. When we had to send the big plane and its crew all the way to Hawaii, as we usually did when the visitor was coming from the Orient, costs mounted rapidly. And of course, if we picked him up in Hawaii, we had to fly him back there at government expense when the time came for him to leave. The sad fact, as most travelers know, is that getting from one place to another is expensive, and the more lavish the arrangements, the higher the expense. When we arranged for a special train to carry Queen Elizabeth from Washington to New York, the bill came close to $4000.

Our State Department usually pays the tab for the first fourteen days of a visit. After that, the visitor's own government is supposed to assume expenses. Guy Mollet's visit was brief and businesslike. He stayed only four days and cost us only about $7000. Chancellor Adenauer stayed six days; the bill was some $8000. President Diem stayed seventeen days, and costs soared over $40,000. Premier Kishi was with us exactly fourteen days; the cost was about $25,000. These figures seem high, but they are small compared to what some governments spend on state visits. During my first year as Chief of Protocol, the United States spent perhaps a quarter of a million dollars on such visits. But this was only a fraction of what the French government spent on a single visit—when Queen Elizabeth came to Paris in the spring of that year.

Car rental, as I have said, was at that time on a basis of $50 per day for each limousine. We never used fewer than five, and sometimes as many as fifteen. Official luncheons and dinners are always elaborate affairs and consequently expensive. Our rule of thumb was $15 per person for an official luncheon. Dinners, with more elaborate food and wines, worked out at $20 per person, or more. Since over a hundred guests were often invited to such dinners, a bill ranging between $2000 and $3000 was not unusual.

The actual preparation and serving of such a meal were always turned over to a professional caterer. The State Department bought its own wines—and paid duty on imported ones, too. This always struck me as a bit odd—Uncle Sam paying himself, as it were. There was a budget for flowers, decorations, music, entertainers, and so on. Once or twice Ruth ran over her flower-budget and worried about it until, by economizing on other dinners, she was back in the black.

We used various buildings in Washington for these entertainments. Sometimes Vice-President Nixon would give a luncheon under the dome of the Capitol itself. If the visitor had any military problem or interests, he might be entertained at the Pentagon, usually at a small luncheon attended by the high brass. At Anderson House, my notes tell me, a typical "upstairs" dinner for thirty-six cost $1500. A dinner for sixty-five downstairs cost $2800. At the Pan American Union, the cost of one fairly elaborate dinner for ninety-five persons was

$3800. Hotels were cheaper; you could have sixty dinner guests at the Carlton for $1550.

And so it went throughout the year. Somebody on my staff once figured that an official visitor cost our government about $100 for every hour that he remained in the United States. I think this estimate is probably too low. Such a figure would not include, for example, the cost of bringing home the American Ambassador in the visitor's country to be on hand for the occasion. Nor the countless man-hours spent in planning such visits. Nor the time—priceless, really—of the President, Vice-President, Secretary of State, and other top government officials who act as hosts on such occasions.

To answer the second question—is it worth it?—I would say yes, the time and effort and money are well spent. We live in the age of the hydrogen bomb, and whether we like it or not, membership in the grim society of bomb-owners is expanding. This means that we need all the friends we can get, and it also means that we must keep in close touch with the uncommitted nations who someday may hold the balance of power on this uneasy planet.

When representatives of such nations come to visit us, I think we should do all we can to make them comfortable. If this includes some expensive dinners and some free airplane rides, so be it. We are selling the United States, and like most salesmen we need an adequate expense account. If you look at the cost from the point of view of the individual taxpayer, it may seem rather high. But if you compare it to the price of a supersonic bomber or an intercontinental ballistic missile, it shrivels down almost to nothing. And if it contributes—as I'm sure it does—to a world in which the bomber never bombs and the missile never strikes, then it is hard to think of a better way to spend the money.

Soon after Queen Elizabeth and Prince Philip returned to England, a teapot tempest arose in the Protocol Division over the slippery business of accepting gifts or favors from visiting potentates. The Constitution of the United States is quite clear on this subject. It says that "no person holding any office of profit or trust shall without consent of Congress accept of any present, emolument, office, or title of any kind whatsoever from any king, prince, or foreign state." The dubious practice of government officials accepting deep-freezers and mink coats from donors with an ax to grind had become quite a scandal in the previous administration. In the State Department, as I have said, the rules required office holders to turn in gifts of any consequence, to be held until their departure from government service. Of course, there was a point at which strict compliance became a bit silly. If a foreign visitor, grateful for help and attention, sent an American official a basket of fruit or a bottle of bourbon, no one expected him to turn it in. In general, the accepted rule was, "If you can eat it, drink it, or smoke it, keep it!"

But when the gift had considerable monetary value, the situation was different. The motives of the donor might be beyond reproach, and yet the reasoning behind the Constitutional prohibition is perfectly plain: nobody serving the United States ought to be beholden to anyone else. The gift in this case was a $3000 automobile bestowed by a grateful King Saud on one of my staff members. The staff member claimed that this was a gift, not to himself, but to his family—and the car was indeed registered in his wife's name. But morally this seemed to me a clear evasion of the rules. In the end, the State Department issued a statement saying that the staff member was guilty of "bad judgment," and he was transferred to another assignment.

The press had a field day with this. "Protocol Boss Boots Aide" cried the *New York Daily News*. "Big Hello Man Bids U.S. Job Good-bye," announced the *World-Telegram*. Siding with "the little fellow," some editorial writers wanted to know why it was all right for President Eisenhower to accept a jeweled sword from King Saud and wrong for a lesser official's wife to receive a new Oldsmobile. At a press conference, the President was asked about the matter. He replied that the law should be obeyed, but that in his opinion it was all a matter of good taste. Anyway, he said, it was the State Department's problem.

The State Department was obviously not very happy with the problem. Secretary Dulles was asked at his press conference to enlighten the reporters as to what the difference was between a wrist watch, an automobile, or a deep-freeze. He replied, somewhat wearily, that the handling of gifts was a matter of great delicacy and difficulty. "If you can determine that the gift is given to obtain improper influence," he said, "it is easy. You can return it. But in many cases the gift is an act of courtesy and friendliness, and to refuse it would create ill will and discourtesy." He added that he often solved the problem by giving a gift of equal value in exchange. This did not satisfy Doris Fleeson, tart-tongued columnist for the *Washington Star*. This, she said, was a solution that might be possible to men of means, but not to others. "The Government," she wrote, "seems unwilling to lay down a policy of no gifts except something as personal as autographed photographs. In every administration the problem recurs, and none tackles it plainly."

There were other repercussions. In Congress, Representative John E. Moss of California demanded that the veil of secrecy be lifted from the warehouse full of gifts received by U.S. officials from foreign donors. When "the veil" was lifted, and the reporters got in, they were rather disappointed. They were shown a few trinkets that, as one reporter said, "would have looked just fine at a church bazaar," and a dusty collection of five or six thousand foreign medals and decorations. The whole furor seemed almost ludicrous in view of the serious problems that were confronting the nation (the Russians had just launched their first Sputnik), and I was glad when it died down and we could get on with our work.

The last major event of 1957, so far as the Protocol Division was concerned, was the visit of His Majesty Mohammed V, King of Morocco. He arrived with his all-male entourage at noon on November 25. It was cloudy and windy at the airport, but the sun came out just as the King's plane landed. Ruth had decided to come out to the airport "incognita" in casual clothes and dark glasses, so that she could take photographs of me introducing the King to President Eisenhower. She noted later in her diary that the King was wearing "a gray nightgown and a little gnome hat." Actually his gabardine robe did look a bit like a nightgown (I was interested to see some of the delegation from the Moroccan Embassy lift the hem of it to their lips as they bowed low before their monarch); his hat looked like an ordinary felt hat with the brim cut off and the top dented in.

The King was a quiet, rather impassive man in his mid-fifties, more at ease speaking French than English. He had brought with him his brother, who was partially crippled, and to whom he seemed very devoted. He also brought one of his sons. The Prince struck me as a somewhat sullen young man. He wore Italian-looking clothes with narrow trousers, and showed little interest in anything or anybody. My impression that he was rather spoiled was to be strengthened before the visit ended. But whether or not the King was an overindulgent parent, judged by American standards, he was still a good friend of the United States—and we wanted to keep him that way.

The usual state dinners went off very well. Since it was Thanksgiving season, Ruth decided that instead of flowers as table decorations, at the Pan American Union, she would fill large cornucopias with all sorts of autumn fruits and vegetables. The day of the party she personally selected all the produce, then spent hours polishing apples and artistically arranging the fruits and vegetables on croton leaves in golden cornucopias. The eighteen of them looked magnificent, but she was a bit chagrined when one of the Moroccans, gazing at them pensively, said to her, "Don't you Americans ever put flowers on your tables?"

Since the King was interested in agriculture, cattle-raising, and irrigation methods that might be transplanted to Morocco, we decided to have him visit sections of our country where the climate and the terrain more or less matched his own. Our first stop was in Dallas, where my mother makes her home. Since we thought he might like to see a famous American department store, we took the King and the Prince to Neiman-

Marcus, where they put on a fabulous fashion show for him. The Prince perked up noticeably at the sight of the pretty models. None of the Moroccans spent a dime, but Ruth had less sales resistance, and so the store's effort wasn't entirely wasted.

My mother gave a reception for the King to which about 150 Dallas people were invited. The King found an attractive Dallas mother and daughter, Mrs. Bruno Graf and Mrs. Joanne Stroud, who spoke fluent French. He enjoyed talking to them so much that he announced that he would not leave early the next morning for the King Ranch as planned. He preferred, he said, to stay in Dallas a while longer and leave when he was ready.

This was a bit embarrassing for me, since the Klebergs and Armstrongs, owners of the famous King Ranch who were personal friends of mine, were expecting the Moroccan monarch the next morning and had made elaborate plans for his entertainment. But the King came from a country where his whims were law, and he was accustomed to having them obeyed without question. There was little I could do but alert our hosts, explain the situation, apologize, and say I would hurry the King along as best I could.

In this I was not very successful. I believe the Prince stayed out late with some of the Dallas models, which didn't speed things up much. I had the planes ready and waiting at the appointed hour, but it was noon before we took off. Ruth, who watched us go, said I looked like an exasperated American homburg in a sea of red fezzes. Thousands of people in Kingsville, Texas, had been waiting hours to see the King; the town was gaily decorated with street signs and American and Moroccan flags. By the time we finally arrived most of the disappointed spectators had gone home.

The enormous King Ranch, comprising about a million acres, fascinated the King as it does everyone else lucky enough to visit it. It has been in the King, Kleberg, and Armstrong families for several generations, and is almost a feudal barony.

Mrs. Henrietta Armstrong and Dick Kleberg were our hosts, the senior Klebergs being out of the country at the time.

The King and his party were escorted to their rooms. We had sent our usual information sheet on what they liked to eat and drink. The King's personal apartment had been newly painted and beautifully prepared, down to the last detail. But suddenly a great hubbub arose, and I was informed that His Majesty was being moved to other quarters that would be "warmer."

Now, when a visiting dignitary is assigned to a suite of rooms, that suite has been very carefully chosen in advance for all sorts of reasons—his personal safety as well as comfort, accessibility to elevators, and so on. To move a king, furthermore, you don't just summon a bellhop and ask him to carry a bag. There are dozens of pieces of luggage, there are aides, valets, secretaries, bodyguards—all of whom have to be moved as well. It causes great commotion and confusion. I couldn't imagine what was happening.

What was happening was that one of the King's underlings, whose name sounded like Snouzzi, had decided that the King would be happier in some domestic staff quarters that were just above the kitchens. This Snouzzi claimed some minor relationship with the King, and would brag about this at the drop of a fez. He evidently took great delight in being the power behind the throne, and somehow he had persuaded the King that the throne should be installed over the kitchen. In some dismay, I went to see His Majesty in his new quarters. It was true that the halls were a bit warmer as a result of all the cooking that was going on, but the whole thing was unnecessary and ridiculous, and I was afraid our hostess was going to be justifiably annoyed. I had visions of a rift between the State Department and the Klebergs that would end years of cooperation and would prevent any other state visitor from ever coming to the ranch.

Just as I was pondering these unhappy possibilities, someone brought word that Mrs. Armstrong wanted to see me. Feeling like a schoolboy summoned to the principal's office, I went to her apartment and found her sitting with her husband on a terrace outside their bedroom. "Henrietta," I said, braced for anything, "I hear you wanted to see me."

"Oh, yes," she said, "I did. Pull up a chair. I understand Moslems don't drink, and I thought that after the long day you've had we might just sit here and have a highball together."

I was greatly relieved, and no drink ever tasted better.

Dinner was scheduled for 8, but it wasn't until about 10:30 that the King was ready to come downstairs. How the chefs were able to delay dinner for more than two hours and still have it perfectly cooked and served must be a King Ranch state secret.

The next morning, wearing riding clothes and a Texas sombrero, the King went out to see some heavy machinery made especially for the King Ranch and designed for clearing rough country. There was one fantastic machine, I remember, that could pull up a fair-sized tree, roots and all, and toss it aside like a matchstick. Then it would fill up the hole and smooth the dirt neatly. The King was fascinated by this monster, and to please him its operators dug up trees by the dozen.

The ranch is well known for its Santa Gertrudi cattle, and we were shown some prize bulls. Its racing stable, equally famous, has some of the finest quarter horses in America. The King had indicated a desire to ride a quarter horse, and his hosts had selected a beautiful animal, wonderfully mannered but with considerable spirit. He was a dark chestnut color, his hide glistening in the sun. The King's eyes lighted up and he walked over to the groom who was holding the horse. With him was his military aide. Everyone waited to see the King display the famed Arab horsemanship, but to the surprise of all, it was the aide who mounted the horse and rode around the corral two or three times. The King watched every move. Finally he mounted the horse and rode him around with great ease and assurance. I couldn't help wondering whether Mr. Snouzzi had warned him that we might try to trick him into riding a bucking bronco.

After we left the King Ranch, our itinerary called for a stop at Omaha, where the King was given a tour of the global headquarters of the Strategic Air Command. He was really startled and pleased when, in order to demonstrate how efficient Air Force communications were, General Thomas Powers, the SAC commander, picked up a phone, called an American air base in Morocco, then handed the receiver to the King and said casually, "Your Majesty, your son wants to speak to you." We had arranged for another one of the monarch's sons to be at our base that morning, and he was standing by to speak to his father. Usually the Moroccans were rather impassive, but this time the King's face really beamed.

The Moroccans had a sense of humor that took odd forms. With the King's entourage were four men who were listed as valets or housemen but whose real function, as far as I could see, was to act as court jesters. One was large and muscular and dark; another was almost as big, but lighter in color. These two, I noticed, always slept just outside the King's bedroom door. The third was a man of average size. The fourth was quite small, with a little black mustache. They each wore bulky pantaloons and a red fez, and each carried a great curved knife. Now and then they would stage mock free-for-alls, batting one another around like the Three Stooges.

On our flight to San Francisco, I remember, this quartet of funny men invaded the VIP compartment of the Presidential plane where I was sitting with the King, the Prince, and the King's crippled brother. They began their usual boisterous horseplay, and I thought the King might object to the noise. But he seemed to enjoy it, watching it all with a slight smile, and sometimes speaking to one or another of them.

Finally, somewhere over the Great Divide, the act reached a rather remarkable climax when the two big men seized the little one, flung him on the floor, and held him there while the third produced a razor and proceeded to shave off the victim's mustache. The little man screamed and struggled, and the King laughed heartily. I laughed a somewhat more nervous laugh, myself, as I had never seen before and certainly will never see again such a performance in a Presidential airplane.

It was in San Francisco that I finally had to settle accounts with Mr. Snouzzi. The King's accommodations were in the Mark Hopkins Hotel, a magnificent apartment with a sensational view of the Golden Gate. His various aides all had their room assignments, but again I learned that Mr. Snouzzi was going around changing everything. The security people were distraught; the hotel people were frantic. Mr. Snouzzi clearly had become, in Mr. Goldwyn's immortal phrase, the most important clog in the machine.

I found Snouzzi in one of the foyers of these private apartments, screaming in French and flailing his arms. One of our big security men, trying to calm him, had him backed up against the wall. At this point I entered the fray, seized Snouzzi by his shirt front, and told him in very un-protocolish terms that if I ever caught him trying to move a person out of his assigned room again I would go straight to the King and request that he be sent back to Morocco, preferably in a box. I added that he had done nothing but make a nuisance of himself, that I was sure the King had no idea of the trouble he was causing, and that he had better cease and desist unless he wanted his head cut off like the jester's mustache.

After that, we had no more trouble with Snouzzi.

From San Francisco we went to Los Angeles, where the King had meetings with various Moslem groups. I remember one group who entertained us at their Moroccan Society building. There were tall candles burning that formed an aisle from the street up to the house, and there were candles burning in every room. As soon as we entered we were given dates in milk, which one had to eat as a token of good will or friendship. It seemed more like Casablanca than the City of the Angels.

The King so thoroughly enjoyed Disneyland that he went a second time and took his crippled brother. He too enjoyed it immensely, especially the Jungle Boat-ride. The Prince meanwhile—not finding American models sufficiently compliant, perhaps—imported his own from Paris. With her in the entourage, it was difficult to get him interested in irrigation and farming problems, especially early in the morning, but we kept on trying.

It was hard to make hard-and-fast plans with the Moroccans because you could never pin them down to anything definite. I heard a rumor that some of the King's daughters might meet us in New York. When I asked His Majesty about this, he smiled gently and said, "We'll see." Actually, the Princesses did arrive—three of them. They were the only females I ever saw who had chairs placed for them in a receiving line so that they could shake hands sitting down. Ruth, speaking fluent French, tried to make friends with them, but found them very hard to talk to.

We had one minor crisis with the Moroccans in New York, when their money-man disappeared. Evidently they had never heard of Travelers Checks—or else they found it easier to keep one faithful follower loaded down with cash. The money-man thought nothing of strolling around with $30,000 or $40,000 crammed into a little black bag which he was never without— in case someone in the royal retinue was smitten with an uncontrollable urge to buy two or three Cadillacs, as sometimes happened.

I was always a bit nervous about this, even though it was neither my money nor my responsibility. And sure enough, one day the money-man suddenly wasn't there. The Moroccans did not seem very worried, but I was feeding myself tranquilizers and about to alert the New York police when he wandered in, quite safe. He had had a toothache, he said, and had been looking for a dentist. No one had bothered him at all.

The King and his children finally departed, and a blessed Christmas lull set in. We were able to see something of our children, for a change, and get a little rest ourselves. It had been a hectic year . . . and we still had a long way to go.

VI

From Caviar to Castro

At the end of my first year as Chief of Protocol, I felt that I had a fairly firm grip on the job. It was demanding and fatiguing, but it offered infinite variety, and I found it very exciting to be close to the men who guided the destinies of nations, to feel the impact of their personalities, hear them talk, and observe their mannerisms. Although the state visits themselves tended to follow a pattern, the individuals involved were endlessly different. Life for Ruth and me was like a kaleidoscope of flashing colors, the combinations always changing, the framework always the same.

The only thing I regretted was having so little time to spend with the children. Fortunately, all three of them were genuinely interested in my job and never failed to question me closely about it whenever they got the chance. Bonnie, our eldest, tended to be interested in the romantic aspects of state visitors: was the Prince handsome, was the Queen happily married? Dede, who has a sharp, incisive mind, was more concerned about politics and practicalities: was the Foreign Minister *really* a friend of the United States, was the Russian Premier's airplane *really* bigger than any of ours? Bucky was less interested in protocol than in hunting and fishing, but whenever I came back from a trip he always wanted to know exactly where I had been, and with whom, and what had happened. This interest made me feel a little less guilty about leaving them so often.

Only once can I remember feeling a real twinge of nostalgia for the less demanding life that I had known before entering government service. Ruth and I had gone to Florida to meet a South American dignitary—it was the President of Colombia, actually, who was arriving at Miami. We flew down to Palm Beach the day before—a standard procedure to make sure that bad weather did not keep us from being on hand when the state visitor arrived.

We spent that night in Palm Beach with our good friends Mary and Bunny Monell. Ambassador Santa Maria of Colombia was with us, and in our honor the Monells gave a large dinner dance for about a hundred guests. Many of these were Washington friends like the George Garretts, the McCullough Darlingtons, and others with whom we had spent much time in Florida, and we had a wonderful evening. The next morning we all had breakfast with the warm sun beating down from a blue sky. Everyone else was wearing sports clothes and making plans for sailing or fishing or tennis. I must admit that getting dressed in dark (though lightweight) city clothes and leaving our friends was a dreadful chore, and on the drive from Palm Beach to the International Airport there was a good deal of groaning and griping with such questions as, "Is it worth it?" and "Why do we have to work eighteen hours a day?"

However, once the Colombian President arrived, we reacted like a pair of old fire horses. The bell started to ring, and we were raring to go.

Almost always, on these trips, there were little humorous episodes that we would relive and chuckle over when we got home. There was the time, for example, when I raised a diplomat from the dead—well, the almost dead. In mid-air, too.

On this occasion, Ruth and I were flying to Hawaii in the *Columbine* to meet an Asiatic Head of State. With us in the plane was the Ambassador from that country, a little man whom I sometimes called (affectionately and privately) the Ambassador from Rhode Island.

On these long trips, Ruth and I always took with us a traveling medical kit with a marvelous assortment of medicines. There were pills to pep you up and pills to slow you down, pills for headaches and hay fever, thermometers, bandages, the works. Ruth is an excellent amateur nurse; the crew of the *Columbine* used to say that "Mrs. Buchanan could deliver a baby, if she had to." I enjoyed no such Dr. Kildare reputation. The sight of blood makes me sick, and I have a horror of hypodermic needles equal to that of the late Admiral "Bull" Halsey, who required a direct order from the Secretary of the Navy before he would submit to his "shots."

In any case, the Ambassador traveling with us was a high-strung little fellow, and the nearer we got to Honolulu the more worried he became about meeting his boss and whether all the arrangements he had made would go smoothly. I tried to persuade him to relax and have a drink, but he said he didn't drink. Ruth and I were tired (those transoceanic time changes can be exhausting) and wanted to take a nap, but this was impossible with the Ambassador from Rhode Island pacing up and down. Finally Ruth got out the medical kit, showed him the sleeping pills, and persuaded him to take one.

A couple of hours later Ruth and I awoke, much refreshed, and began to get ready for our landing. But there was no sign of the small Ambassador. I sent someone to see if he was ready for arrival at Honolulu. Back came word that His Excellency was asleep, and seemed to have no interest whatever in waking up. In fact, no one could awaken him.

I must say, I was a bit alarmed. "Did you give him a whole pill?" I asked Ruth.

"Why, yes," she said, "that's what we always take."

"But he's only half our size," I cried. "You should have given him half!"

In the VIP compartment our friend was stretched out in a bunk, face down, all worries forgotten. I shook him by the shoulder. No response. I shouted in his ear. No reaction. Finally in desperation I pulled down the covers. The Ambassador was as innocent of clothes as a newborn baby. I had heard that it was customary to get newborn babies started with a smart slap. So with a mighty and highly undiplomatic swing, I left a large Caucasian handprint on a small Oriental bottom.

The results were miraculous. Up sat the Ambassador from

Rhode Island, rubbing his eyes. "Had a nice teep," he announced. "Velly nice teep!"

He'd had a velly nice tap, too. But he never mentioned it—and neither did I.

These long trips were fun, but we were always glad to get home. Washington is a lively and stimulating place in which to live. Something is always going on, and people sparkle with bright ideas. I remember the time that Lee Walsh, the wonderfully clever newspaperwoman who was then president of the Women's Press Club, decided that it would be amusing to give a luncheon at which living descendants of all our Presidents would be honored. Every single one was represented, all the way from George Washington to Dwight Eisenhower. Some of the guests were merely introduced; others made brief talks. Calvin Coolidge's son, for instance, told of walking down a New England street as a small boy with his father and coming to a bank. The elder Coolidge stopped, turned to the youngster, and held his finger to his lips. "Shhh!" he said. "Listen carefully. Maybe you'll hear your money working for you!"

John Eisenhower also told an amusing tale about a commanding general who had his son for an aide. At a critical point in some battle, the son was dispatched to the front line with an urgent message for the field commander. He rushed up to him in the smoke of battle and cried, "Daddy says you're to hold this position at all costs!" The battle-stained battalion commander gave him a look. "Oh, yeah?" he said wearily. "And what does *Mommy* say?" The story brought down the house, and I remember thinking that only an unusually well-adjusted person could tell a joke about a situation so nearly paralleling his own.

The ladies of the Washington press corps were always a great help to my department. Crack reporters like Ruth Montgomery of UPI, Betty Beale of the Washington *Evening Star,* Dorothy McCardle of the *Washington Post,* and Evelyn Gordon of the *News* never failed to give full coverage to our state visits and official functions.

Some of our limited free time we spent with members of the

press corps. These people are wonderfully well informed, good company, and some truly interesting evenings were spent re-hashing events, off the record—conversations and discussions which always gave us a different insight into occasions in which we had participated.

There were other evenings that also proved to be fascinating —though in a different way. The Russian Ambassador in Wash-ington in 1958 was Mikhail Menshikov, a handsome and affable diplomat whose cheery demeanor was in such startling contrast to sour-faced Russians like Gromyko that our newspaper boys had dubbed him "smiling Mike." Smiling Mike spoke excellent English and had quite a sense of humor. Once, I remember, at a large Embassy reception I ran into him in the main hallway. He was turning to go to his left into a drawing room; I was going the other way. Said Menshikov, "How do you do? I can see that as usual you are going to the right and I am going to the left!"

For some time Menshikov had been suggesting that I bring my wife to the Russian Embassy for a little private dinner. No politics, he said; just a chance to get better acquainted. I put it off as long as I could, but finally decided that it was part of my job to accept. Perhaps a glimpse into the enemy's camp as it looked to the distaff side of our family might be interest-ing. Here are the entries in Ruth's diary for April 10 and 11, 1958.

April 10: A truly unusual experience this evening; we were invited to the Russian Embassy for dinner. It was more or less a command performance, since Ambassador Menshikov had phoned Wiley's office continually asking for a free night. We finally agreed on this one—7:30—black-tie—a very small dinner, he said. He was so right! It was just ourselves and the Striga-novs, the Counselor of the Embassy and wife.

The evening was appropriate for a cold war dinner, pouring rain, cold and horrible. Arrived in State Department car (in-stead of our own), were let in through barred doors by a sinister character; coats taken by another character not quite so sinister who then led us to the elevator.

Very ornate elevator took us to the third floor, where we walked through austere-looking reception room and into the arms of Menshikov and his wife. They were waiting for us in their private sitting room, a small room decorated rather stiffly with matching sofas at either end, each with coffee table and two chairs on either side. Straight ahead, standing out in the room in front of the windows, were two small console tables, each with a vase of pink roses. I was surprised that they weren't red! Just behind them, against the wall on either side of the windows were two more console tables—a very odd arrangement. Off to one side was a television set. The lights in the room were bright enough to blind one.

We were introduced to the Striganovs, she in a hand-made blue lace dress. She is very young and very Slavic-looking. Madame Menshikov had on a long black evening gown, very simple, with a gold necklace. I was glad I had worn a short, not-too-formal gown.

Out came a maid with a tray of vodka, sherry, tomato juice, and orange juice. I chose the tomato juice, much to the Ambassador's dismay—he immediately tried to make me take the vodka. Wiley took some, and I tasted his. From then on they plied him with vodka and continued to try to get me to taste more. It was obvious that they wanted us "warmed up" a bit.

I sat on one sofa with Madame M. and we ladies talked. The men stayed at the other end of the room and talked. We discussed language, flowers, and flower shows. Finally, when Wiley had downed two ponies of vodka, we were asked to dinner. There on the table was caviar and more vodka. The dining room was terribly simple; it was like walking into a farmhouse dining room. The table had a white cloth, salt and pepper tray in the center, no flowers or candles. China and glassware were very pretty. The Ambassador covered himself up thoroughly with his napkin, and we started in on the caviar, which incidentally wasn't nearly so good as that which the Iranian Ambassador sent me as a farewell gift on Monday.

This time I condescended to take some vodka, and my glass kept being refilled. We discussed caviar and my love for it, and this got the Ambassador off on the story of one Nicholas Nicholaivitch (a parable no doubt) who owned a caviar fishery under the Czarist regime. Under the new regime, said the Ambassador, Nicholas' son works for the state at the fishery. He no longer has all the worries of ownership. He is a free man, makes a good wage, and only pays 10 percent taxes. At this point, Wiley remarked dryly that Americans prefer to own their property and their businesses and are willing to pay taxes for this privilege. Americans know, furthermore, that taxes are necessary to build up our defenses and keep us strong. Menshikov asked, "Whom are you defending yourself against? Certainly not Russia, because Russia doesn't want to fight you. We just want to be peaceful and understanding." Ha!

Dinner went on like this. They really tried to brainwash us, but we gave it right back. We were served white wine with fish, a good red wine with chicken, strawberries and cream for dessert. After dinner, we three ladies again took up our positions on the sofa at one end of the sitting room. We were served brandy, coffee, and fruit—I ate grapes. We discussed sack dresses, diet, children, and the usual female talk. Then Madame Menshikov brought out picture books of Russia for me to look at. At 10:20, when I suggested leaving, she presented me with a lacquer box with a picture of the Kremlin on it and also a picture book of the Hermitage Art Gallery. We thanked them, and the Ambassador and the Counselor took us down in the elevator. The Ambassador explained that he lived on the third floor, and two other families lived on the top fourth floor. They saw us to the front door. It was a fascinating evening, really like a play. I learned to say Kokvinpojevieta (or something like that)! A night among the enemy, really exciting!

April 11: Could hardly sleep last night for dreaming of that weird evening, especially since I'm sure everything we said was recorded and sent back to Moscow. But I'm equally sure that we are on the list of hopeless capitalists, classified as impossible to change!

Four days after our evening at the Russian Embassy—and

Ruth's subsequent nightmares—Vice-President Nixon returned from South America where he and his wife had been reviled, threatened, and spat upon by Communist-led mobs in Venezuela. He was given a hero's welcome at the National Airport in Washington, which he fully deserved. Everyone from the President on down was there to greet him. It was a magnificent spring day and a truly inspiring spectacle.

My department was given the assignment of handling all the details, and we had to work very hard at very short notice. I remember that only an hour or two before the Vice-President's arrival I received a rather brusque phone call from Sherman Adams, the President's "civilian chief of staff" in the White House. He asked me in his tart New England way whether certain details had been taken care of. I told him that they had, but somehow his questions irked me. I am sure that Mr. Adams was a first-class administrator and took a great load off the President's shoulders, but his brusque manner irritated a great many people in the government.

In June, Ruth and I made another trip to Honolulu, this time to meet His Excellency Carlos P. Garcia, President of the Philippines. On the *Columbine* with us was Carlos Romulo and his lovely wife Virginia. He was Philippine Ambassador to the United States at the time. Romulo, a real little dynamo of a man, is one of the most delightful diplomats in the world, intelligent, witty, without a trace of pomposity. I can still see him doing an improvised hula using a blanket instead of a grass skirt. His experiences during the war were fabulous. His escape from Bataan on the last patched-up airplane to leave that island is one of the most thrilling stories I've ever heard.

I always like the story of Romulo's visit to my native state of Texas. Seeing him surrounded by a group of towering Texans, somebody asked him, "How does a little fellow like you feel when surrounded by all these giants?" "Like a dime among nickels," said Romulo instantly with his flashing smile.

We brought the Garcias back to New York via Chicago. Mrs. Garcia and her daughter loved to shop for shoes, and Ruth spent hours with them in various shoe stores. Back in New

York, we ran into a minor protocol problem. President Theodore Heuss of West Germany was also staying at the Waldorf-Astoria. Protocol required that the two presidents meet one another, but the problem was who should call on whom. Pondering this thorny question one night, I suddenly thought of a solution, namely, to ask former President Hoover, who also lives at the Waldorf, to invite both gentlemen to tea. Mr. Hoover graciously consented, and so the two were able to meet on equal terms.

Too many Presidents can lead to a degree of confusion, though. A day or so later President Heuss left the hotel just as President Garcia did. Herr Heuss was sailing for Germany, and I went down to the ship to see him off. My wife, meanwhile, was taking President Garcia to the Empire State Building. My Deputy, Clem Conger, was at the airport, greeting the Prime Minister of Afghanistan.

In the main lounge of the ship, in the midst of making a farewell speech to the departing Germans, I suddenly spotted three of our Filipino group standing in the crowd listening. Obviously, the cars in the two motorcades had gotten scrambled. I quickly ushered the Filipinos down the gangplank and into a hastily commandeered car. A few more minutes and they might have been on their way to Germany.

While in the Philippines, we spent some unofficial time with His Imperial Majesty, the Shah of Iran, who had made a stopover there for a few days' rest prior to continuing on to Washington for an unofficial visit. Later I met him in Boston. He was a darkly handsome, serious-minded man who had a strong belief in an all-powerful Destiny that controls the lives of men. He told me how, as a young man in Iran, he had been riding his horse along a mountain precipice when suddenly the animal stumbled and threw him. "By rights I should have been killed," said the Shah, "but it was not my time to die. Destiny still had work for me to do, and I must try to do it." He was quite a mystic; be believed in mental telepathy, precognition, and such occult things. I got the impression that he had really been in love with his wife, Soraya, and had divorced her with great reluctance—only because he felt his country needed a male heir to the throne and apparently Soraya could not give him one.

Close on the heels of the Shah came the Honorable Dr. Kwame Nkrumah, Prime Minister of Ghana. He was the first representative of one of the new African nations to pay us a state visit. He was a dynamic individual who knew this country well, and had a few shrewd observations to make. The American Black Muslims, he said, were not real Muslims at all; in his opinion they were just a sort of secret society, and a dangerous one at that.

We took the Prime Minister up to see the Hershey chocolate factory at Hershey, Pennsylvania, since cocoa is one of the chief exports of Ghana. We photographed him outside the Lincoln Memorial, and the pictures must have pleased him because one of them turned up eventually on a Ghanian postage stamp.

Most of our visitors from overseas were lively and entertaining people, but now and then we'd get a dud. Then the business of being an affable host became real work. One Far Eastern potentate was an impassive, poker-faced character who never showed any enthusiasm for anything. He simply would not throw the conversational ball back to you. He would reply to a direct question—yes or no—and then sit there woodenly waiting for you to ask him another.

Such people were a trial to everyone, even the President. When Mr. Eisenhower rode back to the airport with this particular visitor someone asked him how it had gone. "Toughest ride I ever had," growled our unhappy Chief Executive. After subsequent meetings, I remember the President shaking his head in bewilderment. "Wiley," he said to me, "doesn't that guy *ever* smile?" But finally, with typical Eisenhower charm, the President discovered a subject that did interest the visitor: hunting—and after that the going was much easier.

Sometimes our visitors had their troubles with us. I remember one such occasion when Queen Frederika of Greece brought her two children to this country on an unofficial visit.

She wanted to take them to the theater in New York and was particularly anxious for them to see *My Fair Lady*, but one of our welcoming officials decided that the play she and her children should see was *The World of Susie Wong*.

Susie Wong was a rather dubious character, to say the least, and the Queen had no desire whatsoever to take her children to see such a play. Every time the suggestion was made she would parry it politely, but the official wouldn't take no for an answer. He kept praising the play and offering to obtain tickets. He must have brought the subject up at least ten times. Finally, in a desperate effort to silence him, I said, "Tell me, have you read any good books lately?" I heard the Queen stifle a giggle, but the official took me quite seriously, and began talking about books.

Later when we were on the train with the Queen between New York and Washington, she asked Ruth and me into her compartment, where I apologized for the obtuseness and persistence of the official. "Oh," said the Queen, "I thought I would burst out laughing when you asked him if he had read any books. To tell you the truth, I had been wondering how to discourage him myself. I even dreamed up a little dialogue in which I would ask him innocently what the play was about. He would have to admit it was about a Chinese prostitute. Then I would look even more wide-eyed and say, 'What is a prostitute, Mr.——?' "

All of which proves that a Queen can have a keen sense of humor, and it was only her long training in protocol that kept her from puncturing that particular windbag with the sharp point of her wit.

Actually, Queen Frederika was one of the most impressive visitors we had during my term of office. She arrived on the *Ile de France* on October 21, 1958, and stayed for several weeks. She brought Princess Sophia and Crown Prince Constantine with her, and Ruth and I—along with New York's Commissioner Patterson—met them at the boat. The children were both very handsome. The Queen was stunning in a light beige full-length mink coat and matching hat. She was wearing ruby and diamond drop earrings and pearls around her neck with a huge ruby and diamond pendant, four or five rings, and two bracelets with diamonds and emeralds. She had a beige-colored poodle named Toodle that matched her fur coat, and Sophia had a dark brown one named Topsy. Ruth, who has a passion for poodles, offered to carry the Queen's dog, and from then on she was more or less official dog carrier.

In Washington I took the Crown Prince to the Pentagon to have lunch with Secretary of Defense Neil McElroy and various high-ranking officers. The Queen was a bit nervous because she knew her son had to make a speech. He made a very good one, and I remember on our return how the Queen clutched my arm and asked, "How did it go? How did my son do?" just like any anxious mother. When she finally went home in December, the Queen took the first transoceanic jet flight—rather adventurous of her, but typical of this dynamic and fascinating woman.

Later in November we had an exciting trip to London. Vice-President Nixon was going over to dedicate an American chapel in St. Paul's Cathedral, and Ruth and I were asked by Secretary Dulles to represent the State Department. We flew to London in the Presidential plane. The weather, as was to be expected in November, was damp and dismal, but we all had a marvelous time. The Nixons stayed at the American Embassy with our Ambassador and his wife—Jock and Betsy Whitney. Ruth and I stayed at Claridge's as guests of the British government, and a car was put at our disposal.

On our first night in London the Nixons were honor guests at a dinner at the Guild Hall. This was attended by Queen Elizabeth and Prince Philip, Prime Minister and Lady Macmillan, the Selwyn Lloyds, the Whitneys, ourselves, and a very impressive group of government officials.

The Guild Hall itself is a magnificent old building, and I was fascinated by the old-world formalities and protocol that still survive. Prince Philip made a short speech full of his characteristic humor. While he was speaking I watched the expression on the Queen's face, and at some of his quips she would smile or occasionally break into quite a hearty laugh.

Prime Minister Macmillan also spoke, but the most impressive speech of the evening was by our Vice-President. Up to this point, Nixon had not been particularly popular in the British press. Most of the people at the dinner knew him only through his political speeches or campaign utterances. The enormous room was absolutely silent when he stood up to speak, but when he finished the applause was tremendous. Lady Dorothy Macmillan, the wife of the Prime Minister, said that never in her life had she heard a better speech. Selwyn Lloyd thought so well of it that he telephoned the British Ambassador in Washington and said that Nixon had made the best speech on the subject of Soviet-Western relations that had been made anywhere. When I think of that speech, and the other notable services that Dick Nixon rendered, it is inconceivable to me that the American people will be content to have him out of public life for very long. His experience and ability are too valuable to waste.

After dinner a little episode proved to me how friendly and democratic Prince Philip can be. My coat had been taken to the cloakroom by some young man who had escorted us to our places. He was to return and pick us up, but didn't reappear. I did have the check for my coat, so made my way to the cloakroom line, which was quite long. I was standing there when Prince Philip came by. Much to my surprise, he spotted me in the line and came over and spoke to me. He was most apologetic about the fact that nobody had brought my coat to me. I was then aware that all the people in the line had quietly moved away to a discreet distance, leaving us alone. The Prince stood there and chatted until I reached the window. Then he left, still apologizing about the inconvenience he thought I had been caused.

Another highlight of this visit was a dinner and reception given by Mr. Macmillan at Number 10 Downing Street, the historic residence of England's prime ministers. The size of the interior surprised me greatly; it was much larger than I expected. There was a maze of reception rooms and one very large room in which we were served an elegant dinner. I had been told that Number 10 Downing Street is badly in need of repair, just as our own White House was a few years ago. But on that occasion it seemed solid enough to last another 200 years.

Perhaps the pleasantest evening of our stay in London was the dinner that the Nixons gave at the American Embassy for Queen Elizabeth. One amusing sidelight on this occasion was the fact that Nixon found that his dinner jacket had not been packed and had to borrow one at the last minute from an American newspaperman.

It was a typical American Thanksgiving dinner, with turkey, cranberry, and so on. Prince Philip did not appear; he had gone to Germany to visit his mother. The Queen seemed more relaxed than I had ever seen her. It was the only time that I had ever seen her in the evening without a tiara. After dinner she chatted with all of us in a most friendly and leisurely fashion, recalling in particular her drive to the airport in New York when people waited up in their pajamas to get a glimpse of her. Young Jimmy Symington's wife played the piano. There was a very informal atmosphere, and the Queen stayed as late as she ever stays at a private function of this kind. After she departed, the party broke up at once.

Betsy Whitney, a wonderful hostess, was very popular in England. Her flower arrangements that night were beautiful. The Whitneys had taken many magnificent paintings and pieces of sculpture from their private collection to embellish the Embassy, and the result was something that any American could be proud of.

There was an amusing case of mistaken identity on our way home from Britain. Our plane landed in Newfoundland to refuel very early in the morning. The Base Commander and a half-frozen honor guard were on hand to greet the Vice-President. I had decided the best place to be was in my nice warm bunk, but Ruth got up and dressed. Pat Nixon had no more desire to face the freezing dawn than I did, so Ruth and Dick came out of the plane together. Ruth was bundled up in a fur coat, and in the semi-darkness everyone assumed she was Mrs. Nixon. At that hour and under those circumstances, people's identity didn't seem to make much difference, so Ruth and Dick were driven all over the base and came back with no one the wiser. Actually Ruth and Pat Nixon do look somewhat alike, and on various other occasions Ruth was mistaken for the Vice-President's wife.

Again the holiday season flashed past, and the endless stream of visitors went on. In January, His Excellency Sr. Dr. Arturo Frondizi, President of the Argentine Nation, arrived in Charleston with his wife. The Frondizis were quiet, modest, and charming. Ruth and Mrs. Frondizi struck up a great friendship, although she would startle Ruth occasionally by stepping aside to let Ruth precede her through a doorway or even try to help her on with her coat—endearing gestures, but hardly in accordance with protocol.

We flew back from Charleston to Washington (we bought a lot of fireworks for Bucky and I was secretly wondering whether the package might blow up the *Columbine* with the Argentine President aboard), and plunged into the usual round of state functions. Later we escorted the Frondizis to Chicago and New York. Ruth took the Argentine President's wife on a tour of some New York stores. She was thrilled by the vast number of things to buy, but—unlike many state visitors—was reluctant to buy anything because of their "austerity regime" at home. Therefore, as a parting gift, Ruth bought her a hat, a wonderful flowered creation that she loved. Later, at a solemn Presidential press conference, Señora Frondizi leaned over to Ruth and whispered, "Do you know what I'm thinking about? I'm dreaming about my wonderful hat!"

The Frondizis went back to Argentina on February 1, but the dizzy whirl in Washington went right on. One day a mysterious character called my home twice and asked if I could arrange for Christine Jorgensen to have a special tour through the White House. My children were convinced that it was some practical joker, but it was not. The same person—Miss Jorgensen's manager—called my office the next day and made the same request, but I turned him down. The protocol of such a request was clearly beyond me.

As St. Patrick's Day approached, so—appropriately enough—did the President of Ireland. This was His Excellency Sean T. O'Kelly, a spry little septuagenarian, who looked like a leprechaun. He bounded off the plane in New York and started kissing all the women in the welcoming party. They were no casual kisses either. Ruth wrote in her diary that the President was "five feet tall and cute as a bug."

He arrived on March 16, a day when President José Maria Lemus of El Salvador happened to be in New York. We arranged for the two presidents to meet briefly, and it was quite funny: all the people from El Salvador had bright green ties with shamrocks over them while none of the Irish party was wearing green at all.

Since President O'Kelly was to arrive in Washington on St. Patrick's Day, we had gone all out on this green business. Some of my staff even wore green socks. I had a green tie. Ruth was wearing a Kelly-green suit. We had even changed the ceremonial carpet at the airport from red to green for the occasion. At a dinner being given by Vice-President Nixon, Ruth had arranged for green flowers, green water in the fountain—even Irish potatoes as part of the decorations. We were all a bit chagrined to learn that the Irish are superstitious about the color and seldom if ever use or wear it.

President O'Kelly, however, remained in top form, making speeches and kissing all the women. Ruth found herself in a conversation that was more than lively. He told her about his first wife who, he said, was intellectual but very shy, especially when they were first married. Women, the seventy-seven-year-old President assured an astonished Ruth, were a good deal harder to undress in those days, because of all the corsets, than they are now. His present wife, he added cheerfully, was the sister of his first one, which made life simpler as he only had to break in one mother-in-law!

Guests like President O'Kelly left everyone in a good humor, but the next month brought a radically different Head of State. On April 15, the new Prime Minister of Cuba arrived in town.

In those days the reaction of the American people to the Cuban leader was very mixed. Some saw him as the savior of his oppressed country, while others thought he might eventually become a menace. Still others regarded him and his beard as a kind of unsavory joke.

Something about furry Fidel evidently tickled my family's sense of humor, because the children decided on the morning of the day I was to meet the Cuban Prime Minister that it would be a great joke if I went to the office disguised as Castro himself. They found an old piece of mink fur and made me a ferocious beard; one of Bucky's old khaki hats was placed rakishly on my head; a pair of dark glasses and a sword cane from the Flea Market in Paris completed the disguise. I must say my entrance into my office caused a sensation.

But Castro was no joke. His seizure of power, as everyone now knows, was a tragedy for Cuba and a threat to the whole Western Hemisphere.

I had watched the whole process with growing dismay. Even before President Batista fled from Cuba on New Year's Day, 1959, it was apparent that despite our official policy of "non-intervention," certain individuals in our State Department were anxious to see Batista ousted and Castro come to power. To speed up this process, these men had done everything they could to prevent Batista from obtaining the arms he needed to defend his regime against Castro's guerrilla tactics. They had ignored—and concealed from their superiors—the extent of Castro's Communist affiliations. They had disregarded the warnings of Arthur Gardner, our former Ambassador to Cuba and a good friend of mine, that while Batista might be a dictator he was at least anti-Communist and pro-United States. Ambassador Gardner had gotten a promise of free elections from Batista, but, alas, this was never allowed to come to pass. Meantime, the pro-Castro element in the State Department sidetracked or buried the increasingly urgent reports from our current Ambassador in Havana, Earl E. T. Smith, that the

Castro revolution was Communist-inspired, Communist-supported, and Communist-led.

At the same time certain journalists, notably Herbert Mathews of *The New York Times,* were busily engaged in convincing the American public that Castro was a combination of John the Baptist and Robin Hood, a man of simple habits and great idealism fighting to free the Cuban people from the chains of a hated police state. With Castro, they insisted, would come reform, democracy, free elections, peace on earth and good will to everybody.

I had no such illusions myself. I had little use for Batista's police state, but I also knew that as far back as 1948 Castro had been one of the plotters behind the Communist uprising in Bogotá, Colombia, a bloody and violent affair. I had come to like and trust the Cuban Ambassador in Washington, Nicholas de Arroyo, who was hoping through a vigorous public relations campaign to change what he said was a Communist-distorted image of the Cuban President. Arroyo, a brilliant architect as well as a diplomat, was a cultured and intelligent man. He believed that if, while piously proclaiming its neutrality, the United States did pull the rug out from under Batista and allow Castro to seize power, we would regret it bitterly.

When I heard the news that Batista had fled, my primary concern was for the safety of Arroyo, his wife Gabriela, and their small son. I knew that inside the Cuban Embassy there were sure to be Castro spies or sympathizers, just waiting for the signal from Havana to take over. There would also be the inevitable opportunists, quick to change sides if that meant saving their skins. Cubans are a passionate and temperamental people. Frankly, I didn't know what might happen.

What happened was that the Castro-ites did take over. Under the leadership of one Emilio Pando, a member of the Embassy staff, they opened and rifled the safes. Pando's wife stationed herself at the switchboard and refused to put through any calls that did not suit her. All personal possessions of the Arroyo family were seized, even the child's schoolbooks. The Ambassador and his family moved out of the Embassy and took refuge first with Arthur Gardner, later at the Shoreham Hotel. The Pando faction refused to let Señora Arroyo take her own clothes. They tried to confiscate Arroyo's personal automobile. They even impounded the family dog. When Arroyo protested, they reminded him ominously that he still had relatives in Cuba.

Fortunately, the personal servants of the family remained loyal to the Arroyos. Their maids smuggled some of their belongings to them by concealing them under their dresses.

I was outraged by our State Department's indifference to the Arroyos' plight. The attitude of the department was that, since the Cuban Embassy was foreign soil, they had no right to intervene in any way. Arthur Gardner and I did what we could on an unofficial basis. Arthur sent a van for the Arroyos' belongings, but they were never released. Both of us stood by for hours in case we were needed. I arranged, ultimately, for the family to have a bodyguard. Word had reached us through intelligence sources that an attempt on Arroyo's life was possible. None was ever made, but perhaps this was because of the presence of the bodyguard, a former Secret Service man.

Within a few days the Castro regime was recognized by the United States as the legitimate government of Cuba. Hindsight, as they say, has 20-20 vision, and it is easy to look back now and point to the fatal consequences of such a step. But at the time only a few people realized what was happening. Admiral Arleigh Burke was one of these; I have been told that he pleaded with Bob Murphy at the State Department to prevent a Castro take-over. But most Americans had been cleverly sold on the idea that Batista was an iron-fisted dictator who ought to be removed, and that any change would be for the better.

In April, with the treatment that the Arroyos had received still rankling in my mind, I heard that Castro had been invited to this country to address the American Society of Newspaper Editors. The State Department, to my knowledge, was not consulted about this; it was simply presented with a *fait accompli*. By this time, Castro's merciless program of executions had begun to alienate many Americans, and there was some doubt as to whether his visit should receive any official recognition at all. In the end it was decided that some gesture should be made, and it was decided that I should meet Castro at the airport, shake his bloody hand, and welcome him in the name of peace and friendship.

The date fixed for his arrival was April 15. I told myself a bit grimly that if I had been able to welcome Khrushchev I should not feel too squeamish about Castro. But then I had had the President of the United States beside me. This time, fortunately perhaps, the President would be out of the city. Secretary Dulles, too, was not available; Christian Herter was Acting Secretary. Ruth said she would drive out to the airport with me, but our security men recommended that she stay in the car. We knew that there would be plenty of enthusiastic Fidelistas on hand, but there was always the possibility that a relative of a firing-squad victim might be on hand, too, intent on putting a knife or a bullet into the visitor and not caring too much who got in the way.

At the airport the confusion was fantastic. Castro had been scheduled to arrive in the late afternoon, but was delayed by a speech he was making in Havana. When we finally got word that he had taken off, it was evident that he would not arrive in Washington until about 9 P.M.

Meanwhile a crowd of about 1500 Castro supporters and Dominican exiles had gathered at the airport. They were equipped with Cuban flags and placards proclaiming such sentiments as: "Fidel, we embrace you with all our hearts." When the plane finally landed (it was a Britannia turbo-prop named *Libertad*), the crowd went wild. Cuban security men let many of them through the barriers, and we were promptly engulfed in a swirling, cheering, gesticulating mob. When Castro stepped out of the plane in his green fatigue uniform, the cheers were deafening. Behind him came his bearded cohorts; it seemed to me that there were dozens of them. Trying to get to the microphones that had been set up, we all became jammed together so tightly that it was possible to feel the concealed weapons—pistols, knives, Heaven knows what sort of military hardware—under the uniforms.

Castro was bigger than I had expected, a tall, solid hulk of a man with piercing black eyes. He had, without any doubt, the crowd-attracting magnetism that many demagogues have. "'Look at his eyes!" I heard one woman say. "Aren't they marvelous?" "He's a saint," cried another, "a saint right out of the Bible!"

Ernesto Dihigo, Castro's new envoy to the United States, was there, a reserved, scholarly-looking man. His wife seemed carried away with enthusiasm; she kept chanting, "Fidel! Fidel!" along with the other happy welcomers. In his remarks to me, Castro was pleasant and polite. He talked incessantly, going off on all sorts of tangents. Now and then he would make a solo dash to the barrier to shake hands with some admirer. The thought occurred to me that if he picked the wrong Cuban, any one of these excursions might be his last. I was relieved when I finally saw him into the car that was to take him to the Cuban Embassy. I was sure that Blanco, who had turned so savagely on my friends the Arroyos, would be waiting with jackal eagerness to greet his new master.

At the State Department, meanwhile, a degree of uncertainty persisted as to just how nice to Mr. Castro we wanted to be. A tug of war was going on between those who had favored the Castro take-over and those who were becoming more and more alarmed by the blood bath in Cuba and the multiplying signs of ruthless Communist methods. Arroyo, who was still in Washington and had his sources of information, told me that hundreds of unreported executions were being carried out. The victims, he said, would be lined up beside a trench scooped out by bulldozers, machine-gunned so that they would fall into the trench, and then—dead or half dead—covered with dirt pushed over them by the blade of the bulldozer, a well-known totalitarian form of mass murder. He added, with a helpless shrug, that no one might believe a former Ambassador of the Batista regime, but that someday the truth would come out.

It was finally decided that the State Department should

give a luncheon for the "savior of Cuba," with Acting Secretary of State Herter as host. We had trouble finding a suitable room at such short notice, but finally the management of the Statler Hotel agreed to accept the dubious honor. We invited various members of the press, and some of the more respectable civilians in the Castro party. But Fidel brought his whole gang. Still in their beards and rumpled uniforms, the uninvited ones flopped on the floor in a corner of the room, chattering, yawning, occasionally scratching, and watching their leader with evident pride and satisfaction.

They made so much noise that it was almost impossible to carry on a conversation with your luncheon partner. Secretary Herter endured it all with good humor, but I felt that something had to be done. Finally I summoned the head waiter and asked him if there wasn't another part of the zoo where these animals could be fed. He was very cooperative and set up tables in an adjoining room where the uninvited guests were fed at the taxpayers' expense—they got their lunch, actually, before we got ours. But the respite was only temporary. As soon as they finished eating, they all came trooping back, big cigars clamped between bearded lips, squatted down on the floor again, and chattered as noisily as ever.

My last assignment where Castro was concerned was to see him off on the train to Baltimore, where he was to address the newspaper editors. He was still talking incessantly, his followers were still milling around, and the wife of his Ambassador was still one step behind him, lost in adoration. The train pulled out at last, and he was gone—so far as I was concerned.

He still remained a headache, however, to our State Department security men who had to follow him to New York and protect him from would-be assassins. The Cubans who had fallen before Castro's firing squads had many friends and relatives in the United States—some of them almost certainly in New York. Any one of them might try to shoot, stab, bomb, or poison the Cuban Prime Minister. At one point, checking for poison, one of our agents sampled the thermos jug from which Castro refreshed himself during his marathon speeches. He told me that it contained a mixture that seemed to be half coffee and half fiery Cuban brandy.

Visits from men like Castro, Khrushchev, and Tito always put a severe strain on our security forces. The safety of the President of the United States is the responsibility of the Secret Service, but once foreign visitors leave his presence, their welfare is the responsibility of the State Department Security Division. This division, headed by John Lynch, contains about twenty men—in my opinion some of the hardest-working and most devoted people in government service. Thanks to their vigilance and skill, no visiting dignitary has ever been harmed while in the United States, although on occasion would-be assassins have been discovered before they could do any damage.

The chief function of the State Department Security Division is to act as liaison between other Federal Intelligence Agencies such as the CIA or the FBI and local police authorities. When a foreign Head of State is scheduled to visit this country, his own security agents arrive ahead of him and confer with our security men. They may bring with them a list of individuals living in the United States who are thought to be hostile to their own chief executive. It then becomes the function of our security men to find out where these individuals are and make sure that they have neither the intention nor the opportunity of harming the visitor.

Often this involves a great deal of paperwork. If the whereabouts of the potential assassin are unknown, a security agent will go to the Bureau of Immigration, ascertain the suspect's place of residence, and if possible obtain a photograph of him so that the agents guarding the visitor will recognize the suspect if he appears. Security men are also trained to watch for people carrying parcels which may contain explosives, or who are wearing bandages that may conceal firearms. If they have any reason to suspect that an attempt is going to be made on the life of the visitor, they will close in around him. They screen all incoming parcels and packages for possible bombs (recently they have started using fluoroscopes for this), check all electrical and plumbing fixtures for possible booby traps, and investigate servants, chefs, and waiters in hotels where the dignitary may be staying. They even make sure that the cables that hoist the elevators have not been tampered with.

Our security men take every possible physical precaution, but mainly they rely on what they call "the psychological deterrent." The theory is that any potential assassin is bound to be in a highly apprehensive state of mind, and that a show of force in itself will often discourage him from making a move. If a sniper behind a tree sees fifty motorcycle policemen escorting the car carrying the visiting dignitary, his instinctive reaction is to wonder how many concealed cops may be watching *him*.

Ninety-nine times out of a hundred such elaborate precautions seem unnecessary, but once in a while they pay off. During Castro's visit to New York, hundreds of spectators were milling around him when a policeman spotted a man carrying a paper bag. He made him open it and discovered a home-made bomb fashioned from a piece of lead pipe. It might or might not have killed Castro, but it certainly would have maimed dozens of bystanders if he had been allowed to set it off.

From time to time, security agents receive tips—anonymous or otherwise—that a bomb has been planted or that an assassination attempt is going to be made. Almost always such tips are false, but they have to be checked out anyway. And it is not enough simply to pass along such information to the local police; the security men do not consider their job done until they have received a report stating that appropriate action has been taken.

At the Presidential Guest House, security men are on guard around the clock when a state visitor is staying there. Each agent keeps a log in which he notes the identity of each visitor and records any unusual incident. Sometimes, if a great many people are going in and out, mistakes can be made. During the visit of King Saud of Arabia, one of our security men spotted an unfamiliar face in the King's entourage. The man was wearing a turban and seemed very much at home. Nevertheless, the American agent asked a Saudi security man to identify him. "I don't know who he is," cried the Saudi agent. "I thought he was one of your undercover men!" The visitor turned out to be an adventurous barber from Long Island who had wrapped his head in a towel and joined the festivities at Blair House just to win a bet from a friend. He was gently but firmly evicted!

When a state visitor goes on a tour of this country, a security man precedes him, checking every place he will stay. The Security Division maintains a file that contains surveys of all the nation's leading hotels. Every survey goes into great detail on every aspect of security, from fire hazards to the reliability of the staff. If the visitor orders a meal in his suite, the integrity of the waiter who carries the tray must be established beyond question. If he eats in the dining room, it is probable that just before he enters the room the security man will remove the salt and pepper, or the rolls and butter, and replace them with similar items from a table chosen at random. In other words, if you want to poison a visiting potentate, you had better arrange to poison everyone in the dining room.

Actually, the security men are not so worried about the political assassin as they are about some dangerous crank or mentally deranged person. Political refugees who have gained asylum in this country are not likely to throw their own lives away in an assassination attempt. The mentally unstable person who has some imaginary grievance and who does not care whether he lives or dies is the one mainly to be feared.

Now and then supposedly reputable persons make remarkable proposals for getting rid of people they consider enemies of the U.S.A. During my term of office a doctor in a Midwestern state wrote a letter to President Eisenhower claiming that he had a foolproof way of getting rid of Mr. Khrushchev during the Russian leader's visit to this country. His proposal, which involved the use of radioactive materials, was so ingenious and so potentially lethal that the State Police in his area were requested to keep an eye on him until the Russian

Premier went home. The police decided that the safest thing to do was put the worthy doctor in jail—which they proceeded to do. When our security men in Washington heard of this, they were appalled and wondered if the doctor might not sue everybody involved for false arrest. The State Police, however, were not concerned. "We have this doctor's letter," they said, "with his signature on it. If he gives us any trouble, we'll simply publicize it. We rather doubt that anyone will want a doctor who is so ingenious when it comes to killing people. So we don't expect to have any trouble." They didn't.

The State Department security men with whom I traveled constantly were always good company, relaxed, friendly, efficient. Besides Jack Lynch and Leo Crampsey, already mentioned, there were men like Joe Rosetti who had what seemed to be an ever-expanding family, the McDermott twins, who looked so much alike that few of us could tell them apart, George Vlk, always good-humored, Frank Madden, another able officer, and many others. Nothing ever seemed to upset these men; no matter what happened they never became confused. "We always expect the worst," one of them said to me. "If it doesn't happen, that's fine, but if it does we are ready for it and know what to do."

VII The Bachelor from Brussels

In my four years as Chief of Protocol, I saw hundreds of VIPs come and go, but only once did I witness the personality and outlook of an important visitor dramatically changed as a result of his visit. It was a remarkable and exciting thing to watch —and be a part of.

The blasé American press was not exactly sold on this visitor in advance. Before he had even arrived, our newspapers were picturing him as a somber, unsmiling monarch who peered distrustfully at the world through horn-rimmed glasses and did not care for what he saw. Gloomy analyses of his personality were offered. Readers were reminded that his mother had been killed in a tragic car crash when he was five. At fourteen, he had been carried into exile by the Nazis. After the war, his father had abdicated in favor of his son—who at that time did not want the job. He was twenty-eight years old and still unmarried. Now he was coming to the United States, but the press predicted that he wouldn't get much fun out of his visit, and neither would anyone else. This was the melancholy preview offered to the American public of Baudouin, King of the Belgians.

This, I knew, was pure nonsense. I had never met the King, but during my years as Ambassador to Luxembourg I had seen a great deal of his sister, Princess Josephine Charlotte, who was married to Prince John of Luxembourg. I had also met Prince Albert, the King's younger brother. I knew that the family was made up of earnest, intelligent people, devoted to a strict concept of duty. I also knew that to some extent the King was a prisoner of the rigid European protocol that made it almost impossible for him to meet his subjects informally, and had kept the press at arm's length.

So I was not at all dismayed by all the gloomy predictions. In fact, I was looking forward to the King's visit. The Belgian Ambassador in Washington, Baron Silvercruys, Clifford Folger, our Ambassador to Brussels, and I agreed that it would be good for Belgian-American relations for the King to see as much of the United States as possible. Consequently, working closely with Jean Bassom-Pierre, the efficient and tireless Minister of the Belgian Embassy, my department had planned the most comprehensive and lengthy itinerary that any visiting monarch had ever had.

It began, in a breathless sort of way, at the crack of dawn on Monday, May 11, 1959. The night before I had gone to Langley Air Force Base, near Norfolk, Virginia, to await the King's arrival from Brussels. His plane was not due until 7 A.M., but unexpected tail winds pushed it along so fast that at 4:10 in the morning Langley got a radio message that the King would be on the ground in twenty minutes. There was a frantic scramble as General O. T. Weyland, head of the Tactical Air Command, and I jumped into our clothes. Without even time to shave, we rushed to the runway just as the royal plane landed. Out of it stepped the King, very wide awake, with a very firm handshake, and profuse apologies for the inconvenience his early arrival had caused us.

He was a tall, slender young man with a warm, friendly manner and a touch of diffidence that I found very appealing. Behind his horn-rimmed glasses, his eyes were a keen, interested blue. As for the rumors that he should have been called "Baudouin the Silent," nothing could have been farther from the truth. He spoke English fluently, and showed a wry awareness of the silken cords of protocol that bound him. "I'd really like to travel incognito," he said with a smile, "but I never get a chance."

Later that morning we flew to Washington, where President Eisenhower met the King at the airport and rode with him to the Presidential Guest House. The housekeeper, Mrs. Geaney, had made the old Blair mansion gay with flowers, a huge arrangement of pink and white peonies in a rare Meissen bowl in the drawing room, a centerpiece of yellow roses and blue bachelor buttons (an appropriate touch) in the dining room under the sparkling crystal chandelier. The King was offered his choice of the so-called "King's bedroom" facing the street, with its massive four-poster canopied bed, or the lighter, more spacious suite at the back of the house. He decided on the latter—a prudent choice that spared him the traffic noises of Pennsylvania Avenue.

I saw the King settled and was about to leave when he asked me to stay for lunch. This was his first state visit to America, he said; he wanted all the advice and reassurance that he could get. What was worrying him most, apparently, was the speech he was to give the following day before a joint session of the Congress. I could see that this might well be an unnerving prospect for a young man of twenty-eight—a major address in an unfamiliar language to the assembled law-makers of the most powerful nation in the world, along with the entire diplomatic corps of Washington. But I assured His Majesty that he would have a sympathetic and attentive audience. Furthermore, I said, once this "blood bath" was over, he would be able to relax and enjoy himself. He smiled a bit wanly at the term; it was plain that he really did consider it a blood bath.

That afternoon, when the press gave a reception for the King at the Sheraton-Carlton Hotel, he handled himself very well. Surrounded by a horde of note-taking reporters and flash-happy photographers, he read a short prepared statement, gently reminding his audience of their responsibility where truth and accurate reporting were concerned. It seemed to him, he said, that some newsmen had a tendency to play up bad news and ignore good. The press, he suggested, should keep in mind the old Belgian proverb: "A hundred bridges that stand make less noise than one that falls." The reporters seemed charmed by this little lecture, and applauded the young monarch heartily.

The dinner for Frondizi

Frondizi and the author leaving Blair House for meeting with President Eisenhower

THE PRESIDENT'S GUEST HO

King Baudoin of Belgium with the Buchanans on way to White House dinner

Mrs. Nicholas Longworth (daughter of Teddy Roosevelt) giving the author her appraisal of the political scene

The President and the Protocol Chief chatting at Military Air Transport field, Washington National Airport, upon return from Gettysburg

Prime Minister Kiski of Japan, with author, and Ambassador Asakai of Japan on left at baseball game in Yankee Stadium

Fidel Castro, Prime Minister of Cuba, arrives in Washington

Secretary of State Dulles,
President Eisenhower,
and the author

General Charles de Gaulle
arrives in Washington

De Gaulle and Wiley Bu-
chanan en route to White
House for meeting with
Eisenhower

Prime Minister Nkrumah of Ghana and author standing in front of the Lincoln Monument where the Prime Minister placed a wreath

[Qu]een Frederika of Greece and her two children, Princess Sophie [an]d Prince Constantine, arrive aboard the *Ile de France*. They are [sh]own with city greeter Richard C. Patterson, Commissioner of the [De]partment of Commerce and Public Events, and Chief of Protocol and Mrs. Buchanan

King Frederick and Queen Ingrid of Denmark with the author
arriving in San Francisco

Secretary of State and Mrs. Christian Herter at farewell dinner to diplomatic corps at the conclusion of the second Eisenhower Administration. Secretary of State shaking hands with Ambassador Carlos Romulo of the Philippines

That evening President Eisenhower gave a state dinner for the royal visitor. I thought the King seemed a bit nervous as Ruth and I escorted him from the Guest House to the White House. But the Eisenhowers soon put him at ease. A special effort had been made to invite people who had firsthand knowledge of the King's homeland. Chief among these was former President Hoover, still venerated in Belgium for the relief program he had directed at the end of World War I. I always felt proud of our White House, small compared to most European palaces, but full of light and music and color and the informal-formal atmosphere that the President and Mrs. Eisenhower created so well.

The next morning the King visited Mount Vernon and laid a wreath on the tomb of George Washington. He tried to appear interested, but he was tense and preoccupied—his speech was weighing heavily on his mind. By noon we were in Speaker Sam Rayburn's office in the Capitol, and precisely at 12:30, wearing the uniform of a Lieutenant General and looking much calmer than I knew he felt, the King faced the Congress.

As I had assured him that he would, he did a magnificent job. With great deliberation he looked around the Senate Chamber until the applause that had greeted him ended. Then after bowing formally to left and right with regal dignity, he began to speak slowly and clearly in English.

He started out by saying that he was a young man from a country that was old when Julius Caesar was writing about it. He touched on the problem of the Belgian Congo; he said he hoped that it would achieve independence as soon as it was ready for self-government. He spoke of world peace, and its critical importance to all people—especially young people. "It takes twenty or more years of peace to make a man," he said. "It takes only twenty seconds of war to destroy him." The Congress was deeply impressed; you could feel the respect and the admiration. The King ended by stressing the ties of affection that bound his people to ours. "Nor shall our confidence in you be misplaced," he said, "for what is written on your coins I have read in the hearts of the American people: 'In God we trust.'"

He sat down to a storm of applause; I had never heard the Congress give anyone such an ovation. Later Sam Rayburn paid him high tribute. "Young man," he said (this was hardly the proper way to address a King, but Mr. Sam was a law unto himself), "in all my years in Congress, I've seldom heard a speech that could match the one you have given us today." The King was grateful, and vastly relieved.

When we got into the car to go back to the Presidential Guest House, I noticed that his shirt was wringing wet, soaked with perspiration. I made no comment about this, but I smiled to myself because it reminded me of a remark once made by an American to King Leopold, Baudouin's father. The American Ambassador at the time, Fred Alger, and his wife had been golfing in Brussels with the King. Susie Alger had a terrific sense of humor. After the match, Leopold was showing them his new sports car, which had one of those folding straw mats on the front seat. "It keeps you from sticking to the leather," His Majesty explained. "Oh," cried Susie with mock amazement, "I didn't know kings sweat!" But they certainly do, and Baudouin's shirt was proof of it.

That night the Vice-President and Mrs. Nixon gave a large formal dinner—114 guests—for the King at the Pan American Union. The weather was hot and muggy, and I thought the young monarch might be tired after the emotional strain and excitement of the day, but he seemed in high spirits.

At about 11:30, I escorted the King back to the Guest House. Ruth came along a few minutes later in our car to pick me up, but I had disappeared. Somewhat puzzled, she asked Mrs. Geaney where I was. "You've heard of people walking the dog, haven't you?" said Mrs. Geaney. "Well, the King and Mr. Buchanan are out walking the security men!"

This was true. The King had announced that he wasn't really tired and would like to take a walk, as he simply had to have some exercise. So the two of us set out through the deserted streets with two somewhat worried security men loping along behind. I say "loping," because never in my life had I tried to match strides with such a fast walker. We halted momentarily at a snack bar where the King bought us doughnuts. Then we raced—I can think of no better word—all the way down to 7th Street. I had left word that we would be back in about ten minutes. After forty minutes, Ruth began to cruise up and down looking for us. She had no luck, so she settled herself resignedly at the Guest House to wait. It was 1 in the morning when the King and I got back. I felt as if we had walked half-way to New York. I also felt as if the King and I had known each other for years.

On his third evening in Washington, the King was to give a dinner for President Eisenhower, followed by a reception at the Belgian Embassy. Just before the dinner I had a telephone call from President Eisenhower. "Do you think it would be all right if I took Barbara to this dinner tonight?" he said. "Mrs. Eisenhower is out in Denver for her mother's birthday."

I assured the President that the Silvercruys would be delighted to have his daughter-in-law. Mrs. Eisenhower and Rosemary Silvercruys were close friends; the Belgian Ambassador's wife, I knew, had a private telephone line to the White House. Barbara and John Eisenhower did not go out socially very often in Washington, but Barbara was a lovely girl with a lot of sparkle—an asset to any party. So that was easily and quickly arranged, and added much to the evening. It also was typical of President Eisenhower to be this modest in making this request.

Actually, an effort to include some pretty girls for the benefit of our bachelor guest was made. The Ambassador asked his stepdaughter, Pat McMahon, and our own debutante daughter Bonnie. He had also asked Milton Eisenhower's daughter, Ruth, but her father sent word that her studies needed attention and that she had better not come—a display of parental firmness that I couldn't help admiring.

Bonnie let me in for some good-natured teasing when she made a deep curtsy on being presented to the King. I was the Chief of Protocol who had said that American women need not bend the knee to royal visitors, wasn't I? Wasn't I master in my own house? And so on. Bonnie explained her curtsy serenely. The Belgian Embassy was technically Belgian soil, wasn't it? Well, then, when in Belgium, do as the Belgians do.

The next morning we flew to Detroit, first stop on the King's transcontinental trip. It was a back-breaking day. We toured the General Motors Technical Center and the Chrysler Corporation engine plant. The King seemed interested, asked intelligent questions, and took a ride in a futuristic General Motors automobile.

But at a press conference late in the afternoon, the reporters all but overwhelmed him with persistent and sometimes too-intrusive questions. He became noticeably ill at ease, and finally said desperately that he never gave press conferences in Europe, and wasn't used to this. As I went to his rescue, I made up my mind that in the future I would have the King meet the press by walking down the line of reporters, shaking hands, but constantly on the move. That way there would be much less chance of his being cornered and harried.

That night the Henry Fords II gave a black-tie dinner for the King at their beautiful home on Lake Shore Road. It was a handsome affair: the King's table, which seated twelve, was covered with a gold cloth and ornamented with tall golden candelabra wound with garlands of gold-sprayed laurel intertwined with red carnations—the gold and red of the Belgian flag.

After dinner there was some dancing, and I was amused to see that even at the Fords', to improvise a dance floor they followed the old American custom of rolling up the rug. The rug in question was an eighteenth-century Aubusson museum piece, but nevertheless it remained rolled up against the wall all evening. Mrs. Edsel Ford, charming mother of our host, thought the King was looking a bit tired. "Now, Your Majesty," she said to him, "you mustn't overdo things. I know you have a lot of these functions ahead of you so you just go along any time you want to." And she gave him a motherly pat on the shoulder.

The King did seem weary as we drove back to his hotel after the dinner. He was still worrying about the press conference, which he knew had gone badly. In fact, he said, almost moodily munching a Life-saver, his whole schedule was too crowded and exhausting. He didn't see how he could survive another day as strenuous as this. There was to be another press conference in Chicago, wasn't there?

I told him that I was sure it would go well if we followed the new technique that I had suggested to him.

"You'll be there, won't you?" he asked anxiously.

I told His Majesty that I had planned to fly to Dallas from Detroit to make preparations for his visit there. But I added that I would go to Chicago with him if that was what he wanted.

The King seemed torn between reluctance to make me change my plans and a strong desire for the moral support that my presence seemed to give him. He looked helplessly at Ruth, who was sitting between us. "What shall I do?" he asked plaintively.

"Just say what *you* want us to do, Your Majesty," Ruth said promptly. "We're all here to help you."

The upshot was that I canceled my flight to Dallas and continued on to Chicago with the royal party. And the press conference there did go better.

One reason I wanted to precede the King to Dallas was that we were planning a private party for him there in my mother's home. I had a strong feeling that if we could just get the King offstage, so to speak, and into the gay, less formal atmosphere of a moonlight garden party with music and dancing and pretty girls, a long-repressed side of the young monarch might be liberated—not just for one evening, but perhaps permanently. In Detroit I had heard him complain that he never met any eligible girls. "What sort would you like?" I had asked him. "Oh, pretty ones," he said with a smile. "And not too intellectual, but I don't like them to be stupid."

I knew there were plenty of pretty ones in Dallas.

We flew from Chicago to Dallas on Saturday morning. My

mother's chauffeur, Jules de Regge, was a native Belgian. I had arranged for him to drive the King, and he was the happiest man in Texas. He jokingly told one of the motorcycle officers in the King's escort that the thirty-mile-per-hour speed limit set for the motorcade was too slow. "You get out of my way, I go swish!" he said. "You go swish, and you and the King will both go to jail," the officer told him cheerfully.

A surprise was waiting at the airport for the King. For about a month, he had told me, he had been taking flying lessons. He had expressed a desire to see an Aero Commander, an excellent small twin-engine plane. So we had one waiting, complete with test pilot from the factory, at the airport. We took off for a short flight: the King, the pilot, a security man, and myself. The King took over the controls and was having a marvelous time. After a while he put the little plane in a steep climb, and soon I heard the ominous beep-beep of the warning signal that meant we were approaching the point where the plane would stall. There was really no danger; the King coolly nosed the plane down and corrected matters. Still, I told my royal friend that I was hoping to show my home town to a *live* monarch. He laughed, and after a little more circling over the city turned the controls over to the pilot for a landing.

That night the King made a speech at a dinner given by the Dallas Council on World Affairs. The next day, Sunday, he was on his own, and for the first time really began to enjoy himself. After going to early Mass at the Cathedral of the Sacred Heart, he flew over to Fort Worth and played a round of golf with the great professional, Ben Hogan, at the Shady Oaks Country Club. Hogan, who had been ill with influenza, got out of a sickbed to coach the young monarch, and praised his game highly. The day was hot, dusty, and windy, but Baudouin enjoyed himself immensely. When he got back to Dallas, he sent me a message scrawled on a card: "My golf was so-so. I like Ben Hogan."

For three days preparations had been going on at my mother's house for the garden party that evening. We wanted a setting really fit for a king, and so we had called in Joe Lambert, in my opinion the greatest landscape architect in America. In Dallas people say, Neiman-Marcus dresses people; Joe Lambert dresses Dallas. Later on, in her syndicated column, Betty Beale described the setting as vividly as if she had been one of the forty-four guests:

The city's top landscape artist, Joe Lambert, was hired to convert the gardens into a dreamland, and he and his crew spent three days doing it. The King sat at a table for twelve under a pink and white striped regency-style canopy that had a white wrought-iron frieze and was supported by white wrought-iron columns. Under his feet was a ruby red rug and overhead was a real crystal chandelier magically hung from the center of the canopy. Pink and white flowers decorated his and every other table.

Stretching out before him was the swimming pool, which was a myriad of candlelight and flowers. Standing in the water were four candelabra holding 15 hurricane lamps each. In the middle of the pool was a white wrought-iron three-tiered fountain that played constantly. And floating about the candelabra and the fountain were artistically spaced clusters of pink and white peonies.

Beside the pool, an outdoor dance floor had been constructed, and beyond it was the backdrop of trees that half encircle the garden. Hanging from some of the limbs of the trees were more wrought-iron hurricane lamps sparkling from the lighted candles hung inside, and on other limbs hung baskets of pink and white peonies with lighted electric candles in the center.

To make the party of 44 an intimate one, an enclosure of French screening was erected, covered with rambler roses and banked with calladium plants.

The chef of the Sheraton-Dallas Hotel and two assistants provided the evening menu: fresh caviar, consommé, filet mignon, hearts of artichoke, white Belgian asparagus imported for the occasion, brie cheese and lettuce salad, and a pink-and-white strawberry dessert.

By 8 o'clock everything was ready, from the small dance orchestra to the red-coated waiters. All day we had worried about the weather, which had looked threatening. But now the clouds began to drift away. Eventually the moon came out, and Joe Lambert's electricians, who stayed on duty throughout the party, were able to dim the lights in the trees imperceptibly as the moonlight grew stronger until it really was a moonlight garden party.

We had asked three of Dallas' prettiest debutantes, and some of the gay young-married set, and so the King did not lack for dancing partners. At each of the smaller tables, one of my three married sisters acted as hostess: Kathleen Tennison, Ava Inglish, and Eva Hall. My brother Avon sat with Ruth. I sat at another table with my mother, Count d'Aspremont Lyndon and Count Duparc, and other members of the Belgian party.

To get things started we arranged for Ruth to have the first dance with the King. She found His Majesty a bit inexperienced, but willing to learn. "I think I've had more hours as a pilot than as a dancer," the King said to Ruth (he'd had about six hours as a pilot!), "so you'll have to push me in the direction you want me to go. Just pull me around!" A royal wish is a command, so Ruth pushed and pulled with enthusiasm. I brought other eager partners by dancing up to the King and exchanging partners in mid-floor, an old American custom that seemed new to him. He kept saying enthusiastically that he had never enjoyed himself so much, that this was the best party he had ever attended. Ordinarily one discounts such polite protestations from one's guests, but I had a feeling the King really meant it.

One of our pretty girls offered to teach everyone a new Brazilian dance. The King lined up and learned with the rest. Trying to put his newly acquired knowledge into practice he was bumped smartly by the Grand Marshal of his own court, the elderly Count Gobert d'Aspremont Lyndon, who was also attempting the dance. The Count started to apologize profusely but the King cut him off gaily: "You've been wanting to bump me for years," he said laughing. "Now you've done it."

The Count looked astonished; it was evident that he had never seen his sovereign in such a merry mood before.

The party went on and on. Every hour or so, the King would ask me if I thought he should go home. "Not if you're having a good time," I would say. "Well, I am," he'd assure me, and danced some more. No one, of course, was supposed to leave until the King did. At 2 o'clock, feeling that her age gave her special privileges, my mother slipped away to bed. At 3:30 the music was still going, but the musicians were playing with their eyes closed. Finally, at about 4 A.M. the party ended. The King kept saying what a marvelous time he had had. Actually, all of us had had a wonderful time watching him have a wonderful time. For the first time in his royally restricted life, a very likable young man had been left alone to have fun. He'd had it.

We had all of two hours' sleep in what was left of the night. By 8 o'clock we were taking off from Love Field, but not before the King had personally written a letter to my mother thanking her for the party. He also sent her a personally inscribed photo of himself. That morning the King inspected military installations at Fort Bliss, near El Paso, and watched a Nike guided missile intercept an aerial target. By lunchtime we were in Los Angeles.

The City of Los Angeles and the local World Affairs Council gave a dinner for the King that night at the Biltmore Hotel. Twelve hundred guests had been invited. I felt that the King still dreaded making speeches before large audiences, and so I frequently reminded him of his magnificent success in Washington. Western audiences, I assured him, were even more friendly and less critical than Eastern ones. He listened to me hopefully, and when the time came he did very well indeed.

Next day, with his speech behind him, the King became a happy tourist. He went to the MGM studios to see how motion pictures were made, and watched such stars as James Cagney, Gary Cooper, Robert Mitchum, and Eleanor Parker at work. He had lunch in the commissary, where he sat between Debbie Reynolds and Glenn Ford. Miss Reynolds, recently divorced from Eddie Fisher, chattered to the King with such animation that the newspapers began referring to her as his date—an inaccuracy no doubt aided and abetted by her press agent. The King seemed fascinated by the world of make-believe in which he found himself, and we reluctantly departed to inspect the X-15 research plane at the North American aviation plant and watch a test-firing of a huge rocket engine at the Rocketdyne testing center.

That night Mervyn LeRoy, one of Hollywood's best-known producers, gave a party for the King. He had invited a truly glittering array of stars: Bob Hope, Jack Benny, Jimmy Stewart, Gary Cooper, Cyd Charisse, Tony Curtis, June Allyson, Dick Powell, Kirk Douglas, and others. The astonishing thing was that the King was able to recognize almost none of these famous faces; he admitted rather sheepishly that he almost never saw movies, and consequently didn't know one star from another. I told him that he could correct this "grievous gap" in his education by having American films shown in the palace. He said he certainly planned to do so in the future.

It was a gay party, despite the momentary blow to so many high-priced egos. Mervyn LeRoy made a clever speech. When he was a newsboy selling papers on the streets, he said, he never thought he'd have a home fit for a King. But here he was, and here was the King, and he considered it one more proof that America was a fabulous country. Jack Benny played his violin for the King; Tony Curtis played the bongo drums. Our good friends Cyd Charisse and Tony Martin were there, so I asked Cyd to give the King some instruction in the rumba. She found a quiet corner and tackled her assignment with enthusiasm while I stood guard to discourage onlookers who might have embarrassed the King. Afterward, I noticed, the toes of Cyd's white slippers looked a bit battered, but she claimed that her royal partner really had a good sense of rhythm. "All he needs is more practice," she said. As for the King, he was having a ball. It was almost 2 A.M. when the party finally ended.

Next day, the King went to Disneyland. He had lunch with

Disney himself, surely one of the authentic geniuses of our time. He rode in the cab of the Disneyland railroad's locomotive, blew the whistle of the Mississippi River stern-wheeler, and took an underwater trip in one of the new Disneyland submarines. He was enthusiastic about everything, especially the fairyland castle at the entrance to Fantasyland. "Much nicer than the castle I live in," he said with a twinkle.

Later, he asked that all of the police and chauffeurs who had escorted him through southern California be lined up. Then he walked down the line, thanking each one with a handshake. He did the same with members of the press. "I want to come back," he said, "and spend more time."

From Los Angeles, we flew to San Francisco. This beautiful city enchanted the King, as it enchants everyone. Nothing was scheduled for our first evening there so we asked some friends of ours, the Edwin Wilsons, to find a girl for the King's dinner companion. They suggested Dolly Fritz, an attractive brunette, and the six of us went out to dinner, then to see a revue. "I really don't know how you keep up this pace," the King said to me at one point. "I'm younger than you, and I find it strenuous." He'd have been startled had he known how exhausted I really was!

It was apparent to me by this time that the King really needed two things: occasional exercise and occasional solitude, and he wasn't getting enough of either. His midnight foot-races with me helped in the exercise department, but during his waking hours there was hardly a moment when he could be by himself. I didn't realize how much he longed for freedom until the next day when we took him on a sight-seeing tour of the city. We had driven across the Golden Gate Bridge and stopped on the Marin County side of the Bay to admire the view. The King had his camera out, like any tourist, but suddenly he decided that he had been escorted long enough. Down the precipitous rocky hillside he went like a mountain goat. No one could keep up with him; he bounded completely out of sight. I was a bit alarmed. Below him were the swift and frigid waters of San Francisco Bay. Policemen and security men scurried around. Walkie-talkies were brought into action. Finally a mounted policeman spied the King almost at the water's edge, snapping pictures and climbing happily over the rocks. He stayed "lost" for almost three-quarters of an hour, then rejoined us members of "the black Cadillac set," looking relaxed and pleased with himself.

His taste of freedom made him want more. "Can't we just get away by ourselves?" he asked me that night. I told the security men not to worry about us (I knew they'd follow us at a discreet distance anyway); then I smuggled the King out of the Mark Hopkins Hotel by going through the garage, and we set out on an incognito tour of the city. No one recognized us. We walked through Chinatown; we rode on cable cars. "Sit down and stop blocking the door," the cable-car operator said to the King. The King cheerfully sat down and stopped blocking the door.

My stay in San Francisco was ended abruptly by the death of John Foster Dulles. I had known that the Secretary of State was very ill, and had told the King that I might have to leave on short notice. "I know you have no choice," he said. "But I hate to see you go. We get along so well and have had such a good time together."

I told His Majesty I would rejoin him in New York as soon as I could. Then I took the next plane back to Washington.

The funeral of Secretary Dulles was one of the biggest and most important in the history of the Capitol. Hundreds of mourners came to pay their final respects to the man President Eisenhower called "the greatest Secretary of State I have ever known." Chancellor Adenauer came from Germany. The Foreign Minister of Japan came. Gromyko flew from Geneva. As far as my department was concerned, it was like trying to handle a hundred state visits rolled into one. We were just about swamped. President Eisenhower thanked me personally for the efforts we made, but when I took the plane to rejoin the King in New York I was depressed and exhausted. I felt that the country had lost a great fighter for the cause of freedom and that I had lost a close personal friend.

During the flight many recollections of this great man came back to me. I remembered his unfailing kindness and courtesy, his patience and his sense of humor. I remembered his habit of doodling as he listened to you, and his extraordinarily illegible signature. ("Daddy," said our seven-year-old Bucky once in great puzzlement, staring at an autographed photograph of the Secretary, "how can such a smart man be such a bad writer?") I remembered his fondness for good food and good wine, how much he always appreciated the little jars of Beluga caviar that Ruth and I would send him from time to time.

But the most vivid recollection of him was a very simple thing. It happened at the airport in Dallas, the morning after the Hungarian Revolution exploded and the Secretary had been up most of the night receiving frantic telephone calls from Washington. His private plane was waiting, and we were driving out to it when he reminded me that his little granddaughter, Edith, who had flown up from her school in San Antonio to see him, was leaving on a commercial airliner at about the same time. He wondered if it would be possible to see her once again.

I was able to arrange this. The child was actually on the plane with my sister, Mrs. Charles Tennison, who was also returning to San Antonio, but they had not yet taken off. We sent someone to bring them to us. And I'll never forget how that little girl's face lighted up, how she ran down the corridor crying, "Grandpa! Grandpa!" how she flung herself into his arms, knocked his hat off and his glasses askew, and hugged him while he swept her into the air. Hungary was in flames, and the threat of atomic war loomed over us all, but this man cared enough about the simple, basic, decent, human things of life to pause in the midst of international crisis and give his love to a child.

When I met the King in New York, he too expressed his sorrow at the death of Foster Dulles.

Shortly after my arrival there was a reception at the Overseas Press Club. The King joked about the "shock treatment" he had received from inquisitive reporters throughout the country. "I've learned a lot about the way you operate," he said, "and I've had to learn fast. I know, for example, that questions about young ladies are not considered indiscreet in the United States. I've been questioned on this subject from coast to coast."

A stubborn streak of modesty remained in him, however. When the time came for his ticker-tape parade up Broadway, he resisted the efforts of Commissioner Patterson to make him sit up on the top of the rear seat of a white convertible so that people could see him better. "That's what Lindbergh did," the Commissioner told him reassuringly. "Yes," said the King unhappily, "but Lindberg had *done* something!" The parade went well, New York showered the royal visitor with confetti and affection, and by the time the fifteen-car motorcade reached City Hall he seemed to be enjoying himself.

For his last weekend in the United States, we had made plans to give the King a glimpse of American sea power in action, followed by a quick tour of Williamsburg and a farewell dinner at the world-famous Longwood Gardens of the Du Pont family just outside of Wilmington, Delaware.

Our naval host was to be Admiral Jerauld Wright, NATO's Supreme Allied Commander Atlantic (SACLANT) whose headquarters were in Norfolk, Virginia. Jerry Wright's command, the first international ocean command in history, stretched from the North Pole to the Tropic of Cancer, and from the Western Hemisphere shores to the coastal waters of the British Isles and the continent of Europe. The protection of Belgium itself was one of Admiral Wright's responsibilities, and therefore we thought the King would be particularly interested in a visit to a big American aircraft carrier.

Actually, it was a fascinating experience for all of us, though marred by tragedy at the end. We flew from New York to the Naval Air Station at Norfolk, where Admiral Wright met us. After a briefing on SACLANT operations, we had lunch aboard the USS *Northampton,* a floating combat information center carrying the world's largest seaborne radar. After lunch, six airplanes carried our entire party, including many newsmen, to the anti-submarine carrier *Randolph* about 100 miles off-shore.

They put on a marvelous show for us. Submarines cruised past us, destroyers fired anti-submarine weapons and anti-aircraft bursts. Helicopters were launched and recovered. We were allowed to attend the preflight briefing of pilots scheduled to take part in the night exercises. Sitting in the briefing room, dimly lit by red bulbs (to prepare the pilots' eyes for night flying), I thought I had never seen a finer group of young Americans.

After dinner in the Admiral's cabin, we all went to the flag bridge where we were to watch the launching of six S2F aircraft. Plans called for one of these airplanes to illuminate a destroyer on the starboard beam of the carrier, while another made a similar run with its powerful lights on the port beam. Everyone was stunned and horrified when one of these air-planes, through some miscalculation, flew too low and plunged into the sea. All three crewmen were killed. The King was dreadfully upset; he seemed to feel that the demonstration had been put on for him, and that somehow he was responsible for the tragedy. I kept telling him that the night maneuvers would have been carried out anyway, which was true, but this did not seem to console him. The whole ship was plunged in gloom. The King asked for the names of the victims, and wrote personal notes of condolence to their families. But the tragedy left us all saddened and shaken.

The next day, helicopters lifted us to Williamsburg, where Winthrop and Jeannette Rockefeller were waiting to greet the King. His Majesty did not care for helicopters as a means of transportation; he told me that one had had to make a rough forced landing with him on one occasion. This time we all arrived without incident, and after a tour around the restored capital of the Old Dominion we flew to Wilmington, where the King was to keep his last engagements in America—tea with Lamont and Pam Copeland, at their beautiful house, and dinner with all the Du Ponts.

It was both a happy and a sad occasion—happy because the King's tour had proved such a success and sad because we were genuinely sorry to see him go. In his last few hours with us, the shadow caused by the death of the airmen seemed to lift, and he was happy and at ease once more, admiring the handsome Du Pont gardens and particularly the magnificent many-colored fountains. Ruth and I were delighted to find that at a war-council of the clan, the Du Ponts had chosen our friend Bunny Du Pont—Mrs. Nicholas R. Du Pont—to act as hostess for the King. They couldn't have made a better choice. Bunny is blonde, vivacious, and dazzling—a real American beauty who is often Ruth's companion at Elizabeth Arden's "Main Chance" in Arizona.

By midnight we were at the airport where the King's plane waited to take him back to Belgium. He made his official fare-wells, then called Ruth and me into the plane to say good-by privately. We really felt as if we were seeing a close friend off to some important overseas assignment. I think the King felt much the same way, for he said many kind and complimentary things. "I just wish," he kept saying, "that I knew how to re-pay you."

Later the King was to send me a handsome, inscribed wrist watch which I turned in to the State Department to hold until my tour of duty ended.

Just before his plane took off, the King told me of a decision he had made. "When I get back to Brussels," he said, "I am going to hold a press conference. I know it's never been done in Belgium, but I think it would be a wonderful thing. I've seen how they work in this country. It would give my people a chance to know me better, and me to know them better."

And, to the astonishment of his subjects, the King did hold a press conference. Formerly, on his return to Belgium from trips abroad, he would land at the airport and have himself driven rapidly—almost furtively—to the Palace. But this time he made a fifteen-mile tour of the city in an open car, smiling and waving to his amazed and delighted people. "It's the American Baudouin!" shouted one Brussels housewife, as flowers rained upon the King.

According to *Life* magazine, Baudouin returned to his country "apparently a changed man." In Belgium heretofore, the magazine said, the King "had worn the manner of a gloomy divinity student" and before his trip, the very suggestion of a press conference would have appalled his courtiers. But he conducted one on the day after his return, mingled with one hundred reporters who downed champagne and cookies."

That press conference was a triumph. The King said flatly that he was not in favor of strict protocol, that he wanted the press to know him better, and that with closer relations it would be possible to avoid all sorts of misunderstandings. "I'll invite you here to the Palace again," he said, "but you must invite me to some of your meetings too." The newsmen could hardly believe their ears. The King affably answered questions ranging from the quality of American food (very good, he said, especially the sweet potatoes) to the allegedly materialistic outlook of Americans (he said that we were a practical people, but fundamentally idealistic—a shrewd and accurate appraisal).

When the meeting broke up, the reporters were walking on air. "Thank you, sire!" cried the headlines the next day. A new chapter in the history of the Belgian monarchy had begun— and I really think it was a moonlight party plus a touch of Disneyland that started it all!

VIII   Beneath the Fanfare: Foreign Policy

In the summer of 1959, Queen Elizabeth and Prince Philip paid another visit to Canada and the United States. They came in the royal yacht *Britannia,* their chief purpose being to open the St. Lawrence Seaway, and we flew up to Montreal to meet them. Both President Eisenhower and Vice-President Nixon represented the United States at the ceremonies. Governor Nelson Rockefeller of New York was also there. There was a good deal of confusion at times. Fog blanketed the river and made it difficult for the royal yacht to move. The Vice-President's flag blew off the limousine in which he was riding with the Queen and had to be retrieved. I added somewhat to the confusion myself, as this little excerpt from Ruth's diary shows (it also shows how masterfully I organized protocol in our own household): "After the usual to-do about curtsying to the Queen—Wiley telling me not to—my wanting to—talking it over feverishly with other ladies—at the last moment, just before I was presented, he whispered to me that I should! But earlier he had insisted that I shouldn't, so I didn't!"

The Queen and the Prince went on to Chicago where we met them again on July 6. The whole city was in a great state of excitement: I have never seen a more enthusiastic welcome. Plans called for a royal barge from the *Britannia* to bring the Queen and the Prince to a floating platform on the lakefront where I was supposed to greet them. The platform bobbed up and down so violently that I had visions of becoming seasick before a hundred thousand people, so as a precaution I swallowed a couple of dramamine pills. When the royal barge did come alongside, the Queen had to make a flying leap across what looked like six feet of open water. Somehow she managed it with her enviable dignity but it was a tricky moment at best.

Riding through the streets of the city, the Queen seemed really thrilled by the enthusiasm of the crowds. It was quite a contrast to the days when Mayor "Big Bill" Thompson of Chicago announced that if the King of England came to town he would punch him in the nose. Mayor Daley, "Big Bill's" more civilized successor, reminded the Queen of this and we all had a good laugh about it. There is nothing fragile, incidentally, about the Queen's laugh. When she feels like it, she can throw back her head and really let it go.

She was very pensive, however, at luncheon. I noticed that she ate almost nothing and seemed less animated than usual. I found out later that she was suffering from a severe toothache and finally had to be treated by a Chicago dentist. But, in the tradition of royalty, she went right ahead and did her job.

Prince Philip was his usual self, full of quips and wisecracks. When we all squeezed into an elevator at the Drake Hotel he remarked, "If someone would just pour a little oil over us, we'd be like sardines." There was a sign in the elevator "Bath Room —6th floor." Said the Prince, "Do you mean to say there is only one bathroom in this big hotel?" The manager hastened to explain that it was a private clubroom named after the city of Bath in England.

The management of the Drake had outdone themselves for the royal visit. They had put down $40,000 worth of new carpeting, had bought a $5000 tea service, and spent heaven knows what on other items. With us in the hotel were the British Ambassador, Sir Harold Caccia, and his wife, Lady Caccia. Nancy Caccia, who has a great sense of humor, kept us all laughing with her complaints about the nylon satin sheets that she had encountered for the first time. She said that she and her husband slithered around on them all night long, and the pillows kept jumping off the bed in a most un-English fashion. Harold also had his troubles. He and Nancy had remained at the hotel during one of the civic functions to attend to some

Embassy duties. When the Queen returned to the hotel, guarded by countless police and security men, the Caccias were watching her arrival from their suite some twenty floors above the main entrance. As the Ambassador peered out, the screen somehow became unhooked from the top of the window frame and started to fall. He managed to catch it, but it was too large to bring in through the window. There he was, with this lethal object poised above the head of his own Queen. He shouted to Nancy for help. Instead of calling the hotel management, Nancy calmly called her social secretary who was in another suite and ordered *her* to summon help. After what seemed to him like an eternity, Harold was eventually rescued from his predicament, but not before he had had dreadful visions of headlines reading, "British Ambassador Drops Screen on Queen!"

The Queen and the Prince left that same evening after a crowded and satisfying day. Her Majesty presented me with a silver cigarette case, saying with a smile that we had already been through the framed photograph procedure. She rode through the streets of Chicago in her lighted car, just as radiant as she had been in New York, reboarded the royal yacht, and the *Britannia* sailed away under a spectacular canopy of blazing fireworks. Some sentimentalist once said that protocol is three parts practicality and one part poetry. I think the proportion is more likely thirty to one, but the visits of the Queen definitely belonged in the poetry category.

After the Queen, as already described, came Khrushchev. No sooner had that hectic visit ended when the President of Mexico, His Excellency Adolfo Lopez Mateos, arrived with his wife and entourage. The Mexicans were lively and charming people, great fun to be with. Ruth and Señora Lopez Mateos became fast friends; Ruth liked and admired her as much as any visitor who came our way during our four years of protocol.

One misstatement in the press served right away to show how tolerant and understanding the Mexican President's wife really was. When we went to Blair House to pick up the Mexican party for the state dinner at the White House, Ruth was wearing a white mink cape. As it happened, Señora Lopez Mateos also wore one that night. When we all came out of the Guest House, Ruth was carrying hers. Seeing the Mexican President's wife in a white mink cape, some society reporter jumped to the conclusion that she had borrowed Ruth's and made this announcement with great fanfare in the next day's paper. It was one of those maddening mistakes that could have been prevented by a single telephone call of inquiry. Ruth was upset, but Señora Lopez Mateos brushed it off with a smile. Such things also happen in Mexico, she said.

In New York, I remember, we arranged for the Mexican President to meet former President Herbert Hoover. Photographers swarmed around as usual, and Mr. Hoover, a bit annoyed, apologized to the visitor. "I don't mind if you don't," said President Lopez Mateos cheerfully. "I do mind," growled our grand old statesman. "They take hundreds of pictures, but you'll be lucky if you ever see a single one in print." I couldn't help sympathizing; as usual, Mr. Hoover was right.

As I have said, it was our job in the Protocol Division to see that no social blunders were committed that might offend distinguished guests, and we relied on careful advance planning to prevent any serious *gaffe*. But during the visit of President Lopez Mateos there was one shocker. I knew nothing about it until the damage was done, but I can still get hot under the collar thinking about it.

It resulted from a temporary breakdown in our communications with the White House, which usually were excellent. Arrangements had been made—so we thought—for Mrs. Eisenhower to entertain all the ladies of the official Mexican party at a White House luncheon. Mary Jane McCaffrey, Mrs. Eisenhower's competent secretary, was in charge of these arrangements. As we understood it, the wife of the Mexican President, her daughter, and the other five ladies were supposed to leave the Guest House a few minutes before 1 o'clock, cross Pennsylvania Avenue, and be welcomed at the White House. It all seemed like a routine affair.

Ruth had not expected to go to the luncheon; she knew that some American ladies had been invited, including Pat Nixon, but had been told that it was to be a small affair—fourteen persons in all. This, too, was standard procedure. If Ruth was needed, she was always ready to go—she considered it part of my job. If not, not. She had asked the Mexican ladies to come to our house for tea that afternoon, so she would be seeing them later in any case.

At about 10:30 the White House called Ruth, told her that one of the American ladies had had to drop out, and asked if she could come on short notice so as not to have a luncheon group of thirteen. She said she would be glad to fill in.

But when she arrived at 12:55, an agitated Mary Jane Mc-Caffrey drew her aside and nodded toward an unhappy-looking little group of Mexican ladies. "You've got to get them out of here," whispered Mary Jane. "They're not expected. We don't have room for them!"

Ruth was aghast. The four Mexican ladies standing there were beautifully dressed and groomed. Obviously, they were expecting to have lunch in the world-famous White House with the wife of the President of the United States. But Mary Jane explained, practically wringing her hands, that only three were expected: the wife of the Mexican President, her daughter, and the wife of the Mexican Ambassador.

Ruth's first reaction was instantaneous. "Set four more places," she whispered. "Stretch the food, somehow!"

This, actually, was the only intelligent solution, but plans at the White House are not always so flexible. In this case, Mary Jane said, the table was all arranged; it was too late to change it.

"Call Wiley!" was Ruth's second reaction.

She knew that this was not just a minor mistake; it was a protocol catastrophe. Among the rejected ladies was the wife of the Mexican Prime Minister. The Prime Minister had been a former Ambassador to the United States. Certainly prime ministers' wives are Very Important Persons indeed, though it was bad enough to turn away any member of the official party. To ask the Prime Minister and former Ambassador's wife to leave was unthinkable. But Mary Jane kept insisting that this be done.

"I'll take them all to lunch at the Mayflower or somewhere," cried Ruth in despair.

"You can't do that," Mary Jane said. "It would leave us with thirteen at the table!"

So in the end, wishing that she could drop through the floor, poor Ruth had to explain that a terrible mistake had been made, that only three of the Mexican ladies were expected at the luncheon. The other four, naturally, smiled bravely and left.

When I heard this, I rushed over to the Guest House to do what I could to atone for this appalling breach of good manners and hospitality. The Mexicans were quite understanding about it. But, being proud Latins, they must have found our performance incomprehensible. As a matter of fact, I did myself. Ruth suffered through the luncheon, explaining to Pat Nixon what had happened. All of us, including Mary Jane, were sick about the whole thing.

The episode brought home to me once again how absolutely essential protocol is to the conduct of foreign policy. Beneath all the fanfare, like a steel wire inside a silken thread, runs a kind of life-or-death awareness that in the last analysis foreign policy is made by human beings, with feelings that can be soothed or flattered or bruised or lacerated. When chiefs of state or their representatives deal with one another, or even when their wives deal with one another, the climate of such a meeting is of supreme importance, and protocol is what determines the climate.

Throughout the four years, no matter where I was, no matter what I was doing, this sense of deadly seriousness underlay my attitude toward my job. When you are responsible for protocol, you are an instrument of your country's foreign policy, and, believe me, the knowledge brings with it a sobering sense of accountability.

Since Mexico and Texas have hundreds of miles of border in

common, and good-neighbor relations are important, we took President Mateos and his party to visit President Lyndon Johnson's Texas ranch.

He was at that time majority leader of the Senate. During President and Mrs. Mateos' overnight stay with Lyndon Johnson a rather unexpected event occurred. Prior to luncheon, much to everyone's surprise, in flew a helicopter containing former President Harry Truman and Sam Rayburn, then Speaker of the House. It landed smack in front of the Lyndon Johnson ranch house, and their arrival coincided to the second with numerous people parading in front of the house with "Johnson for President" placards. We never dreamed that we would participate in the opening phase of the Johnson-for-President boom.

Our Mexican friends finally departed on October 15. We went to Austin, Texas, to see them off and stayed in the Governor's mansion with Price and Jean Daniels. Jean, who is a descendant of Sam Houston, assigned us to a guest room containing the famous Texan's bed, a huge four-poster hung with red damask. It was an historic spot, certainly, but as Ruth pointed out, Mr. Houston must have been a very heavy man. There was a sizable depression in the mattress about six inches deep. I spent the night in this trench quite comfortably, but Ruth kept climbing up the sides and rolling back down again.

The tempo of our life slowed down briefly as the Christmas season approached, but it picked up again with the New Year. In 1960, in addition to my ceaseless travels inside the United States, I was to make two trips to South America and two to Europe.

The first South American trip was a "dry run" for President Eisenhower's visit to Brazil, Argentina, Chile, and Uruguay in February. These survey trips are standard procedure whenever a Head of State travels abroad. The trial run gives the crew of the Presidential aircraft a chance to check on all airport facilities. Medical experts and security experts take the necessary precautions for the President's health and safety. My job was to inspect accommodations for the Presidential party, to make

contact with my opposite number in the protocol depart-
ments of the various countries, and to approve whatever arrangements they had made.

On the trip were Tom Stevens, President Eisenhower's appointments secretary; Jim Hagerty, his press secretary; and
John Eisenhower, the President's son. We were a congenial
group; Tom Stevens and Jim Hagerty are extroverted Irish-
men with wonderful senses of humor. It was Tom, for instance,
who decided—when President Eisenhower's interest in painting
was much in the news—to send do-it-yourself painting kits to
all the members of the Cabinet with a Presidential order to
turn in a finished product to the White House. Most of the
distinguished gentlemen complied, and some of their efforts
hung in the White House during the remainder of the President's administration.

On this trip I got to know John Eisenhower much better and
to like him very much. In Rio, at his own request, John was
given very modest quarters, while Hagerty and I each had a
penthouse. I insisted that John move in with me. After that
we shared rooms on many occasions and had a great time
together.

Plans called for President Eisenhower to land first at Brasilia,
the new and still unfinished Brazilian capital, 900 miles inland
from Rio. My first impression of Brasilia was that it was no
place to bring anyone, let alone the President of the United
States. Most of the streets were unpaved, and the dust was bad.
Every country had been given free ground on which to build
an Embassy, but not much progress had been made. The American Embassy consisted of a trailer parked in an empty lot. I
couldn't help wondering how the Portuguese felt about this,
since they had just completed a magnificent new Embassy in
Rio at a reported cost of $2,000,000. The President's Palace was
spectacular in design, but had considerably fewer bedrooms
than our own White House and almost no bathrooms. It had
been designed by a known Communist, which perhaps left
me a trifle prejudiced. A motley collection of antiquated automobiles honked and clattered through the streets. The whole

place was more like a movie set than the capital of the largest nation in South America.

We went on to Buenos Aires, where I was glad to see President Frondizi again. In Buenos Aires I bought a handsome, expensive alligator brief case which I carried with me constantly. My colleagues thought that it contained valuable state papers, but what I really kept in it was a growing collection of unlaundered clothes.

We visited Chile and Uruguay, checking all arrangements in both places. Our security men thought that President Eisenhower might be greeted by Communist demonstrations in Montevideo, and precautions were taken, but the threat never really materialized. There were a few anti-American signs painted on some buildings, but that was all.

Ruth was not with me on the survey trip, but she was invited to fly down to Rio privately and be there for President Eisenhower's visit. Her hosts were Walther and Elizinha Moreira-Salles, good friends of ours and two of the most attractive people I know. We had known Walther when he was stationed in Washington as Brazilian Ambassador. He is a brilliant and highly cultivated man, a collector of French impressionist paintings and rare books and manuscripts. I met Elizinha when Walter came to Washington on his second tour of duty, and she struck me as one of the most perfect wives for a diplomat that I ever met. She was a very beautiful woman, tall and statuesque, with dark hair and very white skin. She spoke English with a delightful accent and was equally fluent in several other languages. She was a marvelous mimic, had a great sense of humor, and dressed to perfection. Her first year in Washington, her name appeared—along with that of the noted beauty, Nicole Alphand, the French Ambassador's wife—on the international list of best-dressed women. In addition, she was—and is—as well informed on any international topic as any diplomat I know. I was also able to stay with the Moreira-Salleses in Rio, and the four of us had a marvelous time.

President Kubitschek of Brazil with his wife and daughters flew to Brasilia the day before President Eisenhower was to arrive. The city was in a great state of excitement, the streets crowded not only with antique cars but with horse-drawn vehicles of every description. The Brazilian President came to the airport, got word that the American President's plane was late, and returned to the Presidential Palace.' Almost at once we saw the American jet approaching. President Kubitschek came back as fast as he could—I think we sent a helicopter for him, actually—but President Eisenhower's plane was on the ground and waiting by the time he arrived.

The Brazilians had a red carpet ready. Unfortunately, it was about twenty feet too long. The end of it, piled up at the foot of the plane's unloading ramp, was not only unsightly but dangerous, especially for passengers like Chris Herter. I looked wildly around and spotted a GI who had come on the American plane and had descended by another ramp. "Do you have a knife?" I said. "Can you cut this carpet?"

Quick as a flash, the boy pulled out a razor-sharp knife, made one slash, and cut the carpet as clean and straight as if he had been using a T-square. He kicked the surplus behind the ramp just as the door of the plane opened for President Eisenhower to descend. It was one of the neatest bits of work I ever saw, and proved to me once more how resourceful members of the Presidential plane crew always were.

After the welcoming ceremonies, both Presidents climbed into a car for the ride back to the Presidential Palace. At this point one of the wildest scenes imaginable occurred. It looked as if all the taxi drivers in Brasilia, all the ancient cars, all the horse-drawn wagons broke through the police lines and came charging across the field for a closer glimpse of the American President. It made me think of the start of the Oklahoma land rush back in the 1880s. Cars were colliding, radiators were boiling over, horses were rearing, red dust was over everything. It was a security man's nightmare. Fortunately it was a friendly and good-humored crowd, and the Presidents' car finally got through. But it was the most chaotic sight I ever saw in my life.

A mild degree of chaos continued throughout our stay in the

half-finished capital. Accommodations were hopelessly scrambled; it was not unusual to find some exhausted newspaper reporter asleep in the bed in the room that had been assigned to you. Taxis hooted and celebrating Brazilians laughed and chattered in the streets all night long. No one got any sleep.

By contrast, the welcome for President Eisenhower in Rio was splendidly staged. Here our Brazilian hosts really went all out. The President was taken straight from the airport to the magnificent harbor, where a platform had been built over the water. Yachts were flying pennants, the crews of warships were lined up at attention, fireboats hurled great fountains of water into the air. High above, on the mountain, the great statue of Christ looked down through drifting clouds. I saw all this from a helicopter that brought Mr. Herter and me from the airport, and it was a thrilling sight—the most elaborate arrival I've ever seen. Ruth watched it from a seventy-five-foot yacht belonging to some friends of the Moreira-Salleses; she said it was unforgettable.

Festivities planned in Rio were dampened the next day by incessant rain and a terrible air disaster. An American Army plane bringing a Navy band from Buenos Aires to Rio to play at a reception at the American Embassy collided with a Brazilian airliner. Both planes plunged into the harbor. Sixty-eight people were killed; only three survived. The reception was canceled. Our Ambassador to Brazil, John Cabot, was unnerved by the tragedy, but he and his attractive wife gamely went ahead with the dinner at which President Eisenhower was to play host to President Kubitschek. No one mentioned the air crash, but it cast a pall over everything. I remember that dinner was delayed because the seating charts were on the second floor of the Embassy, the upstairs servants would not bring them down, and the downstairs servants refused to go up and get them—a case of carrying back-stairs protocol a bit too far. There were two conspicuously empty places at the table—the parents of a Brazilian boy killed on the Brazilian plane. Rain poured down outside. Everyone did his best, but it was a somber occasion.

Later that evening we joined some friends at a night club called the "Black Horse," where we danced the Brazilian samba —a smoother and less exhausting version of the dance than ours —and were introduced to the curious custom of sniffing a few drops of ethyl chloride sprinkled on a handkerchief. This is supposed to pep you up, and evidently it did: we got home so late that we decided there was no point in going to bed since our plane left for Buenos Aires just after dawn.

The remainder of the trip went very well. In Buenos Aires, Ruth renewed her friendship with Señora Frondizi (she brought the President's wife another hat, but the New York one remained her favorite). I flew with the Presidential party down to Barraloches, a fishing resort farther south, where President Frondizi entertained our President in a handsome, Swiss-style chalet, rustic but very comfortable. The furniture, I remember, was strikingly upholstered in white-and-black horsehide. I also remember that by this time my laundry situation was desperate. At the point when I was due to join the President and had no clean shirt, I saw somebody's clean shirt hung out to dry on a balcony near my room. I simply grabbed it, wore it to the meeting, and then furtively put it back. Laundry problems and lack of sleep were the worst part of these grueling trips—especially the grim necessity of being ready to move on at 5 or 6 o'clock in the morning.

We flew over the Andes in perfect weather, the snow-covered peaks and arid canyons very reminiscent of our own Rockies. President Eisenhower was received with warmth and friendliness everywhere. I wished that Mrs. Eisenhower could have been with us, but she hates flying and so had stayed in Washington.

At each of our embassies—in Rio, Buenos Aires, Santiago, and Montevideo—our ambassadors, their wives, and their staffs made a splendid effort to welcome President Eisenhower and the rest of us. I have often thought, though, that some of our Embassy buildings throughout the world do less than justice to the prestige and dignity of the United States. The British usually outshine us in this respect. The story goes that after World

War II, when the British were bled almost white and were seeking areas in which to retrench and economize, it was proposed that funds earmarked for the purchase and maintenance of their Embassy buildings throughout the world be sharply reduced. But Winston Churchill disagreed vehemently. "Increase those funds," he said, "and I will guarantee that the prestige of Britain will rise higher than ever!" This was done, with results that persist to this day. I have yet to see a British Ambassador in residence who did not have a gleaming Rolls-Royce, symbol of British quality craftsmanship. Their Embassy buildings have an elegance and splendor that are truly impressive. By comparison some of our embassies (such as the one in Lisbon, for example) are pathetic—almost shabby.

Such penny-pinching, it seems to me, ill becomes the richest and most powerful nation in the world. Sometimes, too, there are ready-made solutions just begging to be adopted. In Paris, for instance, several years ago our government bought from the Rothschild family a magnificent building on the rue St. Honoré. This building is almost identical to the British Embassy, which is only a few doors away. Each has a large garden in the rear. The Rothschild building, which has been used for various purposes—none of them very important—would make a splendid Embassy, far better than our present one in Paris. I think we are making a big mistake in not using counterpart funds to turn this grand old eighteenth-century building into an Embassy that would rival any in the city. We should do the same with the former German Embassy, which we also own, in Lisbon.

In April, 1960, a very distinguished visitor from Paris paid us a state visit. This was that towering embodiment of French *grandeur*, General Charles de Gaulle. He did not stay long, and I was unable to accompany him on his visits to New Orleans and San Francisco because the King and Queen of Nepal arrived in Washington the day De Gaulle left and of course I was occupied with them. But I did spend three days with this extraordinary man.

He arrived with Madame de Gaulle in a Caravelle, that

excellent jet aircraft designed and built in France. Despite his reputation for being austere and unbending, the French President—and his wife also—struck me as being simple and unpretentious people, very easy and pleasant to deal with. I thought he had aged a good deal since the last time I had seen him. He brought his doctor with him, as do most visiting heads of state, and a supply of his rather rare blood type in case of emergencies. His sight is bad. I noticed that when he was approaching a flight of stairs he would hold his glasses like a pair of lorgnettes, look at the stairs, judge the distance carefully, then put the glasses back in his pocket and walk up confidently.

Mme. de Gaulle was a motherly type of woman with dark hair, fine skin, simple clothes and jewelry. Mrs. Eisenhower took her on a personally conducted tour of the White House—something she rarely did—and the French President's wife seemed to enjoy this greatly.

There was a state dinner at the White House, and the Nixons also gave a dinner for the French delegation at the Mayflower Hotel. From a floral standpoint, I always thought this dinner was Ruth's masterpiece. In the center of the great horseshoe table she had arranged for Washington florist Walter Charron to erect a whole tree of lilacs and orchids illuminated with pink lights. Tall white wrought-iron vases were overflowing with cascading lilacs. It made one feel that April in Washington could be just as memorable as April in Paris.

The next afternoon the French Embassy gave a tremendous reception for about 2000 people, very lavish and beautifully organized. I remember seeing Elsa Maxwell come through the receiving line. She had been decorated by the French government for her services during the First World War and was a passionate admirer of De Gaulle. He talked to her at some length, and thanked her so warmly and so graciously for what she had done for France that when she left him she was in tears.

It's strange how often the real personality of these great men is hidden behind a kind of artificial image. De Gaulle is often portrayed as stubborn, proud, inflexible, and arrogant—and perhaps he is all these things where the prestige of France is concerned. But he can be democratic and considerate, too. His Chief of Protocol, M. Chancel, told me how he gave a reception in the Élysée Palace in honor of the head butler, who had served there for forty years. M. Chancel also told me of the time at some official luncheon when an unexpected guest caused a food shortage and the harassed staff decided to fix an egg for De Gaulle. The President, who apparently does not care for eggs, looked at his plate with distaste and said to the waiter, "Please get me something else." The plate was hastily withdrawn to the kitchen. But there another waiter saw it, thought that it had never left the kitchen, and triumphantly carried it to the President for the second time. You can imagine, he said, "the reception it got!" I could indeed!

General de Gaulle went on to New Orleans and then to San Francisco, where the turnout for him was the biggest in the city's history. His visit was well timed, because it strengthened the historic ties between France and the United States at a critical moment. Within less than a month of his visit, the General was to prove himself a firm friend and ally of President Eisenhower. This was at the ill-fated Summit Meeting in Paris.

Without doubt, this was the most dramatic occasion during my four years as Chief of Protocol. The tension was building up long before we took off from Washington in the Presidential plane. On May 1, an American spy plane had been shot down over Russia. Khrushchev had reacted with furious denunciations—although such flights had been going on since 1956, and he knew it. It was evident that he would be coming to Paris in an ugly mood.

I must confess that, in my opinion, we did not handle our side of the U-2 incident very well. First we denied that the U-2 was a spy plane. Then we implied that the flight had been made without the President's approval. This left Mr. Eisenhower in a position where he had to take full responsibility for the flights, or else admit that he didn't know what was going on in his own administration.

Regarding the plane incident, I remember, there was much speculation as to what the Russians would do. Some thought they might be easier to handle, now that we had demonstrated our capacity to carry out aerial surveillance. Others thought that the loss of face would force them to make some dramatic effort to regain the initiative in the cold war. I had thought for some time—as I indicated in the first chapter of this book—that the Russians had no intention of letting President Eisenhower visit their country and score a personal triumph behind the Iron Curtain. I was very much afraid that with the U-2 affair we had handed them a ready-made excuse for canceling the invitation.

When we landed in Paris, it seemed to me that the whole city was keyed up and on edge. President Eisenhower was staying at our Embassy Residence, and offices for the rest of us had been set up at the Embassy Chancery. Rigid security was being enforced; it was impossible even to walk down the street outside a building where one of the meetings was being held without all sorts of credentials. I remember very well, on the morning of the first meeting, coming out of our Embassy, hearing a roar of motorcycles and sirens, and seeing a big open automobile swing around the corner. In it were Khrushchev, Marshal Malinovsky, the Defense Minister, and Gromyko. For some reason, Khrushchev was sitting on the jump seat. He was smiling and waving, as he had done in New York, but not getting much response from passers-by. The car was moving fast, and it soon disappeared.

At the critical meeting, as everyone knows, Khrushchev put on a performance worthy of Hitler. He ranted; he raved; he demanded that the United States admit that it had committed aggression, punish those "directly guilty," and promise to make no more flights over Russia. As I had expected, he canceled the invitation for President Eisenhower to visit Moscow. His manner was deliberately insulting; I don't know how President Eisenhower controlled his temper. President de Gaulle, icily polite, called Khrushchev to order. But the damage was done:

the Summit was wrecked, just as Khrushchev intended it
should be.

Later, in the Embassy, I found myself alone for a moment
with our grim-faced President. "Mr. President," I said, "I'd
just like you to know that all of us think your conduct today
was magnificent."

He shook his head slowly. "There are some people," he said,
"who just don't care one bit about peace."

Two days later Khrushchev held a press conference at which
he denounced the United States more violently than ever.
"Thief, coward, aggressor," were some of the epithets he
hurled. But by this time President Eisenhower had flown on to
Lisbon, four days ahead of schedule.

Presented with the unaccustomed bonus of a little free time,
Ruth and I decided to make the most of it. One day we picked
up Elsa Maxwell and the Henry Fondas and drove out to
have lunch with the Duke and Duchess of Windsor at their
"Moulin," a converted mill not far from Paris.

No one in the world, I am sure, entertains more beautifully
than the Duchess. The food, the surroundings, the liveried
servants—all are perfection. Flowers were everywhere, in the
house, in the gardens, on terraces covered by yellow awnings.
Inside, the colors were dramatic and brilliant—chartreuse and
red in the foyer and the living room, upstairs dazzling combinations of orange and green and yellow and red.

We had cocktails in the upstairs drawing room, with huge
windows looking out over a putting green and swimming pool
to a waterfall in the distance. The Duchess took the Fondas on
a guided tour of the house, showing them the Duke's study
with a large map indicating the places where he had made
speeches in England before his abdication and a regimental
drum that had been turned into a coffee table. The guest rooms
had once been horse stalls; they were tiny but delightful, with
the furniture all in scale. Alfeda Fonda was as excited as a
child. I joined the tour myself to see this marvelous place
again.

Luncheon was at two tables, each seating seven or eight

29-10-1961

Déjeuner
~
Omelette du Pêcheur
~
Chateaubriand Grillé
Sauce Béarnaise
Pommes de Terre Gaufrettes
Salade
~
Montego Bay Ice
Rhum Chaud
Petits Gâteaux
~
Fromages

Luncheon at the *Moulin*

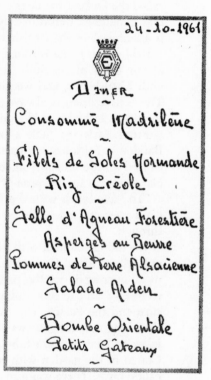

24-10-1961

Dîner
Consommé Madrilène
~
Filets de Soles Normande
Riz Créole
~
Selle d'Agneau Forestière
Asperges au Beurre
Pommes de Terre Alsacienne
Salade Arden
~
Bombe Orientale
Petits Gâteaux
~

Dinner at the Paris residence in
Bois de Boulogne

Two menus of the Duke and Duchess of Windsor

people. The food was unforgettable and the wines superb. Half a dozen liveried footmen with white gloves served us with exquisite formality. There were many dogs about—one sat under the Duke's chair at lunch, and another close to the Duchess. There was a lush green carpet, and Ruth laughingly asked the Duke if the dogs ever mistook it for grass. He replied that sometimes, unfortunately, they did. Obviously loving dogs is a hallmark of the British Royal Family.

I think the Duke is much more relaxed at the *Moulin* than at any other place. Ruth gave him an account of our travels with Khrushchev, and we all talked about the Summit fiasco. The conversation is always stimulating at the Windsors', and the hours flashed past like minutes.

From Paris we took a train up to Brussels to see King Baudouin. Ruth left her passport by mistake in Paris, and this caused a little difficulty at the border. "Madam," said the official, "what is the purpose of your visit to Brussels?"

"To have lunch with the King!" said Ruth calmly. The official's eyes opened wide, he clicked his heels and ushered us through.

We did have lunch with the King, in his private dining room at Lachen Palace. He couldn't have been more cordial, thanked us all over again for the party in Dallas. After lunch he drove us in his Cadillac convertible around the acres of gardens that surround the Palace. The rhododendrons and azaleas were at their height, and the views of the Palace through long vistas of lakes and lawns were fabulous. There was even a miniature Congo in the garden with real live monkeys in the trees and exotic birds. There was also an enclosed swimming pool with a real sand beach, hothouses with orchids and other tropical plants. The King showed us his seven-hole golf course, picked Ruth a sprig of heliotrope, and at the end got out his camera and took pictures of us. It was a wonderful reunion; he made us feel that he enjoyed it as much as we did.

From Brussels we went to Luxembourg, slept in our old bed at the Embassy there, and met many old friends. Many Luxembourgers asked us about Perle Mesta, who had preceded me as Ambassador there, and expressed great affection for her. I remember the time Perle had visited us at the Embassy, driving unexpectedly from Paris. We gave a reception for her at very short notice, and she greeted several hundred people. We thought she would be exhausted, but when Ruth offered to show her to her room she announced that her sister was arriving early the next day in Paris and that she would like to meet her. So off she drove, acting as if Paris were just around the corner instead of five or six hours away. She certainly is a woman of remarkable stamina and energy.

We wished that our little holiday in Luxembourg could have lasted longer, but duty called in Washington. Besides, we were getting homesick for the children, and so we flew home.

In September, I accompanied President Eisenhower to New York for the opening of the General Assembly of the United Nations. This was the session where Khrushchev gained some additional notoriety by taking off his shoe and pounding on the table with it. General de Gaulle should have been there to put him in his place. I know that I, for one, was getting very tired of Mr. K's calculated tantrums.

As was to be expected after the clash at the Summit, Khrushchev and President Eisenhower did not meet. But many other world leaders came to the President's Suite—35-A—in the Waldorf Towers to pay their respects. Tito of Yugoslavia came, a pudgy little man with henna-dyed hair and the coldest, most terrifying eyes I had ever seen. Seeing him reminded me how Secretary Dulles had wryly praised the Yugoslav Ambassador Mates—the ablest diplomat in Washington, he called him, since he seemed able to persuade the American government endlessly to finance and support a Communist regime.

Nehru also came, smaller than I expected him to be, with an inscrutable, brooding expression. He wore his little white Gandhi cap and a rose tucked into the third buttonhole of his knee-length tunic. The Indians, always very jealous of their prerogatives, made it clear that they expected their Prime Minister to have just as much time with President Eisenhower as anyone else. Actually, no one had much time. We would receive the distinguished guests in the rather small foyer, then Tom Stevens would signal with his fingers—two minutes, perhaps three minutes. But most stayed longer.

At one point we had such a crowd that we were forced to use Chris Herter's bedroom as a reception room—and Mrs. Herter had to take refuge in the bathroom! I felt like a juggler trying to keep six balls in the air at once. . . .

But as a matter of fact, that is the way the Chief of Protocol feels most of the time!

IX   Kings, Queens, and Deuces

The last two royal visits of 1960 were among the pleasantest of my entire four years. The royal couples made an interesting contrast, too. First came the talented King of Thailand with his exquisite Queen—dainty, fragile, Oriental. Then came the towering King of Denmark—blue-eyed, rugged, outspoken—with his equally charming and beautiful wife who looked like a Viking princess.

The King and Queen of Thailand came in June, when Congress was struggling to get away from Washington and the Presidential campaign of 1960 was beginning to move into high gear. They had stopped briefly in Hawaii, where the King had had a ride in an atomic-powered submarine. They also spent a few days in Los Angeles, where they had left their four children (the King called them his Thai-phoons) with attendants while they came to Washington.

The King was a slender young man who usually wore dark glasses to conceal the fact that an automobile accident had left him blind in one eye. He was an excellent musician, loved jazz, played the saxophone and the trombone, and had composed and published various popular songs. His wife, Sirikit, was one of the most beautiful state visitors we had ever had. She wore wonderful clothes and jewels. Her wardrobe, designed by Pierre Balmain, was reputed to have cost $75,000. In addition to her beauty she had great warmth and charm, had been educated in Europe as well as in Thailand, and spoke a quaint sort of English with a delightful accent. Like her husband, she was the descendant of kings and queens—and she looked it.

The King brought a present to President Eisenhower that was quite appropriate for an election year—a teakwood and gold elephant. After seeing the terrible-tempered King of Siam as played by Yul Brynner in *The King and I*, I wondered if the present King might be difficult to deal with. On the contrary, he was exceedingly pleasant and well mannered. He had a trick of returning a compliment instantly; if you said something nice to him, he at once said something nice to you. The Queen, too, was quick with a compliment. On their first night in Washington, we were riding from Blair House to the White House for the state dinner being given in their honor by President Eisenhower. The Queen was glittering with gold and diamonds, and I admired her magnificent jewels. "Yes," she said, smiling at her husband, "Queen very lucky have nice husband with grandfather who collected so many jewels." I couldn't help thinking that the King was also very lucky to have such a beautiful wife to wear them.

Guy Lombardo's orchestra furnished the entertainment at the White House that night. The famous orchestra leader had planned to play selections from *The King and I*, but at the last moment we were warned by our Ambassador to Thailand, Alexis Johnson, that this would not be well received. Apparently the King felt that the play treated his ancestors with too much frivolity.

There were many ancient customs that we had to keep in mind. In Siam, or Thailand as it is now called, the Queen must always walk behind the King. No one may be seated higher than he is. Not even the Queen is supposed to touch the King's head.

Traditionally, a commoner is never supposed to touch the King at all, but no one takes this too seriously. At one point, I remember, Mrs. Eisenhower, who suffers from occasional vertigo caused by an ear disorder, reached out and steadied herself by taking the King's arm. Far from being offended, the King was very pleased. "Did you see Mrs. Eisenhower take my arm?" I heard him say later to his wife. "Wasn't that nice!"

The King enjoyed Guy Lombardo's music, but his great idol

in the jazz world was Benny Goodman, and so we arranged for a private jam session in New York at Goodman's apartment. Gene Krupa, Red Norvo, and other famous musicians were to be there. I must admit, I tried to keep the story under wraps—I was afraid it might be thought too frivolous. I was also uneasy because I knew that Mr. Goodman's publicity men would make the most of the occasion if they had the chance. I had been promised that there would be no reporters or photographers, but I got a tip that one of the "musicians" was really going to be a cameraman in disguise. I warned the King about this, but he was anxious to play with such top-level performers, and did not seem too concerned. Sure enough, pictures were taken and released to the press, along with many references by Mr. Goodman to the King and himself as "two Kings of jazz."

In the meantime, Ruth was escorting Queen Sirikit on a shopping expedition. The Queen had heard that it was possible to have face powder specially blended to match any skin color. She was anxious to see this cosmetic marvel, so Ruth took her to Saks, the great department store on Fifth Avenue. Just inside the door they passed the jewelry counter, and a lovely coral pin shaped like a rose caught the Queen's eye. It had a dew-drop made of diamonds nestling on it, and was very attractive—also quite expensive. As I have already mentioned, Queens do not carry money on their royal persons; an attendant carries it for them. In this case, the money-man was held up in traffic and had not arrived. Having made her choice, the Queen moved serenely to the sweater counter. Ruth explained to the jewelry saleslady that she was dealing with the Queen of Thailand and suggested that the pin be sent to the Waldorf C.O.D. The saleslady said that it was too expensive an item for such a procedure. Feeling a bit frantic, Ruth then told the saleslady to charge the pin to her own account, and hurried after the Queen, who was now buying some very costly sweaters. Fortunately, at this point the money-man arrived and paid all the bills.

Entranced with a store where it was possible to buy just

about anything, the Queen had her face powder blended, then went on to the shoe department, where she bought a pair of beige shoes. It was such fun to try to match things, she said; all her Balmain creations came ready-matched, but this way she could do it herself. Most women, Ruth thought, would be very happy to have Balmain do their matching for them!

Before they left for Europe, the King and Queen were honor guests at a dance given for them by Governor Nelson Rockefeller at the Rockefeller estate in Tarrytown. A marquee was set up in the garden, Benny Goodman furnished the music, and before the evening was over the King had taken his place in the orchestra and was adding his royal talent for jazz to the occasion.

After saying good-by to the picturesque couple, we returned to Washington where I shortly had a telephone call from Dick Nixon. The President, he said, had offered him the use of Camp David for the Fourth of July weekend, and he and Pat wanted Ruth and me to join them there. Just the four of us, he said. It would be his last chance to relax before the Republican Convention met in Chicago. I agreed that it would be a fine idea.

Camp David consists of a main lodge, rustic but very comfortable, and several detached cabins each named after a different kind of tree—such as aspen, maple, and so on. These command a magnificent view of the Maryland countryside. The camp was staffed by Filipino servants, and reminded me of a very luxurious hunting lodge. We drove up in the Nixons' Oldsmobile. I had a few qualms about being driven on the Fourth of July weekend by a man who almost always had the services of a chauffeur, but my fears were groundless. Now and then people would glance at us, and it was amusing to see them do a double-take and report excitedly to one another, "You know, I believe that was Richard Nixon driving that car!"

We had three lazy, carefree days, swimming in the pool, walking in the woods, driving golf balls in front of the main lodge. The Vice-President's nomination at Chicago was assured; he was already working on the acceptance speech that was so enthusiastically received by the delegates at the Convention. I remember his telling me thoughtfully that of all the possible Democratic candidates, Kennedy would be the hardest to beat. But he felt sure that he could do it.

The only serpent in our little Eden turned out to be an inquisitive black snake that crawled out on the terrace where Pat and Ruth were sunning themselves. They fled into the lodge where I was reading and demanded that I do something about it. I informed one of the Filipino boys, who alerted the commandant of the camp. He promptly arrived in a jeep, with reinforcements. By this time, the snake had vanished. Later it reappeared, was captured (alive) with a couple of bamboo rakes, and carried far into the woods—the innocent victim of twentieth-century bureaucracy in action.

The rest of the summer passed quickly. We took a week off and went to the Convention at Chicago, a fascinating experience. Various foreign dignitaries made brief appearances in Washington: the Crown Prince and Princess of Japan, King Hussein of Jordan, and the Prime Minister of the Congo, Patrice Lumumba. Meantime, the political campaign grew hotter and hotter, and people in Washington talked of little else.

The last royal visit during my term as Chief of Protocol came in October when the King and Queen of Denmark flew from Copenhagen across the North Pole and landed in Los Angeles. Ruth and I flew out to meet them in the *Columbine* with Count Knuth-Winterfeldt, the Danish Ambassador, and his wife Trudy. The Danish King was a regal-looking man, tall and virile, with a quick sense of humor. He smoked a lot, but did not drink at all. The Queen, who is the daughter of King Gustav of Sweden, spoke perfect English. She was one of the few women we met who was capable of making a graceful impromptu speech when the occasion required one.

The King and Queen broke the ice right away. When we drove in from the airport, Ruth and I took them to their apartment in the Ambassador Hotel. The King smilingly handed me a box with a Danish decoration in it. "This is for you," he said. Rather startled at being given a decoration before I had done anything to deserve it, I said that I hoped I would prove worthy of it. "Well," said the King with a laugh, "if you do anything I don't like, I'll just take it back."

Ruth had been warned that the Queen hated gloves, and so was in a quandary as to whether to wear them herself. Riding in from the airport with the Queen, she noticed that Her Majesty was wearing just *one* glove—on her left hand—and carrying the other. So she and Trudy did the same. Later, when she got to know the Queen better, they agreed to carry gloves but not wear them.

The King was a bluff and hearty person who did not stand on ceremony, though in important matters of protocol he could be very punctilious. On his second night in Los Angeles, I remember, he wandered out into the hotel corridor in his pajamas. The policeman on duty, startled by this apparition, asked him sharply who he was and what he was doing. "I'm the King you're supposed to be guarding," said the King affably, "and I'm looking around!" This sort of thing amused His Majesty but in state ceremonies he was the essence of royal dignity. He did not like to be questioned about the tattoos that he had acquired as a young officer in the Danish Navy, and he did not care for loud or raucous jazz music. One of his enthusiasms, I discovered, was a British automobile that he had, a Bentley. Since I had a Bentley myself, this gave us something in common. Ruth told the King how around the State Department Douglas Dillon, who also owned one, and I were known as "the Bentley boys." This amused the King, who began privately to refer to himself and me as "the Bentley boys."

I soon found that the King was full of a restless energy and hated to be idle. The Queen was equally tireless. We took them to Disneyland, which they loved, and to an orchid farm, since orchid-raising was a hobby of the Queen. We flew them across Los Angeles in a helicopter, and the King was fascinated by the intricate pattern of the freeways and the number of private swimming pools that he could see from the air. We paid a visit to a Danish home for the aged, and it was touching to see how thrilled and grateful these elderly people were when their King and Queen shook hands or stopped to talk with them. Once again I was impressed with the conduct of royalty on such occasions. They know how to make total strangers feel for a few moments that they are interested in their problems and nothing else in the world. This is no easy thing to do; it takes years of training and self-discipline.

From California we flew to Chicago. I knew that sooner or later some reporter was going to ask the King about his famous tattoos and here it happened. It was a lady reporter, actually, and she asked the King where his tattoos were. "Where you'll never see them," said the King sharply, and that was the end of that.

We took the King and Queen to the Chicago Museum of Science and History where a luncheon had been planned for them in the simulated farm. There were waiters in farm costumes, artificial trees, and amplified farm noises played over the public address system. Our table was covered with a red-checked tablecloth. We were served chicken fricassee and dumplings, home-made bread, pickled peaches and beets, and pumpkin pie—a delightful change after the endless succession of formal meals. At one point, the King sent me his place card with a plaintive note written inside: "Please can I powder my nose after all this?" This reminded me of the advice that King Edward VII is supposed to have given his son George—then Prince of Wales. "The most important lesson a King can learn is this: Never pass up an opportunity to 'refresh' yourself!"

Victor Borge entertained the King that night at a dinner given by the Danish-American Society at the Blackstone Hotel. He was extremely amusing, as always, and also played some serious music which I thought the King preferred to his clowning.

Speaking of clowning, I was guilty of some of it myself. In this I was aided and abetted by Eigle Wern, then Deputy Grand Marshal (now the Grand Marshal) of the Danish Court. Eigle was a most attractive Dane, dark-haired, energetic, absolutely tireless, with a sparkling sense of humor. He and his wife Gretna, whom we met later in Denmark, are a wonderful couple, typical of all that is best in the Danish people.

On our first night in Chicago, the King and Queen went for a drive around the city. While they were gone, Ruth and I took the rest of the Danish party to the Camellia Room of the Drake Hotel where there were music and dancing and a very attractive singer named Diana Trask. I believe she was an Australian girl; she certainly was a pretty one. In our group was one of the King's aides, a tall, slim, and elegant Danish Major. Perhaps after four years I was a little tired of being the ultra-correct Chief of Protocol. Anyway, the idea occurred to me of playing a little joke on our friend the Major. A couple of conspirators joined me in the plot—Eigle was one, Ruth was another. We arranged for our waiter to bring a note to the Major, apparently sent by Miss Trask, asking him to call her on the telephone after the show.

The waiter carried out his assignment perfectly. The note was discreetly handed to the Major. It was marvelous to see how he read it with an impassive face, folded it, put it in his pocket. Good manners made it impossible for him to show any impatience, but as time passed it became evident that he was wishing fervently that all of us would get tired, go to bed, and leave him to explore this intriguing situation.

Finally the party did break up. As soon as he was alone, the Major called Miss Trask's apartment in the hotel. By now it was about 2 in the morning. The singer was still awake, but her secretary answered the phone. When the Major identified himself and said happily that he had had a note requesting him to call, the puzzled secretary checked with Miss Trask. The singer said wearily that the caller must be just one more tiresome admirer; she had written no such note. When this gloomy information was relayed to the Major, he was so abashed that he hung up.

But now the secretary and Miss Trask grew curious. The caller had said he was a member of the Danish royal party. They checked with the hotel telephone operator and learned that the call had, indeed, originated in one of the royal apartments. So everyone went to bed intrigued and puzzled.

Next morning I happened to see Miss Trask and her secretary in the coffee shop. I went over, introduced myself, and confessed all. They were much amused. By now the King and Queen were also in on the joke. In the elevator there was a rather spectacular picture of Miss Trask. The Queen called this to the attention of the Major. Didn't he think she was a most attractive girl? The Major said solemnly that he did. We all had to struggle to keep from exploding with laughter.

But it all worked out very well. The next night Miss Trask came over to our table, was introduced to the King and Queen, and danced several times with the Major. They were still dancing dreamily when the rest of us went to bed, and I later learned that they went on from there to various other night spots and got home about 4 in the morning.

From Chicago, we flew on to Washington. It was on the *Columbine*, I remember, that I noticed the King examining a book of matches with an insignie stamped on them. "That's the President's seal," I told him. "Really?" he said. "Where's his whale?" To make an instantaneous play on words in a foreign language is quite a trick, but it was no great effort for His Majesty.

We arrived in Washington on a brilliant October day. President Eisenhower was there to meet the King and Queen. The limousines were waiting for the ceremonial ride back to the Guest House. I knew it was the last time I would ride in such a parade, and so I tried to make myself remember it all as vividly as possible—the King tall and impressive in his uniform, the Queen dazzling in her American-beauty red coat dress and matching hat with black bird-of-paradise feathers, our President's welcoming smile, the honor guard, the ride through the sun-drenched streets lined with the friendly crowds. The King said that he was sorry we would no longer be under one roof. I was sorry, too; we had all become great friends. This perhaps was not apparent to those who saw us in public, where every move is dictated by protocol. But when you sit around late at night and have a bottle of Danish beer (or in the King's case orange juice), with the ladies slipping their shoes off tired feet and piling their tiaras in glittering heaps on the table (we all called them their "diamond hats"), the formalities drop away and a genuine warmth and affection take their place.

My mood of nostalgia persisted through the state dinner at the White House—the last one I would attend as Chief of Protocol. Ruth and I had become a bit jaded with state dinners at times, but now, gazing at the familiar portraits and the glitter and sparkle of the gold service and the profusion of purple orchids and harmonizing purple carnations, I knew that I would miss the excitement and pageantry of it all.

Actually, I was responsible for the presence in the White House of part of that gold service. Much of it dated back to 1819, when President James Madison made his famous trip to Paris and purchased it and many other treasures. But some of it was left to the White House during the Eisenhower administration by the late Margaret Biddle, who had mentioned this legacy to me several times. Her magnificent gift was still in Paris when I went there with President Eisenhower for a NATO meeting. Some pieces were dutiable, some were not. Since there were no funds for packing and shipping them, the whole matter seemed to be hanging fire, and so I decided to take some action. I arranged for the Biddle legacy to be brought to the American Embassy. Then I asked General Robert Schultz, one of the President's aides, why the whole thing could not simply be put on the back-up plane that always followed the Presidential plane and returned to Washington. With his usual efficiency, General Schultz arranged this, with no fuss or red tape whatever. Technically, perhaps, this made me a smuggler, but at least I was smuggling on behalf of my own country, and was delighted to be one.

Although we were now living at home and they were in the Guest House, we continued to see King Frederick and Queen Ingrid every day. Always looking for exercise, the King asked me if I knew of a pool where he might swim. I suggested the White House pool, but when he learned that this was indoors he seemed disappointed, even though it was October. "I hear you have an outdoor pool," he said. I assured him that he was welcome to our pool, if he wanted to try that. He accepted with enthusiasm, and came out the next day. He had a fine swim—and only one complaint. "You need more ash trays," he said. I never did tell him that we had had the pool closed for the winter, and had a frantic rush trying to get it refilled and some of the garden furniture dragged out of storage in time.

I took the King for a private tour of Washington in my Bentley and found that he was quite a stickler for traffic regulations. Once, when I stopped for a red light, he pointed out that my front wheels were over the white line. A few blocks farther on, I made the same mistake. "There, now," sighed the King, "you've done it again!"

From Washington we went to New York, where the King spoke to the General Assembly of the United Nations, the Queen and Ruth went shopping, and I gave a little farewell caviar party for all our Danish friends. Once more there was a presentation of royal photographs, once more a private farewell inside the royal airplane, and our last state visitors departed. We were sorry to see them go, but Ruth and I agreed that we couldn't have ended the long parade on a happier note. The Danish visit had been the beginning of a really wonderful friendship.

In October, with the end of the administration approaching, all of us submitted our resignations as is customary. In November came the election, disappointing to all loyal Republicans like ourselves, and heartbreakingly close. We had an evening with the Nixons immediately afterward, and I marveled at his good humor and good sportsmanship.

The end of my term of office was now rapidly approaching, but one pleasant duty remained. At the end of any story, I'm told, boy should get girl. My last official function was to represent the United States on an occasion where boy did get girl—and since the boy was a King and the girl was a Princess it was quite a storybook romance.

It was in the late summer of 1960 that we began to hear

rumors that our friend Baudouin, bachelor King of the Belgians, had fallen in love with a Spanish Princess named Fabiola. Soon the rumors were confirmed and a December wedding date was announced. Shortly thereafter a Belgian official asked me if there was any chance of my attending the wedding as official representative of the United States. He said that the King would be pleased if this could be worked out.

Actually, Secretary Herter was already planning to fly to Paris to attend a NATO meeting, stopping off one night in Brussels for the wedding festivities. Then I was to replace him as the official U.S. representative to the wedding. So arrangements were made for Ruth and me to fly to Brussels with Chris and "Mac" Herter and Secretary of the Treasury Bob Anderson and his wife Ollie, who were also on their way to the NATO meeting.

We were to stay at the American Embassy with our Ambassador, Bill Burden, and his wonderful wife Peggy. Peggy, I learned, had arranged to borrow a stunning diamond tiara from Harry Winston, the jeweler, to wear at the wedding. She had planned to have it sent over in the diplomatic pouch, but the person in charge of these arrangements learned that I was flying to Brussels and asked me if I would take it. When I said I would, he brought it around, elaborately wrapped and sealed. He was rather startled when I took off the wrappings and stuffed it into my brief case. When he questioned the wisdom of this, I opened the brief case and showed him that it already contained Ruth's own diamond tiara and another that she had borrowed from Van Cleef and Arpels, the jewelers in New York. So when I finally boarded the plane for Brussels I had thousands of dollars' worth of precious stones rattling around in my brief case.

Of all the glittering social events that I attended during my years as Chief of Protocol, the Baudouin wedding was the most lavish and spectacular. Just about every royal family in Europe was represented: Princess Margaret Rose of England and her husband, the former photographer, Anthony Armstrong-Jones; King Olaf of Norway; Prince Axel and Princess Margaret of

Denmark; Queen Juliana and Prince Bernhardt of the Netherlands (who praised the Netherlands Ambassador to Washington, Herman van Roijens, and his wife Ann); the Archdukes Otto
and Charles of Austria; the Grand Duchess of Luxembourg to
whom I once had been accredited, and whose country, with
its connections with the Bourbons and Hohenzollerns and the
House of Orange, has been called the cradle of European
royalty; many titled Spaniards including the Marquis of Vill-
averde, resplendent in the white and gold uniform of a Knight
of Malta (his wife is the daughter of Spain's Chief of State,
Francisco Franco); and many dignitaries from all over the
world.

The truth is, royalty is far from extinct in Europe. Most of
these people know one another, visit one another, sometimes
lend one another jewels or even clothes. Those who still retain
estates are generous with their hospitality to others not so
fortunate. It was King Farouk of Egypt, I believe, who said
that soon there would be only five monarchs left: the kings of
spades, hearts, diamonds, clubs—and the King of England. But
I can't agree with this. It will be a long time before royalty
vanishes from the scene in Europe—and it is interesting to note
that the countries in which the Communists have made the
least headway are those in which a King or a Queen still reigns.

By this time, after four years of faithful diary-keeping, Ruth
was getting heartily tired of writing down her impressions.
But she was still at it, and I think her account of our trip to
Belgium for the King's wedding reflects very accurately the
hectic atmosphere of excitement and fatigue and splendid confusion that we had come to know so well.

Here is her narrative, somewhat condensed, as it begins at
our farmhouse in Virginia the morning of the day we were
supposed to fly to Brussels:

Had planned to get away by 9, so got up at 8, but of course
no one got organized. It was snowing when we woke up. We
didn't get too excited about this, just thought it was the first
light snow. But by the time we got on the road at about 10:30
it was really coming down. We had no chains or snow tires,

and so got stuck on the first steep hill. A nice Virginian pushed us until we finally came to a gas station and were able to buy some chains. The children were excited about the snow and furious that they couldn't stay and be really snowbound, but we just had to get back to D.C. as we were leaving at the crack of dawn in Secretary Herter's plane for King Baudouin's wedding. Finally arrived home about 2:30. Had been on road for five hours—exhausted—and so much to do. I still had a few presents to wrap and mail, plus all my packing.

We got to bed about 1 A.M., but had to set the alarm for 4. White House car came for us at 5—don't know how it ever made it or how we then made it to Andrews Field, but we did. Parkway looked like Siberia—snow all over—abandoned cars everywhere. At airport other members of Herter party began to collect. We were due to take off at 6:30. I sat and talked with Mac Herter and Ollie Anderson, discussing the election, mainly, until 8:30 or 9:00 A.M. Finally the pilot announced we couldn't possibly take off until 7 P.M., a ten-hour delay. Snow was continuing to fall—runway couldn't be cleared as fast as it fell. Andersons offered us a ride back to city, so we took it but got stuck in a snowdrift and were picked up by Herters as their car passed ten minutes later. We seem to be perpetually stuck.

At home we went back to bed, but Wiley was just too tired and too keyed up to sleep. At 4 P.M. airport called to say we would definitely take off at 7 and board plane at 6:15, so at 4:30 we braved snowy roads again, got to Andrews Field and actually boarded plane. Walk out to plane on field was worth your life—slick from snow and stiff winds blowing loose snow at you. It really *was* like Siberia. Guess we're crazy to fly in such weather but I figured if the Secretaries of State and of Treasury could, we could.

We really had a hilarious ride to Brussels. The Herters, Andersons, and ourselves were in the VIP part of plane. We had drinks, then dinner; afterward decided to sleep because we would arrive in Belgium at 4 A.M. our time which is 10 A.M. theirs. No time for rest there, so it was now or never. Since there are only two beds in the VIP compartment, Ollie had had the Air Force put sleeping bags aboard for those without berths. Mac and Chris Herter had the beds, so Ollie, Bob, and I each took a sleeping bag and slept on floor in VIP compartment. Wiley went back to a chair in other part of plane. I passed out sleeping pills—then slept till 1:30, woke up with stiff back, and just had to get up and walk about. Made up my face, then came back and got some water from kitchen, then rested in my bag until others woke up for breakfast at 2:30. They all kept remarking on how wonderful I looked after sleeping in that bag. (What they didn't know was that I had been awake an hour and had combed my hair and made up my face!) I still felt awful though—three hours of sleep a night isn't enough for me. After breakfast we arrived in Brussels on a typical Belgian day, cold, damp, and gray, but at least no rain.

Various dignitaries were at airport to meet us but no Prime Minister (which appeared in paper as an intentional slight because Herter had greeted Lumumba in D.C. this summer and allowed him to stay at the President's Guest House where King has stayed). At our Embassy Wiley and I had our old room where we used to stay when we visited the Algers—the paneled room off the library—it felt like home to us. We unpacked and redressed for day—no time to rest. The Secretary received a decoration in the drawing room presented by Belgian Ambassador Dufresne in small ceremony; then we walked across park to building where he greeted all of Embassy staff.

Back at Embassy we had about twenty minutes to rest before lunch. I lay down on bed and could hardly stay awake. Burdens had about eighty people for lunch. We received with them in front hall by staircase under their fantastic collection of paintings; some are really gorgeous, especially the Monet, which is a dream.

Luncheon was delicious, but too rich for me. However, I didn't mind too much as after lunch I had a three-hour nap—thank goodness!

All dressed up really fancy for evening. Peggy Burden wore

borrowed Winston tiara which we had brought over, and I wore borrowed Van Cleef one—lent my own to Mac. She wasn't too anxious to wear one, but we convinced her she should. Guess Mac was glad she did. Never saw so many tiara-ed people in all my life. Anybody without one was practically undressed. Peggy said she felt like a Christmas tree when we started out—later decided we were underdressed by comparison.

At the Palace, there was a whole contingent of Spanish all glittering in diamonds—they really had them!

Wiley and Bill were included in the Royal dinner party, but we wives were not—the dinner guests being limited to actual representatives of governments. While we waited Peggy and I wandered from one enormous Palace room to another, chatting from time to time. She introduced me to lots of ambassadors' wives. We stood and walked and shared a chair once or twice from 9:30 till 11:30 when finally the Royal Party dinner broke up and the King and his fiancée appeared. We all formed an aisle about two or three deep on each side. The King and his fiancée walked slowly along, speaking to certain people as they passed. I managed to get myself in the front row. The King's aide spotted me, so when King came along he stopped him in front of me. He introduced me to Fabiola who is really "fabulosa"—absolutely perfect for him and he is mad about her. He wouldn't let go of her arm and kept gazing at her with such adoring looks. She is much prettier and younger-looking than her pictures. Wore a gorgeous gown of yellow lace over yellow satin—it was exquisite—and her tiara of emeralds and diamonds (gift from Spanish government) was really fit for a Queen. She said very little; King explained to her who I was and what a wonderful trip we had had, then they turned to go on. King turned back to me and asked so solicitously, "It hasn't been too warm in here has it, waiting all this time?" I told him it didn't matter, everything was perfect.

After that Peggy and I wandered into other rooms, as King and Fabiola had gone into ballroom to start the dancing. We were looking for Wiley and Bill. Peggy spotted Bill and soon took him home. Wiley and I stayed on and saw lots of old friends. I talked with Prince Jean and Princess Josephine Charlotte, King Baudouin's sister. Was greeted excitedly by Prince Don Juan Carlos, who was with Prince Charles of Luxembourg. Juan Carlos asked immediately where Bonnie was and gaily told what fun he had had with Bonnie and her friends in America. He looked very handsome and more mature than when in the States. Kept introducing me as Lady Buchanan. Europeans simply never understand Mrs.!

Later Wiley and I saw King Baudouin and Fabiola again. He stopped in front of us and pointed us out to her, saying, "See this happily married couple. They're always together." I thanked His Majesty and wished them the greatest happiness possible.

Jean Bassompierre introduced us to Princess Margaret Rose and Anthony Armstrong-Jones. Wiley and I stood and talked to them for a while. We told her how we had traveled with her sister and Prince Philip. At first she said distantly, "Which time?" Then when we explained on all her visits to the States she became a little more cordial. Wiley was telling her about greeting Queen Elizabeth on that bouncing barge in Chicago. Margaret said, "Oh, I'm glad to hear your version of the story —did my sister really jump that great distance?" Margaret was in a lavender dress, her tiara was the one given her by Queen for her wedding. Later I heard she was forty-five minutes late for the Royal dinner because of the hairdresser. Some young man came up and asked her to dance, but she glanced possessively at Tony and said, "No, I'm rather clinging to him tonight."

Tony was better-looking in person than in photos—his hair is a bit bleached on top—he's quite handsome and much taller than I expected. I've always heard how short he is. This is not true; he towers over Margaret, who is barely five feet. She didn't let us talk too long, soon took him off to dance. We chatted some more with Prince Jean and Josephine Charlotte, then decided we had better go home. Got home about 2:30 or so. It was really a storybook night. I've never seen so many royalty at once or such glorious clothes and jewelry. Queen Juliana's diamonds were terrific. She certainly has a regal air about her.

Wedding Day of King Baudouin and Fabiola—Gray Brussels day, cold but at least not raining so that was something to be thankful for. Wiley and Bill had to get into white-tie early and leave the Embassy at 8:40 to go to civil ceremony at Palace. We women weren't included in that; had to be dressed in long dresses, hats, and gloves at 10. My Dior outfit really looked perfect for the occasion and my blue paradise feather hat was certainly the right choice. I wore my new Xmas sable jacket and felt luxurious! Got to church easily and quickly; think we were among first to arrive. Found our chairs up on protected platform to side of altar—perfect for viewing bride and groom but couldn't see congregation at all, or watch the royalty march in dressed to the hilt. On TV sets below our platform we watched the civil ceremony at Palace. It was perfect and of course we got to see all the other royal personages and what they were wearing, but still never saw them in person. Wiley did, of course, and was just staggered by their costumes. Paola really looked stunning—like a movie star— many of them wore mink or sable hats. Princess Margaret Rose wore an orange outfit with feathered toque.

King and Fabiola walked down aisle arm in arm and at one point he wrapped his hand around hers—so they could hold each other up, I guess! They came up onto altar and we could see them perfectly; also could see darling little bridesmaids in turquoise velvet and white fur and little boys in maroon velvet —they looked adorable. The Queen was a sight to behold; her Balenciaga gown was exquisite—white satin with white mink around neckline and just below long torso around hips—full skirted from there down; also train was bordered in white mink. She wore a short tulle veil from diamond tiara (which had been Queen Astrid's)—funny she didn't have Spanish or Belgian lace. She looked lovely but a bit white and wan. Since it was a High Mass and Communion she and the King probably hadn't eaten since last night. Ceremony went on and on. An old shaky Cardinal read part of service; two men had to help him up and down. Twice King reached in his pocket and handed Fabiola smelling salts which she put in her glove. Really don't know how they stood the ordeal—we could at least sit or stand or kneel when we got tired or even take our shoes off. King spoke to her several times asking if she was all right, I'm sure. He couldn't keep his eyes off her—they are so in love! Finally it was all over.

Afterward there was a huge reception and buffet, but we had to leave early to catch a plane to Paris.

We flew to Paris, were met by Embassy car. After we got settled at the Ritz we took a long walk on rue St. Honoré; then up onto Champs Elysée and ended up in Lido Arcade where I ate scrambled eggs and cocoa; it certainly tasted good after all that rich Belgian food. . . .

So ended one of the last entries in Ruth's diary, and it seems to me that this is quite a good place to end our story, with boy getting girl in Brussels and the weary but happy wedding guests eating scrambled eggs and drinking cocoa in Paris.

Actually, it was just about the end. Back in Washington, I gave the traditional reception for the diplomatic corps at Blair House on Inauguration Day and handed over the reins to my successor in the new administration, Angier Biddle Duke—an excellent choice for the job.

Looking back down the long red carpet, remembering all the vivid personalities who had walked it with me, I found myself wondering if there was any mysterious element of personality that they shared, any character trait that set them apart from ordinary people. In a way, of course, their high office set them apart. Royalty was born to it; commoners had to achieve it on the basis of brains and drive and ability. But in either case, the office often conferred a kind of dignity and grandeur on the man. Sometimes the chief characteristic of a dignitary was energy, as in the case of President Mateos of Mexico.

Sometimes it was an aura of personal greatness, as in the case of De Gaulle. Sometimes it was a regal charm, as in the cases of the Queens of England, Denmark, and Greece. But always there was *something*, some indefinable stamp of excellence, some sense of mission, some quality of determination or selflessness that made the person willing to undergo fatigue and deprivation of family life and sometimes even personal danger in order to be of service to his country and to know the excitement and responsibility of such high calling.

But to this haunting question, as I said in the beginning, there is no final answer. Human personality is so complex and so mysterious that in the end all attempts at analysis fail, and one is left with a sense of bafflement and awe.

Wonderful as the experience was, I would not care to live through my four years as Chief of Protocol again. On the other hand, I would not have missed the experience for anything. During my journey down the longest red carpet in the world I had given much of myself, but I had gained far more. To represent the United States of America and its President is a great honor for any man. I shall cherish it for the rest of my life.

January 3, 1961

Dear Wiley:

I cannot allow the final days of our governmental service
together to pass without expressing to you my thanks for
the significant contribution you have made to the work of
this Administration.   Because in your most recent post
you have done so much for my personal comfort, conven-
ience, and safety, I owe you a special word of appreciation.
An unprecedented number of visits to this country by Heads
of Government and of State has brought an innumerable
number of difficult problems to the Chief of Protocol.
You -- and your charming wife -- have performed magnificently.

For your service to your country and to me, I am ever-
lastingly grateful. As we go our separate ways -- but,
I like to think, each of us continuing to work to forward
the principles and policies we have supported over the
past years -- you have my very best wishes for a future
as rewarding and productive for yourself and for our
country as the recent past has been.

With warm regard,

Sincerely,

Dwight D. Eisenhower

The Honorable Wiley T. Buchanan, Jr.
Chief of Protocol
Department of State
Washington, D. C..